최신 ② 10회분

토익급상승
Part 5&6

실전문제집 + 해설집

저자 **니오어학원장 임동찬**

토익 인텐시브과정으로 유명한 니오어학원을 운영하고 있습니다.
지난 2000년 초반부터 지금까지 토익강의와 30여 권의 토익 교
재를 집필한 우리나라 토익계의 산증인입니다. 독자와의 직접적인
소통을 중시하는 니오강사는 카카오톡(neoteacher)과 페이스북
(https://www.facebook.com/neotoeicteacher/)을 통해 독자들
의 토익 고민을 실시간으로 해결해주고 있습니다.

최신 토익 급상승 ❷
Part 5&6 10회분[실전문제집 + 해설집]

저 자 임동찬
발행인 고본화
발 행 반석출판사
2019년 1월 20일 초판 1쇄 인쇄
2019년 1월 25일 초판 1쇄 발행
홈페이지 www.bansok.co.kr
이메일 bansok@bansok.co.kr
블로그 blog.naver.com/bansokbooks

07547 서울시 강서구 양천로 583. B동 1007호
(서울시 강서구 염창동 240-21번지 우림블루나인 비즈니스센터 B동 1007호)
대표전화 02) 2093-3399 **팩 스** 02) 2093-3393
출 판 부 02) 2093-3395 **영업부** 02) 2093-3396
등록번호 제315-2008-000033호

ISBN 978-89-7172-888-8 (13740)

최신 ② 10회분

토익 급상승
Part 5&6

실전문제집 + 해설집

반석출판사
Bansok

저자는 지난 20여 년 동안 토익시험을 치르면서 실제 경험의 중요성을 느껴왔습니다. 많은 학생들이 이런 경험적인 요소를 무시한 채 막연히 토익을 공부하지만 이는 효율적이지 않습니다. 처음에는 저 역시 토익에 문외한이었지만, 많은 경험을 쌓으면서 토익 전문가가 되었습니다.

저자는 학생들이 가능한 한 많은 문제를 풀어보면서 실전감각을 익히는 게 점수 획득에 유리하다는 확신을 가지고 있습니다. 본 교재에 실린 문제들은 실제 토익시험에 출제된 기출문제를 변형해서 만들었기 때문에 시중의 어떤 실전문제집보다 수준이 높습니다. 특히 저자는 여러 차례 실전문제집을 발간해왔습니다. 이런 경험을 토대로 만든 본 교재의 파트 5, 6 문제들로 공부를 한다면 단기간에 고득점 획득이 가능할 거라고 확신합니다.

이 책의 특징은 다음과 같습니다.

- 최신의 신토익 출제 경향과 난이도를 반영했습니다.
- 토익 파트 5, 6 실전문제 10회분(460문제)이 실려 있습니다.
- 저자의 카톡과 페이스북을 통해 토익문제 고민을 실시간 해결해드립니다.
- 💬 카톡 neoteacher ⨍ 페이스북 https://www.facebook.com/neotoeicteacher/

끝으로 가족이라는 이름으로 희생만을 강요하는 건 아닌지, 항상 미안함이 앞서는 아내와 아들에게 감사와 사랑의 마음을 전하면서 이 글을 마칩니다.

저자 임동찬

목차

머리말 — 4   이 책의 특징 및 활용방법 — 6

Actual Test 01~10

Actual Test 01
Part 5 — 8
Part 6 — 11

Actual Test 02
Part 5 — 15
Part 6 — 18

Actual Test 03
Part 5 — 22
Part 6 — 25

Actual Test 04
Part 5 — 29
Part 6 — 32

Actual Test 05
Part 5 — 36
Part 6 — 39

Actual Test 06
Part 5 — 43
Part 6 — 46

Actual Test 07
Part 5 — 50
Part 6 — 53

Actual Test 08
Part 5 — 57
Part 6 — 60

Actual Test 09
Part 5 — 64
Part 6 — 67

Actual Test 10
Part 5 — 71
Part 6 — 74

정답 및 해설

Actual Test 01 — 80
Actual Test 02 — 98
Actual Test 03 — 116
Actual Test 04 — 134
Actual Test 05 — 152

Actual Test 06 — 170
Actual Test 07 — 188
Actual Test 08 — 206
Actual Test 09 — 224
Actual Test 10 — 242

정답표 — 260

이 책의 특징 및 활용 방법

1. 신토익 출제가 예상되는 파트 5,6 10회분(460제) 제공!
2. 전체 문제에 대한 해석과 꼼꼼한 해설 제공
3. 저자의 카톡과 페이스북을 통해 토익문제 고민을 실시간 해결

TALK 카톡 neoteacher   **f** 페이스북 https://www.facebook.com/neotoeicteacher/

『최신 토익 급상승 ❷ 파트 5&6 10회분』은 그동안의 기출문제들을 분석하고 앞으로 출제가 예상되는 문제들을 모아서 파트 5, 6 문제 10회분을 제공합니다. 또한 전체 문제에 대한 해석과 꼼꼼한 해설을 제공합니다. 많은 문제를 접하는 것과 동시에 이 책이 제공하는 해설을 꼼꼼하게 리뷰하는 것이 토익 파트 5, 6 점수를 빠르게 올리는 지름길임을 잊지 마세요. 또한 문제를 풀다 막히는 부분이 있으면 위의 카톡이나 페이스북을 통해 실시간으로 질문하세요! 니오토익이 실시간 해결해 드립니다.

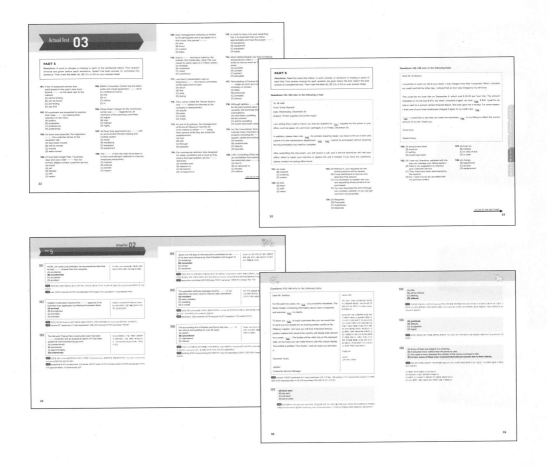

최신 ❷ 10회분

토익 급상승
Part 5&6

Actual Test 01~10

PART 5

Directions: A word or phrase is missing in each of the sentences below. Four answer choices are given below each sentence. Select the best answer to complete the sentence. Then mark the letter (A), (B), (C), or (D) on your answer sheet.

101. ------- to the swimming pool is exclusively for hotel guests and the pool is open during summertime.
(A) Accessing
(B) Accessed
(C) Access
(D) Accesses

102. Air Brazil will ------- a new policy that requires two crew members to be in the cockpit at all times.
(A) implement
(B) acclaim
(C) convince
(D) renovate

103. Vancouver's ------- has improved in the past couple of years following challenges largely based on the global economic crisis.
(A) economic
(B) economical
(C) economy
(D) economizes

104. Please note that in case of insufficient registered participants, the tour ------- and you will be fully refunded.
(A) to cancel
(B) has cancelled
(C) cancelling
(D) will be cancelled

105. PHLD's design team has created the most innovative and ------- tools in the Northern Irish market today.
(A) precision
(B) precise
(C) preciseness
(D) precisely

106. Mr. Richard will be spending three years as chief consultant of a global consulting firm after seventeen years of ------- motivational seminars for managers.
(A) participating
(B) leading
(C) instructing
(D) proving

107. The conference hosted by the Association of Language features several ------- speakers who are experts in the field of phonetics.
(A) notably
(B) notable
(C) notes
(D) noting

108. Hospice I.L.U.E. is a community-based registered charity that strives ------- the quality of life for people facing life-threatening illness or grief.
(A) to enhance
(B) enhanced
(C) enhances
(D) is enhancing

109. Scott Gilchrist is highly respected ------- his colleagues for his devotion and willingness to share his knowledge.
(A) plus
(B) in
(C) to
(D) by

110. These forms must be filled out completely before your ------- at Osaka International Airport customs desk.
(A) arrival
(B) priority
(C) attention
(D) account

111. Due to the Thanksgiving holiday, though recycling items are normally collected on Tuesday, collection will be on Thursday -------.
(A) high
(B) alike
(C) instead
(D) seldom

112. We provide services in promoting any products of manufacturers, starting with an ------- of potential clients.
(A) analysis
(B) to analyze
(C) analyzed
(D) analyze

113. It is a ------- for all Public High schools to conduct at least two annual evaluations.
(A) speculation
(B) acquisition
(C) requirement
(D) training

114. Spring-hill Inn, which has a magnificent ocean view, is located ------- across the street from a white sandy beach.
(A) direct
(B) directly
(C) directive
(D) directness

115. For optimal performance and appearance, C&C sliding doors must be installed ------- great care.
(A) with
(B) for
(C) during
(D) in

116. This weekend the assistant chef, Mr. John Smith, will supervise the dinner service in Ms. Mayer's -------.
(A) absence
(B) absences
(C) absent
(D) absently

117. RASP National Transportation ------- passengers with a long-distance bus service to and from Melbourne, Brisbane and Sydney.
(A) provides
(B) collects
(C) commutes
(D) accommodates

118. ------- Sankai Electronics' stock price has increased recently, the company's board of directors is worried about the slowdown in the appliance industry.
(A) As soon as
(B) So that
(C) Although
(D) Despite

119. With around sixty thousand visitors coming every month, La Défance is a ------- busy tourist spot during the holiday season.
(A) particularly
(B) formerly
(C) generously
(D) popularly

120. The latest poll shows that a ------- of voters are in favor of the presidential candidate from the Democrat Party.
(A) rate
(B) majority
(C) point
(D) summary

GO ON TO THE NEXT PAGE

121. Many specialists ------- that the merger of the two stationery companies will be completed within the next month.
(A) predict
(B) predicting
(C) predicts
(D) predictable

122. Flight 927 to St. Anthony took off one hour ------- than scheduled on account of heavy snow in the New Orleans area.
(A) later
(B) lately
(C) late
(D) latest

123. CFPB Loan Services has conditionally approved your loan application, though we are still waiting for ------- of forms mentioned previously.
(A) receiving
(B) recipient
(C) receipt
(D) to receive

124. Bear in mind that the results of official tests are only valid for a limited ------- of time.
(A) value
(B) amount
(C) setting
(D) venue

125. U&M has ------- its decision on a cleanup plan for the sediments of the Luice River.
(A) finalized
(B) consumed
(C) hosted
(D) designed

126. This two-day career fair is an excellent opportunity for ILS students to meet with ------- from more than 100 companies.
(A) recruit
(B) recruitments
(C) recruiting
(D) recruiters

127. ------- of the sales representatives is evaluated monthly on the basis of the number of products sold during the past month.
(A) Their own
(B) The others
(C) Each one
(D) All

128. Wellington Point is a nature park of ------- meadowlands and forests, located in Moreton Bay within easy reach of city residents.
(A) vast
(B) ethical
(C) final
(D) economic

129. Hundreds of emails and web-forms arrive daily from customers and must be appropriately responded to ------- strict time limits.
(A) past
(B) throughout
(C) near
(D) within

130. ------- is allowed to enter the company building after 7:30 P.M. unless accompanied by security personnel.
(A) No one
(B) One another
(C) Whoever
(D) Somebody

PART 6

Directions: Read the texts that follow. A word, phrase, or sentence is missing in parts of each text. Four answer choices for each question are given below the text. Select the best answer to complete the text. Then mark the letter (A), (B), (C), or (D) on your answer sheet.

Questions 131-134 refer to the following notice.

Attention Associates!

The Capebile Group's continuing lecture series on policy design and implementation is adding a new voice. Ms. Berna Hopper, the former house speaker and head of the budget committee, will present her views on the future of American growth.

Coming from years of experience as a senator and having sat on many powerful committees, Ms. Hopper is a welcome ------- to our series. -------.
                   131.   **132.**

The talk will be given ------- September 18th at 3:30 in the main auditorium. As this is sure to be
               133.
a very popular talk, please make sure to sign up for it in advance ------- admittance.
                                         134.

131. (A) case
    (B) addition
    (C) instance
    (D) attendee

132. (A) She will discuss the relationship between investor confidence and governmental policies.
    (B) It had an impact on our policy formulation.
    (C) She used to design innovative systems over the last 10 years.
    (D) She regularly participated in the seminar held by The Federal Government.

133. (A) as
    (B) in
    (C) on
    (D) to

134. (A) ensures
    (B) ensured
    (C) ensuring
    (D) to ensure

GO ON TO THE NEXT PAGE

To: ron.portwell@ymail.com

From: gian@greatgraphics.com

Subject: For your job application

Date: January 2, 2020

Dear Mr. Portwell,

We have reviewed your letter of application and réesumée, and we want to set up an interview for the position you have applied for. Based on your letter, you are seeking an immediate full-time job as graphic designer. -------, we would like to offer you an apprenticeship for three
135.
months, from January 15 to April 14. -------.
136.

Sometimes applicants who have successfully undergone their apprenticeship are offered -------
137.
positions upon completion, and they are encouraged to take advantage of this opportunity.

If you wish ------- an apprenticeship, please reply to this e-mail as soon as you can.
138.

Gian Smith, Manager

Great Graphics Company

135. (A) As a result
(B) In addition
(C) However
(D) Rather than

136. (A) During this period, you will be able to enhance your skills and obtain practical experience in the graphic design field.
(B) You demonstrated your qualifications as a designer during the interview.
(C) If you accept this offer, your career as a chief designer is set to begin next month.
(D) You need to submit some samples of your work to be eligible for this.

137. (A) persistent
(B) durable
(C) sturdy
(D) permanent

138. (A) pursued
(B) pursuing
(C) to pursue
(D) pursues

Questions 139-142 refer to the following announcement.

Nominations for Student Volunteers

------. Faculty members, staff and students can all nominate ------ students by completing the
  139.   **140.**
necessary form and submitting it to the Registrar's Office. The form must include the activities
that the nominee has undertaken as a volunteer.

The Awards Committee ------ all the nominations in January. The candidates will be ranked
                              141.
------ the services that they performed at school and in the community. An awards ceremony
  142.
will be held in February during the school festival.

The deadline for nominations is December 25. Guidelines and forms for nominations are now
available at the Registrar's Office and on the school website at www.southvillhigh.org.

---

139. (A) South Vill High School held the
        Annual Festival last week.
    (B) We are seeking qualified faculty
        members to join our school.
    (C) South Vill High School is accepting
        nominations for Outstanding Student.
    (D) We are in need of volunteers who
        will be responsible for setting up the
        booths.

140. (A) graduate
    (B) qualified
    (C) licensed
    (D) numerical

141. (A) reviewing
    (B) reviewed
    (C) will review
    (D) to be reviewed

142. (A) since
    (B) due to
    (C) for
    (D) based on

GO ON TO THE NEXT PAGE

Mr. Smith

Chapter Chairperson

This is in reference to the memorandum which prescribes the deadline for the submission of monetary claims, dated January 9, 2020, and issued by Brandon Moore, our Finance Manager.

-------. All claims submitted after the deadline will not be accepted by the accounting division.
143.

Please be ------- that February 2, 2020 the accounting division received a form for the payment
144.
of expenses for the fuel consumption of Frederick Merck, the company driver, by attaching the receipt issued by Afrilco Gasoline Station for the period of December 16-31, 2019. -------, you
145.
are asked to justify the delay of the submission of the form to head office ------- 5 days from
146.
receipt of this letter.

Yours truly,

Christopher Perez

Overall Accountant

143. (A) He can extend the deadline as long as you report that it is not possible to complete the project.
(B) As stated in the memo, the due date for all monetary claims was on January 25, 2020.
(C) There was a change to the procedure in processing the claims.
(D) Please note that our company has a financial aid system for employees who have difficulty with finance.

144. (A) noticed
(B) ensured
(C) informed
(D) said

145. (A) Instead
(B) On the other hand
(C) Nevertheless
(D) As a result

146. (A) until
(B) into
(C) within
(D) during

PART 5

Directions: A word or phrase is missing in each of the sentences below. Four answer choices are given below each sentence. Select the best answer to complete the sentence. Then mark the letter (A), (B), (C), or (D) on your answer sheet.

101. As Mr. Lim used Luxe software, he recovered the data that he had ------- erased from his computer.
(A) accidental
(B) accidentally
(C) accidents
(D) accident

102. Kaplani Corporation received the ------- approval of its business loan application by National Australian Bank.
(A) prompt
(B) promptness
(C) promptly
(D) prompts

103. The Norwich Theme Park construction plan has been ------- reviewed, and an analytical report of it has been posted at www.bonheurcity.go.com.
(A) consecutively
(B) exclusively
(C) approximately
(D) extensively

104. Jacob Lim will stay on the executive committee for the ------- of his term and will serve as Vice President until August 14.
(A) remaining
(B) remainder
(C) remain
(D) remained

105. The upgraded software package recently ------- in our laboratory has been used to improve daily operations.
(A) installed
(B) been installed
(C) installing
(D) to install

106. The accounting firm of Nimbin and Byron Bay has ------- in tax returns and auditing for over 50 years.
(A) signed
(B) specialized
(C) maintained
(D) offered

107. Despite ------- competition, in recent years all the VAMOS subsidiaries have continued to achieve steady growth in the British market.
(A) short
(B) strong
(C) positive
(D) perfect

108. It is important to consume generous amounts of vegetables since they contain antioxidants that will make your skin -------.
(A) healthiness
(B) more health
(C) healthier
(D) health

GO ON TO THE NEXT PAGE

109. All items purchased online before 5 P.M. will be delivered ------- two business days to addresses across Switzerland.
(A) since
(B) besides
(C) between
(D) within

110. Perth City Council has started receiving ------- for the Perth Volunteer of the Year award.
(A) nominates
(B) nominate
(C) nominated
(D) nominations

111. ------- has been recorded about the products made by Luxy Textile Company in the mid-twentieth century.
(A) Little
(B) Few
(C) Who
(D) Anyone

112. Dr. Jason's ------- comes from his 35 years of working in the pharmaceutical and biochemical industry.
(A) indication
(B) expense
(C) impression
(D) expertise

113. Notice of your ------- to take a vacation must be given to the company no less than 4 days prior to your vacation.
(A) policy
(B) intention
(C) proposal
(D) direction

114. Although the requisition for the processing equipment was sent four days ago, we have ------- to receive confirmation of its approval.
(A) still
(B) nor
(C) yet
(D) even

115. The construction of a new bus terminal in Neo Town, that was set to start this year, -------.
(A) has been postponed
(B) postpones
(C) will have postponed
(D) is postponing

116. Highly ------- musicians can easily be hired from universities or orchestras when they need to fill the vacant positions.
(A) qualified
(B) potential
(C) apparent
(D) enclosed

117. Representatives from Maxtopia Publishing ------- a welcome reception in the IBS Building next Friday at 6:30 P.M..
(A) will be hosting
(B) will have hosted
(C) hosted
(D) will be hosted

118. Although Raymond plays a trivial role in the opera, his passionate song leaves a ------- impression on audiences.
(A) lasted
(B) lasting
(C) lastly
(D) lasts

119. A plumber from Horrin Maintenance will arrive at the Q&G Building at 9:00 A.M. tomorrow to ------- the water pipe problem.
(A) invite
(B) commend
(C) assess
(D) proceed

120. All products are ------- inspected and tested before shipment from the factory.
(A) largely
(B) thoroughly
(C) highly
(D) steeply

121. Author Andrew Rixson, who has sold over 10 million copies of Au nom de la rose, is busy working on the sixth ------- of the series.
(A) installation
(B) instalment
(C) installer
(D) install

122. A one hour guided tour is available for groups of 15 or more and the price is $ 28.00 ------- person.
(A) with
(B) per
(C) by
(D) despite

123. The Shown Pen Inc., is known for its tractors and other farm machines, but ------- of us are familiar with modern farm equipment today than ever before.
(A) fewest
(B) fewer
(C) few
(D) a few

124. The College Office will start its process for reviewing each of the applications ------- the deadline for submitting applications has passed.
(A) now that
(B) how
(C) neither
(D) whether

125. Our experienced team can work together to put a quality finish on any house in a ------- short time.
(A) surprise
(B) surprised
(C) surprisingly
(D) surprising

126. Viva Net today announced that the company will not ------- its agreement with the Cable Network Epix next month.
(A) proceed
(B) attract
(C) avoid
(D) renew

127. Northern Construction Inc. has received several awards ------- its efforts to promote energy efficiency.
(A) off
(B) away
(C) for
(D) across

128. Four copy machines that ------- to copying manuals are being set up in the marketing department.
(A) dedicate
(B) dedication
(C) had dedicated
(D) will be dedicated

129. After all, advancement within the company is ------- decided by the individual employee's achievements and performance.
(A) deeply
(B) largely
(C) continually
(D) formerly

130. All four parties agree to the terms of the contract and sign the document in support of each -------.
(A) another
(B) the other
(C) others
(D) other

GO ON TO THE NEXT PAGE

PART 6

Directions: Read the texts that follow. A word, phrase, or sentence is missing in parts of each text. Four answer choices for each question are given below the text. Select the best answer to complete the text. Then mark the letter (A), (B), (C), or (D) on your answer sheet.

Questions 131-134 refer to the following letter.

Dear Mr. Sardina

For the past two years, we ------- you a monthly newsletter, The Motor Dealer, containing
     131.
information about many companies and services ------- to clients.
                                              132.

To show our ------- to loyal customers like you, we would like to send you two tickets for an
           133.
evening pottery exhibit at the Pillsbury Capitol. I am sure you will love it because famous pottery

makers from around the country will display their artwork for a week. -------. The tickets will be
                                                                      134.
valid only on the stamped date, so we hope you can make time to visit this unique display. The

exhibit is entitled "The Andrei." and we hope you will enjoy it.

Sincerely Yours,

Jayden

Customer Service Manager

131. (A) have sent
(B) are sent
(C) will send
(D) are to send

132. (A) offer
(B) will be offered
(C) offering
(D) offered

133. (A) gratitude
(B) attitude
(C) recognition
(D) regret

134. (A) Some of them are subject to a small fee.
(B) It attracted more visitors than the previous year.
(C) You need to hurry because the number of the visitors is limited to 500.
(D) In fact, some of them even received international awards due to their talents.

Questions 135-138 refer to the following e-mail.

From: Sam Smith

Sent: Wednesday, April 3

To: Office staff

Subject: Chair Replacements

Hello, staff

This email is to let ------- know that we will finally be replacing the worn out office chairs we
                        135.
have been using for years. -------. Please note that we do not have the ------- to replace every
                            136.   **137.**
chair in the office, so please do not request a new one if you are still comfortable with your
present one.

Requests can be made by ------- the form on the company website. New chairs will be
                        138.
purchased next month and will replace the old chairs no later than May 14. If you have any
questions or special requests, please contact me.

Emily Hunts

Office Furniture Appropriation Officer, Extension 2382

---

135. (A) you
    (B) your
    (C) your own
    (D) yours

136. (A) The accounting department assigned us funds to be given to outstanding employees.
    (B) Office chairs were made by a unique local artisan.
    (C) If you feel your chair is in need of a change, please submit a request by no later than April 30.
    (D) You need to fill out the form to be considered qualified for the position.

137. (A) charge
    (B) cost
    (C) budget
    (D) expense

138. (A) complete
    (B) completed
    (C) completing
    (D) completion

GO ON TO THE NEXT PAGE

Questions 139-142 refer to the following e-mail.

To: calone@teleworm.us

From: jenkins@dayrep.com

Subject: Career Application

Date: February 9

Dear Mr. Calone,

Having read over your application and accompanying letter explaining your interest in joining
------- firm, we would be very interested in speaking to you in person.
139.

We see you hope to join our company as a manager. Normally, we would not entertain such
requests. -------, after reviewing your background experience, we remain open-minded.
140.

The competition between our rivals has become intense -------, and somebody with your skill
141.
set could be very useful in helping us hold on to our market share. We hope to speak to you
by no later than Wednesday, February 11th. We realize that you are located in Seattle and
our headquarters are in Chicago. -------. She will provide you with information on the soonest
142.
available airplane ticket, which we will of course pay for.

We look forward to seeing you.

---

139. (A) our
(B) ours
(C) us
(D) ourselves

140. (A) However
(B) Thus
(C) Therefore
(D) Afterwards

141. (A) promptly
(B) shortly
(C) lately
(D) currently

142. (A) Our headquarters are very
conveniently located near the subway
station.
(B) Please contact my secretary, Mrs.
Emma,
at 555-0134.
(C) In case of emergency, you can
contact me directly not my assistant,
Mrs. Emma.
(D) We will assist you with the travel
costs.

Dear Sir,

Our office officially received your letter last Tuesday, September 26. We appreciate your noble intention for holding this kind of program.

However, the ------- you requested for your medical services is not available on that date
        143.
because there are already activities that ------- there. We appeal to your management if you
                                144.
could possibly postpone your medical project to the next day, or decide to change venues.
-------.
145.

We deeply apologize for this inconvenience. We are ------- of having your radio station serve as
                                            146.
our partner in upholding our commitment to help other people.

Thank you very much.

Sincerely yours,

James Carter
City Representative

143. (A) vehicle
(B) time
(C) place
(D) equipment

144. (A) schedule
(B) scheduled
(C) has been scheduled
(D) are scheduled

145. (A) We are so sorry to refuse your participation this time.
(B) We consider your proposal very useful for producing our new radio program.
(C) There will be no exception to the participants.
(D) This way, you can still continue to host your activities.

146. (A) appreciating
(B) appreciated
(C) appreciative
(D) appreciation

PART 5

Directions: A word or phrase is missing in each of the sentences below. Four answer choices are given below each sentence. Select the best answer to complete the sentence. Then mark the letter (A), (B), (C), or (D) on your answer sheet.

101. A list of restaurant owners that participated in this year's slow food festival ------- on the desk next to the cabinet.
(A) will be finding
(B) can be found
(C) are finding
(D) can find

102. All customers are requested to express their meal ------- by marking their selection on the menu.
(A) prefers
(B) preferable
(C) preferences
(D) preferential

103. As snow was expected, the organizers ------- the customer dinner to the reception hall.
(A) have been moved
(B) will be moved
(C) moved
(D) were moved

104. If it has been longer than 7 business days and your order ------- has not arrived, please contact customer service via email.
(A) yet
(B) already
(C) still
(D) nearly

105. MARU Convention Center has the latest audio and visual equipment ------- all of its conference rooms.
(A) into
(B) on
(C) before
(D) in

106. Eloise Peter's design for the community center was ------- regarded by all members of the planning committee.
(A) higher
(B) high
(C) highest
(D) highly

107. All River Side apartments are ------- with an environment-friendly heating and cooling system.
(A) equip
(B) equipping
(C) equipped
(D) equipment

108. The ------- of the new task force team is to find more efficient methods to improve employee productivity.
(A) mission
(B) attitude
(C) benefit
(D) reason

109. Each management workshop is limited to 20 participants and is accepted on a first-come, first-served -------.
(A) view
(B) focus
(C) custom
(D) basis

110. Due to ------- decisions made by the brilliant CEO Eddie Max, Myer Flex has raised its yearly sales to 3 million dollars.
(A) strategic
(B) contented
(C) voted
(D) unanimous

111. Luis Nam's presentation was so impressive ------- the transit committee swiftly approved his plan.
(A) which
(B) that
(C) what
(D) during

112. Terry Johns visited the Taiwan factory only ------- before he returned to his company's headquarters.
(A) exactly
(B) easily
(C) briefly
(D) widely

113. As one of its policies, the management of Bruce Art Museum reminds all of its visitors to refrain ------- using their camera while they are inside the establishment.
(A) from
(B) with
(C) through
(D) between

114. For commercial vehicles, tires designed for winter conditions are a must as they ensure that bad weather will not ------- deliveries.
(A) interfere with
(B) depend on
(C) fall behind
(D) correspond to

115. In order to have a fun and rewarding trip, it is important that you dress appropriately and have the proper -------.
(A) equipping
(B) equipment
(C) equipped
(D) equip

116. Most meteorologists say that increasing temperatures make it ------- for sea levels to rise as much as 10cm in some areas.
(A) possible
(B) durable
(C) perfect
(D) allowable

117. Remodelling of Sunrise Gallery will ------- begin as soon as a construction company is chosen.
(A) lately
(B) previously
(C) probably
(D) almost

118. Although laptops ------- desktops for the past several years, desktops certainly still dominate the modern office workstations.
(A) have been outselling
(B) are outsold
(C) will be outselling
(D) would have been outsold

119. As City Councilman, Rick continues to oversee many important city building projects including the ------- opened aquatic centre and central park.
(A) recently
(B) unanimously
(C) directly
(D) typically

120. LINC Consulting Office staff members are prohibited from parking their cars in the restricted area ------- prior approval.
(A) due to
(B) as opposed to
(C) except
(D) without

GO ON TO THE NEXT PAGE

121. The CEO of Kanasaki Bicycle rides ------- bicycle to work three or four times a week from the west side of Australia.
(A) him
(B) he
(C) his
(D) himself

122. The coupon holders should note that these are non-transferable coupons, which can only be used by the owner, ------- must provide identification when redeemed.
(A) who
(B) which
(C) whom
(D) whose

123. Nokis Mobile has launched a new application that ------- its customers to a get a discount on their bills if they are willing to view advertisements on their mobile phones.
(A) allowed
(B) was allowed
(C) will allow
(D) allow

124. Employees at Brady Plum Inc. should complete sixteen training sessions so as to gain ------- to the company's database.
(A) access
(B) advance
(C) approach
(D) routine

125. Star Bike is a nation-wide distributor selling high quality, yet ------- bicycling products.
(A) unaware
(B) inexpensive
(C) undecided
(D) incomplete

126. KP Package Design and its staff are ------- researching new technologies and ways to improve existing ones.
(A) continual
(B) continue
(C) continues
(D) continually

127. Ms. Peche believes that she is the most ------- person to lead the research project because she has twelve years of prior experience.
(A) qualifying
(B) qualified
(C) qualification
(D) qualifiable

128. This product has been successful in the Asian market but should be changed to ------- the European market.
(A) call out
(B) demand
(C) update
(D) appeal to

129. Preliminary data from Jason Travel Research indicates ------- in Massachusetts has been steadily regaining popularity since September 2019.
(A) tourism
(B) toured
(C) tours
(D) tourists

130. Many travel agencies are increasing their ------- because the airline companies are limiting commission to their vendors.
(A) rating
(B) to rate
(C) rated
(D) rates

PART 6

Directions: Read the texts that follow. A word, phrase, or sentence is missing in parts of each text. Four answer choices for each question are given below the text. Select the best answer to complete the text. Then mark the letter (A), (B), (C), or (D) on your answer sheet.

Questions 131-134 refer to the following article.

------- .
131.

------- a Ph.D. in petroleum extraction, Mr. Smith began working in the industry with some of the
132.
biggest companies more than a decade ago. He established ------- by discovering new, highly
133.
profitable methods of oil extraction in deposits long considered depleted.

------- he has joined Collin Minerals, he can again use his unique methods to tap North
134.
America's vast energy reserves, which until now have remained locked deep beneath the earth.

131. (A) Simon Smith has been appointed
head of exploration of Collin Minerals,
a pioneering firm in oil energy
markets.
(B) Collin Minerals announced Simon
Smith's decision to resign.
(C) Collin Minerals has expanded into oil
energy markets in Europe.
(D) There were a lot of challenges in
pioneering oil markets.

132. (A) To complete
(B) Completed
(C) Having been completed
(D) Having completed

133. (A) he
(B) his
(C) his own
(D) himself

134. (A) So that
(B) Since
(C) By the time
(D) Although

GO ON TO THE NEXT PAGE

Harriot Hanson

2043 Terra Cotta Street

Fairmount, MN 58030

USA

We ------- received your email in which you expressed interest in becoming a member of our
135.
exciting sales team. We are always looking for talented and eager people to join our workforce

and would be ------- to look over your application.
136.

All sales representative applicants are asked to mail us their resumes and cover letter -------
137.
why they wish to join our team. We will contact you to schedule an interview shortly thereafter.

-------. Please take a sufficient amount of time to prepare for the interview.
138.

Sincerely,

Jessie Swanton

Sales Department Manager

Qframe Inc.

135. (A) kindly
(B) closely
(C) recently
(D) regretfully

136. (A) pleased
(B) pleasing
(C) pleasant
(D) please

137. (A) updating
(B) planning
(C) notifying
(D) explaining

138. (A) We already knew about previous careers.
(B) You are scheduled to start your work on September 9.
(C) We would like to know what skills you can bring to our sales department.
(D) Interview strategies will be addressed in those sessions.

Questions 139-142 refer to the following memo.

As our new office space ------- customers the ability to see our floor, management has
                              139.
determined that the employee dress code should be revised to reflect the professionalism we
wish to convey.

-------, starting immediately, all employees will be required to wear business attire when in the
140.
office. For men, that means a suit and a tie. Women must wear a skirt and blouse.

Casual Fridays are now cancelled. Furthermore, tags with your name and title must be worn at
all -------. -------.
    141.   142.

139. (A) giving
(B) given
(C) has been given
(D) will give

140. (A) Therefore
(B) Instead
(C) On the other hand
(D) Moreover

141. (A) time
(B) times
(C) timing
(D) timed

142. (A) From now on, you should present
your name tag to the security guard
to enter the facilities.
(B) These will be provided by your
supervisor.
(C) Also, some of the safety regulations
will be revised by next week.
(D) Your personnel information should be
updated accordingly.

GO ON TO THE NEXT PAGE

According to some records, the average oil production at major oil companies went down from the expected 6.5 to 3.29 million barrels of oil per day. -------. As a result, prices have increased
143.
tremendously, ------- in a global economic crisis. -------, car companies are cautiously -------
144.   **145.**   **146.**
about the future. Despite the change in oil prices worldwide, car manufacturers are not directly affected by it because many car owners nowadays are driving energy efficient vehicles.

143. (A) This is because of the increasing number of the travellers who use airplanes.
(B) However, many experts expect that their production rate will be accelerated.
(C) Oil is a useful resource in operating airplanes.
(D) Therefore, the supply of oil is insufficient to meet international demand.

144. (A) resulted
(B) resulting
(C) results
(D) have resulted

145. (A) Nevertheless
(B) In addition
(C) After that
(D) To this end

146. (A) confident
(B) optimistic
(C) frustrated
(D) confused

PART 5

Directions: A word or phrase is missing in each of the sentences below. Four answer choices are given below each sentence. Select the best answer to complete the sentence. Then mark the letter (A), (B), (C), or (D) on your answer sheet.

101. Since 2019, Mr. Leon has ------- as the Vice President, and is the person most responsible for all aspects of marketing.
(A) served
(B) regarded
(C) involved
(D) implemented

102. ------- Nexus Corporation is the smallest construction company in the province, it is the most successful.
(A) Until
(B) So
(C) How
(D) While

103. The ------- of Ray's restaurant and Sohee's Cafe has led to a higher number of visitors to shops in the area.
(A) popularize
(B) popularly
(C) popularity
(D) popular

104. The president of Jake Motors has ------- that the company has improved worker productivity significantly while reducing operating costs.
(A) applied
(B) joined
(C) notified
(D) announced

105. Heal Literature Monthly's new advertising campaign has resulted in a ------- 45 percent increase in the number of subscribers over the last five months.
(A) rigid
(B) receptive
(C) remarkable
(D) perpetual

106. Those who have been let go of are reminded to go to the personnel office ------- their last day of work to return all hotel property.
(A) into
(B) from
(C) before
(D) around

107. Please contact the company's security manager when preparations ------- for the installation of the new central cooling system.
(A) be made
(B) made
(C) have been made
(D) will make

GO ON TO THE NEXT PAGE

108. Ms. Eloise watches all our gauges ------- so that she can ensure accurate humidity records.
(A) personalize
(B) personable
(C) personally
(D) personal

109. With just two weeks remaining before South Bank's annual festival, the organizing committee has ------- to decide the parade route.
(A) already
(B) yet
(C) finally
(D) never

110. ------- the firm's work schedule is now posted on its website, we will no longer distribute paper copies.
(A) Besides
(B) Regardless of
(C) In the event of
(D) Since

111. The new software program can ------- organizations to share information more quickly and efficiently.
(A) refuse
(B) acquire
(C) except
(D) enable

112. Customers at our Hamilton branch know that our warehouse always has products ------- want in stock.
(A) them
(B) their
(C) themselves
(D) they

113. Aside from some minor setbacks with the design team, the first edition of the book is ------- to be printed.
(A) readiness
(B) readily
(C) ready
(D) readies

114. ------- company regulations, female employees who will go on maternity leave must obtain their supervisor's permission two weeks in advance.
(A) In accordance with
(B) On behalf of
(C) As soon as
(D) Prior to

115. ------- the product that was delivered not be the correct one, please send it back to us in the original packaging or bring it to a retail outlet for exchange.
(A) If
(B) Should
(C) Had
(D) Whether

116. The price of coffee beans doubled, and coffee chains increased ------- prices accordingly to cover the costs.
(A) their
(B) themselves
(C) them
(D) they

117. ------- editing content for Limited Publishers, Showna Kim is a correspondent for the Weekly Head newspaper.
(A) Together
(B) Moreover
(C) Otherwise
(D) In addition to

118. According to National Gas Agency, the gap between demand and supply will ------- decrease and then the price is likely to rise.
(A) recently
(B) soon
(C) extremely
(D) lately

119. According to our policies, requests for changes to the membership account must be submitted ------- writing within 30 days.
(A) on
(B) through
(C) in
(D) at

120. If you plan to visit the civic center downtown, taking one of the public transportation systems such as the bus or subway is much more ------- than driving as parking is very expensive.
(A) economics
(B) economical
(C) economy
(D) economically

121. Mr. Eddie Retuna will have to complete all remaining work in the project -------, because her supervisor, Ms. Watson, is going on vacation next week.
(A) herself
(B) her
(C) she
(D) hers

122. It is important that you make ------- records of all transactions and make sure that they are kept safe and in an orderly manner.
(A) accurate
(B) distant
(C) caring
(D) refunded

123. Deposits received after 5:30 P.M. on business days ------- credited to your account on the next business day.
(A) being
(B) will be
(C) was
(D) to be

124. Please note that this document serves only as a guideline and Northern Service should ------- be contacted for full details and an accurate quotation.
(A) than
(B) exactly
(C) always
(D) evenly

125. Tickets to Shark's concert sold so fast that the concert hall was moved from C.P Theater to Metro Concert Hall to ------- a larger audience.
(A) conduct
(B) accommodate
(C) develop
(D) broadcast

126. Computer technology has made it possible for businesses to process information more ------- and at a faster rate.
(A) efficiency
(B) efficient
(C) efficiencies
(D) efficiently

127. Tippi Hedren Arts is ------- to have such tremendous talent as instructors.
(A) fortunate
(B) obvious
(C) encouraging
(D) skilled

128. Food that is produced ------- is one of the best choices for the environment and requires less transportation.
(A) locally
(B) locals
(C) locality
(D) local

129. The overseas manager will approve issuance of a company cellular phone for any foreign sales ------- who signs up for one.
(A) representative
(B) representatively
(C) representation
(D) represent

130. A project plan is currently being prepared for a 13-kilometer ------- of the new road from Leichard to Stich.
(A) stretch
(B) proximity
(C) journey
(D) duration

GO ON TO THE NEXT PAGE

PART 6

Directions: Read the texts that follow. A word, phrase, or sentence is missing in parts of each text. Four answer choices for each question are given below the text. Select the best answer to complete the text. Then mark the letter (A), (B), (C), or (D) on your answer sheet.

Questions 131-134 refer to the following e-mail.

To: All staff

From: Emily Reynold

Date: Wednesday, December 26

Subject: Printer supplies and printer repair

I am writing this e-mail to inform you that the deadline for ------- supplies for the printer in your
131.
office, such as paper, ink, and toner cartridges, is on Friday, December 29.

In addition, please take note ------- for printers requiring repair, you have to fill out a form and
132.
submit it to the maintenance department. -------. ------- cannot be processed without receiving
133. **134.**
the documentation you need to complete.

After submitting the document, you will receive a call, and a service technician will visit your
office, either to repair your machine or replace the unit if needed. If you have any questions,
please contact me during office hours.

131. (A) order
(B) ordered
(C) ordering
(D) orders

132. (A) that
(B) them
(C) with
(D) when

133. (A) Without it, your requests for the
reimbursement will be denied.
(B) It was distributed to anyone who
attended that session.
(C) It is necessary to explain why you
are requesting those printers to be
purchased.
(D) You can download the form through
our company website, or you can get
one from me personally.

134. (A) Requests
(B) Proposals
(C) Substitutes
(D) Materials

Dear Mr. Anderson,

I would like to verify my bill at your resort. I was charged more than I expected. When I checked my credit card bill the other day, I noticed that an item was charged to my bill twice.

This could be my boat ride on September 8, which cost $ 50.00 per hour ride. The amount indicated on my bill was $ 870, but when I checked it again, my total ------- $ 820. I paid for my
135.
ride in cash to a woman named Amanda Baeck. She even gave me a receipt. For some reason, I think one of your hotel employees charged it again to my credit card. -------.
136.

-------, I would like to ask that you make the necessary ------- to my billing to reflect the correct
137.   **138.**
amount of my bill. Thank you.

Yours truly,

Robert Henry

135. (A) should have been
(B) must be
(C) will be
(D) could have been

136. (A) I was not, therefore, satisfied with the way you manage your billing system.
(B) Here is my suggestion to improve your customer service.
(C) They must have been well trained by the experts.
(D) So, I want it to be all cancelled with my previous orders.

137. (A) Even so
(B) Instead
(C) In view of this
(D) In case

138. (A) charge
(B) adjustment
(C) access
(D) replacement

GO ON TO THE NEXT PAGE

Questions 139-142 refer to the following job announcement.

Intersil Corp.

Marketing Manager

-------. The ideal candidate must be able to assist the marketing team in ------- promoting the
139.   **140.**
company's products to potential customers.

Qualified applicants must possess a bachelor's degree in marketing or a related field. Marketing
related graduate study is preferred. At least five years of work experience, excellent market
analysis skills, superior communication skills, and the ability to handle a variety of assignments
------- are required for the position.
141.

Intersil Corp. only accepts online applications. Interested candidates can ------- their réesumée
                                                                          142.
and salary expectations to Andea Bucket mkelly@Intersil.com before October 30.

139. (A) We are pleased to offer you a
marketing manager position in Intersil
Corp.
(B) Intersil Corp. is planning to open a
second branch in Texas.
(C) Intersil Corp. is accepting
applications for the position of
marketing manager.
(D) Intersil Corp. appreciate you applying
for the Marketing Manager position.

140. (A) effective
(B) effectively
(C) effectiveness
(D) effect

141. (A) simultaneously
(B) potentially
(C) inconclusively
(D) patiently

142. (A) place
(B) forward
(C) renew
(D) calculate

Questions 143-146 refer to the following article.

For many years, Oklahoma City has been the capital of theatrical plays. This might be because many students choose a theatrical course or other related majors in college. A few years after graduating, these people are now ------- their achievements in the field of entertainment.
143.

Truly, the quality of shows has gradually increased over the years, with plays ------- than ever
144.
with audiences. In fact, famous plays such as Ms. Taylor's The Crusade and Mr. Joshua's The Korean Way have received several awards and constructive reviews from international critics.
-------. For instance, Ms. Juana Wood directed a show that lost $ 100,000.
145.

-------, many stage directors still become rich and famous because of their talent in directing.
146.

143. (A) recognized for
(B) transferred to
(C) promoted to
(D) criticized by

144. (A) popular
(B) more popular
(C) more popularities
(D) more popularly

145. (A) They are renowned for critically acclaimed novels.
(B) In addition to them, there are a lot of creative and reputable directors.
(C) However, a few shows received negative opinions from many critics.
(D) After graduating, many people have decided to begin their careers as stage directors.

146. (A) In spite of that
(B) Whereas
(C) As far as
(D) In other words

PART 5

Directions: A word or phrase is missing in each of the sentences below. Four answer choices are given below each sentence. Select the best answer to complete the sentence. Then mark the letter (A), (B), (C), or (D) on your answer sheet.

101. Before stepping out of the office, Mr. Morbos ------- his budget proposal for the next fiscal year on his supervisor's desk.
(A) waited
(B) remained
(C) left
(D) offered

102. Following are the various suggestions that ------- by survey respondents.
(A) had been indicating
(B) were indicated
(C) has indicated
(D) are indicating

103. While the headquarters is -------, most work at Wide Steel Corporate should be conducted at the Wony Office Building.
(A) to renovate
(B) renovation
(C) being renovated
(D) renovate

104. The regulations revised by the manager of the marketing department list all the ------- which employees should observe in case of emergency.
(A) guidelines
(B) facilities
(C) functions
(D) inquiries

105. In some cases, we may need to cancel items from your order if they are discontinued and we have ------- in stock.
(A) none
(B) most
(C) finally
(D) even

106. When leaving for a vacation, give your coworkers ------- instructions about how to take care of the sales calls in your absence.
(A) clear
(B) blank
(C) entire
(D) repetitive

107. The recent increase in interest rates has made it more difficult for consumers to ------- home loans.
(A) implement
(B) cement
(C) obtain
(D) review

108. ------ buying products online is convenient, most consumers continue to value the experience of shopping in store.
(A) Rather
(B) Regarding
(C) Except
(D) Although

109. Place the copies of the receipt on Mr. John's desk when ------- are done copying them.
(A) yours
(B) your own
(C) you
(D) yourself

110. On account of recent price increases, nonessential purchases of all office supplies ------- until further notice.
(A) will be deferred
(B) have deferred
(C) have been deferring
(D) are deferring

111. Transport England has released new safety guidelines ------- the use of drone aircraft, which people use for recreation.
(A) either
(B) for
(C) and
(D) so

112. The project team members have come up with a slight ------- to an existing solar technology to make it even more efficient.
(A) modification
(B) modifying
(C) to modify
(D) modified

113. In accordance with company regulations, hospitality expenses are not considered ------- for reimbursement.
(A) considerable
(B) useful
(C) complete
(D) appropriate

114. Unfortunately, the stadium is located on a red train line and not ------- enough to a grand station.
(A) closer
(B) closed
(C) close
(D) closest

115. The Department offers support to children who have a disability, through a ------- of programs targeted to meet their specific needs.
(A) deposit
(B) range
(C) manner
(D) kind

116. Dessert may be added as an option for an additional ------- to the set menu prices.
(A) money
(B) information
(C) charge
(D) interest

117. Joe has been a key contributor to our company's growth and we would like to thank him publicly for his years of service and for ------- dedication.
(A) himself
(B) he
(C) him
(D) his

118. The Texas Redevelopment Authority recently approved Journey Development's proposal ------- a parking lot in South Texas into a vibrant residential and commercial complex.
(A) transformation
(B) is transforming
(C) have transformed
(D) to transform

119. Please keep in mind that all product orders are ------- to cancellation unless payment is received at least seventy two hours prior to the shipping date.
(A) subject
(B) eligible
(C) reluctant
(D) likely

GO ON TO THE NEXT PAGE

120. ------- in Paris, Paris Airlines operates flights all over France as well as some international destinations.
(A) Remained
(B) Based
(C) Stored
(D) Moved

121. If you need to make any ------- to your order, you can remove an item in the cart by clicking the 'X.'
(A) conversions
(B) commissions
(C) announcements
(D) adjustments

122. Heat and humidity can ------- lots of items, such as electronics, musical instruments, and antique furniture.
(A) damages
(B) damage
(C) damaging
(D) damaged

123. Directors have to address a few barriers if they want their employees to work together -------.
(A) productively
(B) productivity
(C) productive
(D) productiveness

124. In case of emergencies such as fire, all hotel guests are requested to stay in their rooms ------- directed to evacuate by hotel employees.
(A) while
(B) unless
(C) whereas
(D) unlike

125. We regret to inform you that K4 Shuttle Service is not ------- for lost or stolen items.
(A) responsibility
(B) response
(C) responsive
(D) responsible

126. The specific terms and conditions of agreement for the merger of the two giant auto makers are ------- under consideration.
(A) more current
(B) current
(C) most current
(D) currently

127. Miyaki, who along with the three other assistant superintendents ------- attends every board meeting, did not attend the last meeting.
(A) typically
(B) equally
(C) recently
(D) well

128. The device is one of the most important systems of a modern wind turbine, and it requires considerable -------.
(A) maintained
(B) maintains
(C) maintenance
(D) maintain

129. To ------- the registration process on your first visit, you may fill in your information below prior to coming in to our office.
(A) relieve
(B) acquire
(C) expedite
(D) equip

130. ------- better serve our valued customers in Europe, we are pleased to announce the opening of our branch office in Germany.
(A) In order to
(B) With regard to
(C) Notwithstanding
(D) Due to

PART 6

Directions: Read the texts that follow. A word, phrase, or sentence is missing in parts of each text. Four answer choices for each question are given below the text. Select the best answer to complete the text. Then mark the letter (A), (B), (C), or (D) on your answer sheet.

Questions 131-134 refer to the following article.

Maryland (June 2) – During the Summer Festival, the city government is planning to ------- the
131.
entry of vehicles into the National Capital Park where the festivities will be held.

From June 7 to 11, no vehicles will be allowed to enter the park except for buses. This rule will
be in effect during the whole duration of the festival in order to prevent traffic congestion -------
132.
the National Capital Park.

-------. Another option to reach the venue is to use the public transportation system, ------- to
133.   **134.**
accommodate a great number of local and foreign tourists expected to come to witness the
festival highlights.

131. (A) restrict
(B) make
(C) take
(D) enhance

132. (A) between
(B) on
(C) around
(D) after

133. (A) As a result, you should find alternative
routes to commute to your work
during that period.
(B) To this end, authorities decided to
extend the operating hours of the
public transportation.
(C) Therefore, drivers and passengers
who use private vehicles should park
their cars outside the park and walk
to the National Capital Park.
(D) There are many ways to participate in
the festival as a volunteer.

134. (A) equipment
(B) is equipped
(C) equipped
(D) equips

GO ON TO THE NEXT PAGE

Questions 135-138 refer to the following letter.

Dear Sir:

This is in reference to the news article in Every News on January 13 related to the sale of a stolen motor vehicle at the QM Motors Incorporation.

QM Motors Incorporation is a registered and well-established company that ------- by all laws of
135.
the country and is engaged in used car sales. Through the years, QM Motors Incorporation has constantly conducted business in accordance with the provisions of the law and has maintained the highest degree of legal and ethical standards in the conduct of its business. -------, QM
136.
Motors Incorporation has never engaged in a transaction contrary to the law, such as that ------- in your newspaper. A large number of QM Motors Incorporation customers can testify to
137.
our high level of professionalism.

-------. We would like to restore the excellent reputation of QM Motors Incorporation.
138.

Thank you very much for your attention to this matter.

Sincerely yours,

Ms. Charlotte Stanley
Counsel Officer
QM Motors Incorporation

---

135. (A) abides
(B) complies
(C) observes
(D) conforms

136. (A) Since then
(B) Even so
(C) For this reason
(D) In contrast to this

137. (A) was printed
(B) printer
(C) printed
(D) to be printed

138. (A) Most of our investors are among our regular customers.
(B) So, let me recommend a professional technician for the position.
(C) We are offering them loyal customer benefits as a token of our appreciation.
(D) Therefore, we request that you publish a retraction and apology in your newspaper column.

Questions 139-142 refer to the following advertisement.

Trendy Hotstyle, the newest magazine to be published in Geralton, welcomes freelance writers to contribute articles ------- local events. To be a contributor, a college degree is not required, but excellent writing skills are necessary.
139.

The magazine will also pay for articles submitted by experienced writers and ------- with high quality submissions.
140.

-------. However, permission of the author will be asked first before an important part of the
141.
article ------- by the editors.
142.

For more information, feel free to send an e-mail to editor@trendyhotstyle.com.

139. (A) pertaining to
(B) belonging to
(C) submitted to
(D) subscribing to

140. (A) these
(B) those
(C) both
(D) whose

141. (A) As always, the magazine will edit submissions to ensure that the grammar is correct and the meaning is clear.
(B) The magazine has a right to keep all profits from distribution.
(C) Articles submitted should contain at least 300 letters.
(D) Payments will be credited to their accounts by the end of the month.

142. (A) was changed
(B) is changed
(C) will be changed
(D) will be changing

GO ON TO THE NEXT PAGE

Questions 143-146 refer to the following e-mail.

TO: Erick Miller <miller@mail.net>

FROM: Mark Denver<mdenver@tsd.org>

DATE: Monday, March 10

SUBJECT: Training Classes

Dear Mr. Alexander,

We would like to thank you for ------- for two of our training courses. Your enrollment for the
143.
oil sampling class for March 27 has been confirmed. -------, due to the unfortunate fact that
144.
only a few people enrolled in the May 1 class you wish to enroll in, we have to remove it from

the schedule. Our policy requires us ------- classes that have not reached at least 40 percent
145.
capacity. -------. Ms. Oswin will be teaching the same class, and there are still openings for that
146.
class. If you wish to register, please inform us by sending me an e-mail as soon as you can.

143. (A) applying
(B) subscribing
(C) contributing
(D) approaching

144. (A) Therefore
(B) Instead
(C) In that case
(D) However

145. (A) cancel
(B) canceled
(C) to cancel
(D) that cancel

146. (A) For that reason, we changed the instructor.
(B) The class you enrolled in is scheduled to be opened next month because of the instructor's health problems.
(C) But as the class schedule indicates, there is another date.
(D) You should have registered for the class which was suitable for your level.

PART 5

Directions: A word or phrase is missing in each of the sentences below. Four answer choices are given below each sentence. Select the best answer to complete the sentence. Then mark the letter (A), (B), (C), or (D) on your answer sheet.

101. Daily News Quantified ------- business news and market data from over 2,300 of the most market-impacting daily news items.
(A) analyzes
(B) analyze
(C) to analyze
(D) analyzer

102. Generally speaking, scientists have developed four ------- methods of determining the age of the earth.
(A) difference
(B) differences
(C) differently
(D) different

103. We are always ------- to deliver our products in the London Tube area at a time that is convenient for you.
(A) complete
(B) rich
(C) ready
(D) skilful

104. You can take this medication ------- as directed by your physician.
(A) finely
(B) mistakenly
(C) only
(D) closely

105. From 10 A.M. to 2 P.M., scenic boat rides ------- the Seine River will be offered for free at the city's waterfront.
(A) below
(B) among
(C) apart
(D) along

106. A filter removes harmful foreign substances from the water -------, so further purification processing is not required.
(A) chemicals
(B) chemist
(C) chemical
(D) chemically

107. All arriving passengers are required to have valid travel ------- including passport and visa.
(A) documented
(B) document
(C) documents
(D) documenting

108. Direct Deposit is now mandatory for all employees, so if you have not yet submitted a direct deposit request form, you must do so -------.
(A) immediately
(B) formerly
(C) clearly
(D) almost

GO ON TO THE NEXT PAGE

109. To ------- safety on the job, each employee is expected to use all personal protective equipment provided.
(A) ensure
(B) protect
(C) insure
(D) assure

110. Lakeview Pictures offers internships to applicants ------- want to acquire work experience in a photo studio.
(A) themselves
(B) whom
(C) whoever
(D) who

111. The questionnaire indicated that businesses in the food industry are ------- optimistic about future prospects.
(A) fairly
(B) fair
(C) fairest
(D) fairness

112. ------- the heavy rain, more than a hundred people formed in a long line in front of the store on the opening day of our new Brisbane store.
(A) Despite
(B) Nevertheless
(C) Due to
(D) Because

113. Customer reports of damaged goods must be made ------- two working days from date of delivery, or a claim cannot be processed.
(A) against
(B) since
(C) within
(D) into

114. Network connections which clearly ------- and speed up working procedures are a must in the industrial world today.
(A) simplify
(B) simple
(C) simplicity
(D) simply

115. W&W is a company ------- strong-willed, driven individuals are rewarded and recognized.
(A) then
(B) where
(C) which
(D) that

116. There has been a ------- improvement in agricultural productivity, which has increased incomes for a number of farmers.
(A) multiple
(B) crowded
(C) respective
(D) marked

117. To repair your transmission problems, you must have a great deal of echanical -------.
(A) timing
(B) decision
(C) importance
(D) expertise

118. Alexix Muttoni, who works at the ------- acclaimed Madrine's Coffee, is the recipient of this year's Outstanding Barista Award.
(A) critically
(B) criticism
(C) critical
(D) criticized

119. We have to wait ------- evaluate Mr. Wilson's ability until we have heard back from all his co-workers.
(A) toward
(B) to
(C) on
(D) for

120. When applying for reimbursement of travel expenses ------- less than $ 18, don't itemize it in your report.
(A) totalled
(B) being totalled
(C) will total
(D) totalling

121. The feasibility of constructing a connecting bridge between the two islands has been ------- researched and the results have been posted at www.contractors.org.
(A) permanently
(B) consecutively
(C) extensively
(D) roughly

122. El Najhad is a three-time recipient of an award at Oxford for ------- in teaching economic history.
(A) excellent
(B) excellence
(C) excelled
(D) excel

123. Yamakasi Motors guarantees its repairs for four years, so feel free to contact the service desk if you have ------- problems.
(A) any
(B) many
(C) no
(D) all

124. The president of the company ------- the opening ceremony which will be held in the conference hall of the Lakeview Hotel.
(A) attends
(B) attended
(C) will attend
(D) will be attended

125. The housing shortage this year in Beaverton County is more serious than ------- experienced last year.
(A) this
(B) those
(C) these
(D) that

126. Environmental activists have advocated the use of more diverse energy sources ------- solar, wind and hydrogen power.
(A) equally
(B) similarly
(C) likewise
(D) such as

127. The candidate for the Hawk Media manager position will ------- excellent communication skills and a positive attitude.
(A) assign
(B) state
(C) review
(D) possess

128. According to the U.K. Department of Labour, employees must receive additional pay when ------- work in excess of 38 hours a week.
(A) they
(B) them
(C) their
(D) theirs

129. After much -------, the committee would like to recommend the following project to be funded.
(A) deliberated
(B) deliberate
(C) deliberately
(D) deliberation

130. At the A.U. Postal Service, mail is sorted by automated equipment, therefore, it is important for your mail to be addressed -------.
(A) corrected
(B) correctly
(C) correct
(D) correcting

GO ON TO THE NEXT PAGE

Directions: Read the texts that follow. A word, phrase, or sentence is missing in parts of each text. Four answer choices for each question are given below the text. Select the best answer to complete the text. Then mark the letter (A), (B), (C), or (D) on your answer sheet.

Questions 131-134 refer to the following e-mail.

From: Mary Fitzherbert

To: Maria Clare

Date: December 8

Subject: Change of plans

Hi, Maria

I was informed earlier today that I have been chosen to attend a mortgage advisor training seminar which ------- on Fridays in March and April from 9:00 A.M. to 12:00 P.M. -------, I will
131.   132.
not be able to cover for you on Fridays after all. However, I can still fill in for you on some of the Tuesday hours while you are out of the office as we have already agreed upon.

I will be on vacation leave this week, so Peter and I have discussed this matter already today.
-------. Please send Peter an e-mail if this ------- is okay with you.
133.   134.

131. (A) was held
(B) are held
(C) will be held
(D) held

132. (A) As such
(B) Because
(C) Instead
(D) Furthermore

133. (A) But he was also scheduled to fly to the Arizona headquarters on those Fridays.
(B) We decided to recruit a new assistant to help promote our mortgage products.
(C) He mentioned that he can fill in for you on those Friday hours as well as the Tuesdays he originally volunteered for.
(D) He said that it is possible to work overtime on Tuesday.

134. (A) flight
(B) arrangement
(C) compensation
(D) replacement

Questions 135-138 refer to the following article.

Airline Merger Leaves Passengers Perplexed

San Francisco (November 10) - A merger of two airlines caused confusion after the computer system for the joined companies failed. Chaos broke out when only the names of passengers of General Airlines appeared on the screen.

As a result, boarding passes had to be issued manually to those who booked with Vita Air, and ------- were rescheduled. -------.
    135.   **136.**

This shows that despite prior experience, no precautionary measures were put in place ------- the same kind of mishap from happening again.
                                                             137.

"Computer analysts are ------- the cause of the problem and will submit a complete report
                                138.
soon, along with a recommendation," said the airline spokesperson.

135. (A) workers
    (B) tickets
    (C) flights
    (D) bills

136. (A) However, as soon as we implemented a new program, scheduling conflicts no longer occurred.
    (B) Passengers who have complaints regarding this problem may claim proper compensation.
    (C) You need to provide us detailed information to claim your lost bags in the airport.
    (D) This problem has been encountered by several airline companies that have merged.

137. (A) to prevent
    (B) to be prevented
    (C) prevents
    (D) preventing

138. (A) removing
    (B) investigating
    (C) contacting
    (D) protecting

GO ON TO THE NEXT PAGE

To: Josephine Charms

From: International Organization of Seafarers

Date: January 4

Subject: Approval of Your Application

Dear Josephine,

Welcome and thank you for joining the International Organization of Seafarers. This organization ------- the rights and promotes the welfare of people working on sea vessels.
139.

Our ------- mission is to extend help to seafarers who encounter problems while in foreign ports.
140.
We provide them some means to contact their families, transportation so that they can visit shopping areas or medical facilities, and counselling when needed.

------- the services mentioned, we have a web site that features up-to-date information on
141.
international laws and policies. Also, -------.
142.

We welcome the opportunity to assist you and safeguard your welfare. Thanks again for joining our organization.

---

139. (A) supports
(B) supporting
(C) supported
(D) having supported

140. (A) previous
(B) primary
(C) early
(D) eager

141. (A) Aside from
(B) In spite of
(C) Due to
(D) According to

142. (A) You can find the form that needs to be completed before you join.
(B) If you want to see that information, you should enroll as a member of the association.
(C) We have attached a document that explains the benefits of membership in this association.
(D) These are requirements for the access of confidential documents.

Questions 143-146 refer to the following letter.

Defaunt- Nestene Banking Corporation

December 22

Rebecca Moore

3rd Avenue

Geraldton, West Australia 6530

Dear Ms. Marzonia,

You might have read in yesterday's newspaper that Defaunt Savings Bank and Nestene Finance Corporation are joining forces to serve you more efficiently. As of December 10, these two institutions -------.
     143.

Our new name is Defaunt-Nestene Banking Corporation. -------. -------, you can anticipate an
                                                        144. **145.**
increase in the range of products you can use.

Please take time to read the brochure that comes with this letter so that you can familiarize yourself with some of our new -------.
                                      146.

For more information with regard to all of our products, visit our web site (www.dnbc.com). We always look forward to serving you.

---

143. (A) will merge
  (B) can merge
  (C) have merged
  (D) is to merge

144. (A) We assure you that no changes will be made to your accounts.
  (B) Our new headquarters will be located on the site where the former city hall was.
  (C) Nestene has lost its business to competitors over the last three years.
  (D) We are in consultation with the union to increase work hours.

145. (A) However
  (B) For instance
  (C) As such
  (D) Furthermore

146. (A) offerings
  (B) employees
  (C) locations
  (D) titles

PART 5

Directions: A word or phrase is missing in each of the sentences below. Four answer choices are given below each sentence. Select the best answer to complete the sentence. Then mark the letter (A), (B), (C), or (D) on your answer sheet.

101. ------- to the Moharvi Building should first register at the main security desk.
(A) Visiting
(B) Visitors
(C) Visit
(D) To visit

102. Our clinic is located inside David Johns Mall which has ample parking spaces and is easily ------- by public transit.
(A) accessibility
(B) accessibly
(C) access
(D) accessible

103. Mishellan Library will be ------- from November 2 until December 22 while renovation works are carried out.
(A) paused
(B) closed
(C) nominated
(D) expired

104. The recently revised safety regulations ------- all the engineers wear safety helmets while working in the factory.
(A) assume
(B) mandate
(C) investigate
(D) organize

105. The addition of three assembly lines to its existing manufacturing plant is ------- of the growth occurring at Jake Corporation.
(A) substance
(B) evidence
(C) support
(D) appreciation

106. The latest software significantly ------- the number of hours needed for employees to finish the task.
(A) reduction
(B) to reduce
(C) reduced
(D) reducing

107. Applicants for the position of production manager must hand in a letter of ------- from previous supervisors.
(A) recommend
(B) recommending
(C) recommended
(D) recommendation

108. While the road is under construction, commuters are advised to use ------- when driving at night.
(A) cautions
(B) caution
(C) cautious
(D) cautiously

109. Errors found early in the development process can be fixed ------- easily than those identified toward the end.
(A) most
(B) more
(C) right
(D) very

110. Lampeter Inc. has ------- that applicants who have minimum 5 years of experience and knowledge of statistics will be considered for the managerial position.
(A) distinguished
(B) specified
(C) connected
(D) hired

111. The Tilamook Land Trust is dedicated to working ------- with landowners to conserve land for wildlife, scenic views, and local communities.
(A) cooperated
(B) cooperatively
(C) cooperate
(D) cooperative

112. Semiconductors were America's third-leading manufactured export in 2019 ------- only airplanes and automobiles.
(A) among
(B) toward
(C) without
(D) behind

113. Telecom network operators are expected ------- more than $ 50 billion from LTE 4G services in 2019, according to recent telecom market research.
(A) generating
(B) will generate
(C) generated
(D) to generate

114. Your reservation may be cancelled with a full refund, ------- notification of the cancellation is received in writing.
(A) provided that
(B) together with
(C) regardless of
(D) according to

115. When you register, you will have the opportunity to enter your ------- flight details on the registration form.
(A) preferentially
(B) preferred
(C) prefer
(D) preference

116. Romanson has a ------- of expertise across a number of sectors and the board is delighted with his appointment as new Chief Executive Officer.
(A) height
(B) fame
(C) wealth
(D) field

117. Each luggage tag is made of durable plastic with a flexible strap that can be ------- attached to any bag.
(A) security
(B) securely
(C) securing
(D) secure

118. The applicant must provide academic transcripts, three letters of recommendation, and three writing samples ------- the completed application.
(A) along with
(B) moreover
(C) however
(D) in addition

119. Everyone involved was greatly ------- of the new equipment that was needed to help the new trees thrive.
(A) appreciated
(B) appreciation
(C) appreciate
(D) appreciative

120. You can save ------- three percent on heating costs for every one degree you lower the thermostat.
(A) approximately
(B) consecutively
(C) substantially
(D) meticulously

GO ON TO THE NEXT PAGE

121. All employees are responsible for a safe and efficient working environment with ------- on a cooperative attitude with fellow workers.
(A) emphasized
(B) emphasize
(C) emphasizes
(D) emphasis

122. If your computer does not switch on, consult page 8 of the user's manual ------- calling a customer support center.
(A) along
(B) though
(C) during
(D) before

123. Research shows that parents who are artists often encourage ------- children to play a musical instrument.
(A) themselves
(B) their own
(C) them
(D) theirs

124. Leonardo Cario was nominated as Outstanding Employee of the Year after his marketing strategy led to an ------- 35 percent increase in company revenue.
(A) extraneous
(B) unprecedented
(C) anxious
(D) imminent

125. Food products must be handled and cooked in a ------- that keeps them from getting contaminated or spoiled.
(A) manner
(B) performance
(C) type
(D) behavior

126. Please e-mail your summary from this morning's board meeting to all managers ------- the end of the day.
(A) on
(B) of
(C) in
(D) at

127. To assemble the purchased wooden desk, you must ------- the instructions in the enclosed manual.
(A) feature
(B) follow
(C) look
(D) direct

128. If ------- enrolls in the management workshop, the session may be rescheduled.
(A) no one
(B) one another
(C) some
(D) few

129. Grocery stores in the area have started selling a wider variety of organic fruit and vegetables in ------- to customer demand.
(A) respond
(B) response
(C) responded
(D) responsive

130. Our call center is open 24 hours a day and our service crew can help you ------- you encounter car troubles.
(A) whomever
(B) whoever
(C) whatever
(D) whenever

PART 6

Directions: Read the texts that follow. A word, phrase, or sentence is missing in parts of each text. Four answer choices for each question are given below the text. Select the best answer to complete the text. Then mark the letter (A), (B), (C), or (D) on your answer sheet.

Questions 131-134 refer to the following information.

Part 3, Section D: Handsfree calling

The Altman Tablet PC has the capacity to store ------- 64GB of information.
131.

You can use your voice to give commands to your tablet PC by pushing the button that looks like a microphone. Different voice commands will appear, like finding maps, searching the Internet, or sending e-mail. -------. Commands must be given by one person because if there **132.** are several people recording, the tablet PC will not recognize ------- voice.
133.

Speak slowly and clearly when giving commands because if the words are not -------, the tablet **134.** PC will not do as ordered.

131. (A) up to
(B) as to
(C) except
(D) without

132. (A) To use the Internet, say the word or phrase that you are looking for and a web page will open.
(B) You need to be familiar with a new commander.
(C) What you have to do is just type the title of books you want to search for.
(D) However, the tablet PC doesn't have these features at all.

133. (A) its
(B) your
(C) more than one
(D) apart

134. (A) distinct
(B) technical
(C) identical
(D) prospective

GO ON TO THE NEXT PAGE

To: Rucino Publishing Employees

From: Abigail Greene

Subject: Annual Employment Survey Request

Date: August 13

We hope that all the expectations you have for every ------- of your employment at Rucino
135.
Publishing have been met, but we also know that our company still has room for improvement.

In line with this, we request you submit your annual feedback about our benefits, rules and

regulations, management and administrative systems, products, and marketing approaches.

The HR team requests that you complete the questionnaire for ------- satisfaction ------- August
136. **137.**
17. -------. To access the questionnaire provided by DDB Consulting on its web site, click here.
138.
Please be reminded that, as always, all your responses remain confidential, as the forms bear

no identifying information and are directly sent to third-party consultants. They will analyze all

the responses from the forms submitted and render their suggestions to our HR department.

Abigail Greene

HR Team Manager

135. (A) aspect
(B) phase
(C) pace
(D) team

136. (A) job
(B) customer
(C) application
(D) statistics

137. (A) to
(B) until
(C) within
(D) by

138. (A) This is to ensure the experience of
employees at Rucino Publishing is a
satisfying one.
(B) The results from the survey will be
utilized for improving our customer
service.
(C) Moreover, it is mandatory for you to
attend the safety course provided by
DDB consulting.
(D) Along with it, at least two references
from your previous supervisor are
required for the application.

Questions 139-142 refer to the following article.

Toronto (September 4) - The City Parking Authority ------- new powers by the City Council to
                                                  139.
tow away any cars they deem to be impeding the flow of traffic.

Traffic has recently become so bad in the city core that for about 6 hours a day between
Monday and Friday cars come to a complete standstill. As Mayor Trumbee put it, "With no room
for traffic, we are going to aggressively ------- the parking laws already on the books." -------.
                                          140.   **141.**

It is hoped that the new subway line set to open next year will make the city ------- more
                                                                              142.
commuter-friendly as well.

139. (A) have given
(B) has been given
(C) will give
(D) giving

140. (A) retain
(B) perform
(C) comply
(D) enforce

141. (A) Therefore, we are soliciting any
proposals to reduce commuting
hours.
(B) That means that you won't be able
to park your car without risking a 150
dollar ticket and a tow.
(C) However, you can be exempt from
fines.
(D) You need to arrange alternative
routes.

142. (A) so
(B) such
(C) few
(D) much

GO ON TO THE NEXT PAGE

Questions 143-146 refer to the following e-mail.

FROM: Information Center <info@bestinvestcorp.com>

TO: employees@bestinvestcorp.com

SUBJECT: Corporate Upkeep

Access to e-mails and electronic calendars of the company will be ------- between 5:00 P.M.
143.
and 7:00 P.M this Thursday. The Information Technology Department will be conducting their
scheduled system maintenance on all related electronic applications.

In the coming week, the client management databank ------- as well. Upon using your
144.
computer, you will be prompted to download the updated version of the software. -------.
145.

If you have problems with upgrading or are not able to ------- the update, you can call the
146.
Information Center for help.

---

143. (A) convenient
(B) unavailable
(C) deserving
(D) allowable

144. (A) to be reorganized
(B) will be reorganized
(C) reorganized
(D) was to reorganize

145. (A) Whether to upgrade or not has yet to
be decided.
(B) It should be renewed annually to
extend your subscription to our anti-
virus services.
(C) There will be restructuring after the
acquisition.
(D) All instructions associated with the
new software are attached in this
e-mail.

146. (A) perform
(B) assume
(C) cover
(D) turn out

PART 5

Directions: A word or phrase is missing in each of the sentences below. Four answer choices are given below each sentence. Select the best answer to complete the sentence. Then mark the letter (A), (B), (C), or (D) on your answer sheet.

101. If Jeannette Glover from Torret Corporation arrives at the airport, please inform ------- immediately.
(A) my
(B) mine
(C) me
(D) I

102. Please contact Mr. Scott if you need ------- with your enrollment.
(A) assisted
(B) assist
(C) assistance
(D) assistant

103. Recent advances in telecommunications have made it convenient for cell phone users to send clear images to other users -------.
(A) easy
(B) easier
(C) ease
(D) easily

104. Fire Chief Jason Nick will retire on September 28, and Ted Miller will serve as interim chief ------- a replacement is named.
(A) outside
(B) within
(C) until
(D) from

105. Confusion remains over whether the tour group had ------- to be in the area of the Sahara Desert.
(A) request
(B) permission
(C) decision
(D) cost

106. Nomper Tech's main objectives are to increase its share of the market in computer sales, and to ------- its range of products.
(A) diversify
(B) diversely
(C) diverse
(D) diversity

107. Because of a ------- conflict, the CEO of Yodobashi Steel Inc. regrettably declined the offer to speak at the local business conference.
(A) scheduled
(B) scheduler
(C) schedule
(D) schedules

108. Later this month, the Olympic Committee is expected to narrow down the list of U.K. cities being ------- as an Olympic host.
(A) categorized
(B) known
(C) remained
(D) considered

GO ON TO THE NEXT PAGE

57

109. Any big merchandise bought at Jamy Hardware requires ------- handling so as not to damage product components.
(A) careful
(B) grateful
(C) previous
(D) typical

110. Liverpool is one of the safest British cities to live in according to a report ------- in the April issue of BK's magazine.
(A) publish
(B) to publish
(C) publishing
(D) published

111. We use production machines imported ------- France and automated quality control systems to ensure all our products are of high quality.
(A) from
(B) about
(C) abroad
(D) against

112. Efforts to ------- work procedures at our Paris plant may lead to lowering production costs.
(A) simplify
(B) contact
(C) proceed
(D) overweigh

113. Raw material prices rose ------- again last month, but most economists expect a sharp decrease in the coming months.
(A) seldom
(B) previously
(C) slightly
(D) highly

114. ------- the firm's official Code of Conduct, employees must obtain their supervisor's permission in advance when taking a day off work.
(A) In accordance with
(B) As well as
(C) Agreeing
(D) On behalf of

115. Harro Ranter has successfully completed the educational program and is now ------- for a promotion to general director.
(A) possible
(B) considerable
(C) decisive
(D) eligible

116. After starting work at Eastern Express Railway, Michale Richards ------- to serve as its vice-president for twelve years.
(A) met with
(B) pick up
(C) arrived at
(D) went on

117. The Mathematics Dialogue promotes mathematical research in Germany and acts as a ------- for discussing issues related to mathematical education.
(A) forum
(B) vision
(C) round
(D) variety

118. Mr. Watson Smith, the Managing Director gave a welcome speech, and took the opportunity to introduce the newly ------- Marketing Manager, Ms. Showna Lim,
(A) appoints
(B) appointing
(C) appoint
(D) appointed

119. The Metro Pole center has more than 150 volunteers, ------- are students participating in various activities to improve awareness of environment.
(A) the reason
(B) following as
(C) most of whom
(D) because of them

120. In order to receive the appropriate visa, all ------- documents and forms must be forwarded to the embassy two weeks prior to the intended departure date.
(A) skilled
(B) compared
(C) required
(D) interested

121. If Nokio continues its steady decline in sales, it will ------- be the leading electronics provider in the market.
(A) anymore
(B) not enough
(C) other
(D) no longer

122. Make sure to fill out the application form completely before ------- it to our office.
(A) to submit
(B) submitted
(C) submitting
(D) submission

123. Beverages can be obtained from vending machines located ------- the office building.
(A) without
(B) throughout
(C) with
(D) into

124. Jeremy Hicks and other top executives will meet on Saturday to discuss new business plans and marketing -------.
(A) initiatives
(B) deadlines
(C) explanations
(D) conversations

125. At the reception for new employees, the food will be served ------- the firm's president finishes his speech.
(A) most
(B) away
(C) almost
(D) once

126. ------- traffic problems are frequent on this road, the San Francisco Transportation Department has decided not to put in a traffic signal.
(A) Although
(B) So that
(C) Both
(D) In case

127. Any application for a building ------- must be submitted to the Municipal Inspector in writing.
(A) to permit
(B) permits
(C) permit
(D) permitting

128. ------- the tremendous success of Dr. Lowang's aesthetics clinic, she is planning to open another salon on the east side of town.
(A) Resulted
(B) As a result of
(C) Resulting
(D) To result

129. Many prominent professors accepted Ms. Leon's ------- for a report on effective educational methods.
(A) approval
(B) renewal
(C) contact
(D) proposal

130. ------- wanting to enroll in the Nice EXPO have to confirm their arrangements with Ms. Eloise.
(A) This
(B) Them
(C) That
(D) Those

GO ON TO THE NEXT PAGE

PART 6

Directions: Read the texts that follow. A word, phrase, or sentence is missing in parts of each text. Four answer choices for each question are given below the text. Select the best answer to complete the text. Then mark the letter (A), (B), (C), or (D) on your answer sheet.

Questions 131-134 refer to the following letter.

Dear Mr. Nicole,

We received a letter from you on June 2 ------- an estimate of the costs involved in ------- the
131. **132.**
building at 3656 Covington Avenue into a residential condominium. -------. Enclosed is our
133.
calculation of the conversion cost. RENO Home Builders offers competitive rates, which include

labor and material costs. We ------- to give our clients complete satisfaction.
134.

The building conversion can begin as early as June 30. Before starting the project, we require a

20% deposit and a signed contract.

Thank you for choosing RENO Home Builders. We look forward to hearing from you soon.

Sincerely,

Simon Luke

131. (A) requests
(B) requested
(C) requisite
(D) requesting

132. (A) relocating
(B) converting
(C) furnishing
(D) constructing

133. (A) Unfortunately, we consider it
impossible to demolish the existing
condominium.
(B) We conducted an onsite assessment
on June 8.
(C) We have been in business for the last
30 years.
(D) You need to vacate the building
before repair works begin.

134. (A) charge
(B) respond
(C) agree
(D) strive

Questions 135-138 refer to the following notice.

Corporate Museum Cards

The city museum is extending admission privileges to the corporate community. Employees of any organization in our city are entitled to receive a corporate card. -------. Government
135.
employees and nonprofit organizations are exempt from these fees.

Corporate cards are intended for employees and up to 2 family members, who are ------- to free
136.
admission to the museum throughout the year.

------- a corporate card, simply visit the city museum. Applicants must show photo identification
137.
to confirm their ------- status. The annual fee for the corporate museum card must be paid at
138.
the time of application.

If you have any questions about the corporate card program, please contact us at corporatecards@citymuseum.com.

---

135. (A) This card must be presented at the
      gate.
    (B) Card holders can use the fitness
      center at no cost.
    (C) There is no entrance fee to the gallery
      in celebration of it 10th anniversary.
    (D) The annual fee for each card issued
      to an employee of an organization is
      $10.00.

136. (A) encouraged
    (B) eligible
    (C) allowed
    (D) entitled

137. (A) Receive
    (B) Received
    (C) To receive
    (D) Receipt of

138. (A) employment
    (B) residence
    (C) investment
    (D) reference

GO ON TO THE NEXT PAGE

To: Karina Bhat

From: Ken Suzuki

Subject: Job application

Date: March 19

Dear Mr. Bhat,

I saw Tracker's job posting in the Bratton Post. I am writing to apply for a suitable position at your new factory in Bratton. Please allow me to introduce myself and to present my -------.
139.

My experience and various skills would serve as an excellent contribution to your company's growth. I am fluent in the Indonesian language, which is my native language. I am also proficient in English, ------- university in Sydney, Australia. There, I studied and graduated with a degree in
140.
Accounting. Over the last three years, I ------- at several companies as an accountant. -------.
141. **142.**

Thank you for taking the time to read this letter. I hope to hear from you soon regarding my enclosed application.

Sincerely,

Ken Suzuki

139. (A) demonstrations
(B) credentials
(C) positions
(D) samples

140. (A) attendant
(B) attended
(C) having attended
(D) attentive

141. (A) am employed
(B) have employed
(C) have been employed
(D) employed

142. (A) As I noted in my résumé, I would like to be considered for a managerial position at Tracker.
(B) I'm so delighted to start my career with such a reputable company like yours.
(C) So I would like to keep working on that project.
(D) Jim Harrison, my direct supervisor, nominated me for this promotion.

Questions 143-146 refer to the following e-mail.

To: Matthew Moy

From: Williams Reed

Date: Friday, November 3

Subject: News

Dear Matthew,

Thank you very much for organizing my trip to Madrid last week. I had a wonderful time, and it was a pleasure to meet our new clients.

During my stay, you ------- interest in relocating to Berlin to be closer to your mother. -------.
                         143.   **144.**
We are looking for sales associates who have at least five years' experience and an educational background similar to yours. The work itself is very similar to what you have been doing in Madrid.

The openings will be ------- posted at the end of next month. If you are interested in one of the
                      145.
positions, please let me know ------- I can tell Miranda Leary, who is in charge of recruitment, to
                              146.
schedule an interview with you.

Kind regards,

Williams Reed

143. (A) focused
(B) appeared
(C) applied
(D) expressed

144. (A) There are better jobs available in other companies in Berlin.
(B) In my childhood, my family also lived in Berlin.
(C) I am happy to inform you that our Berlin office has a total of four openings.
(D) To provide your background and qualifications, please submit resumes along with the job application form.

145. (A) public
(B) publicly
(C) publicize
(D) publicity

146. (A) as soon as
(B) since
(C) now that
(D) so that

PART 5

Directions: A word or phrase is missing in each of the sentences below. Four answer choices are given below each sentence. Select the best answer to complete the sentence. Then mark the letter (A), (B), (C), or (D) on your answer sheet.

101. Mr. Gilitsh had to change his schedule for the business trip to Miami because he arrived ------- for his flight.
(A) lately
(B) later
(C) late
(D) latest

102. When ------- have finished encoding all the data, store the file in our shared drive.
(A) yours
(B) you
(C) your
(D) yourself

103. The paper shredder in the conference room on the third floor needs to be ------- because it runs too slowly.
(A) replacing
(B) replaced
(C) replace
(D) replaces

104. ------- of the employee benefits of the Holguin Publishing Company is a $ 150-gift card towards book purchases.
(A) One
(B) Every
(C) Some
(D) All

105. Vamos Corporation ------- staff members five additional days for vacation if they have worked for the company for more than eight years.
(A) grant
(B) granting
(C) grants
(D) are granted

106. All scissors manufactured by Dixon, Inc. come apart ------- to allow sharpening and thorough cleaning.
(A) effortlessly
(B) attentively
(C) accurately
(D) exactly

107. Before laying a carpet, employees of Bonheur Clothing accurately measure the exact ------- of the rooms.
(A) figures
(B) styles
(C) dimensions
(D) rates

108. Mr. Jaime has asked that employees ------- the benefits and the risks seriously before investing in the start-up company.
(A) considers
(B) consider
(C) is considering
(D) considering

109. Customer service representatives of Maxo Cable Company should promptly ------- to all inquiries regarding the recently updated cable channels.
(A) respond
(B) conduct
(C) collect
(D) invite

110. We offer a ------- range of career opportunities for highly motivated professionals dedicated to improving product quality and customer service.
(A) competitive
(B) diverse
(C) various
(D) several

111. ------- leading medical organizations recommend breaking up sedentary time in the office, most workers still have no choice but to sit at their desks all day.
(A) Although
(B) Nevertheless
(C) But
(D) Only if

112. As construction work becomes more ------- on the use of complex equipment, the construction workers are expected to have enhanced competency in understanding technology.
(A) depends
(B) dependable
(C) dependent
(D) depend

113. NAU airports have excellent facilities for keeping ------- goods within the optimum temperature range between four and five degrees Celsius.
(A) constructive
(B) confusing
(C) perishable
(D) plentiful

114. While many shoppers remain ------- cautious, gift spending is expected to rise 23 percent from last year.
(A) financed
(B) financing
(C) financial
(D) financially

115. For users of previous versions, a discounted upgrade offer is ------- until the end of the year.
(A) beneficial
(B) complicated
(C) frequent
(D) available

116. The restaurant Fresh Food is very popular for a variety of delicious ------- inexpensive food.
(A) yet
(B) once
(C) despite
(D) because

117. Please ------- reference books to the second floor so they will be available for the next user.
(A) return
(B) renew
(C) research
(D) replace

118. Upon receiving your shipment, inspect the content to determine if it may ------- have been damaged while in transit.
(A) possibilities
(B) possibility
(C) possible
(D) possibly

119. It is necessary for all tour visitors to wear the life jacket provided and listen ------- to the safety procedure.
(A) attention
(B) attentively
(C) attends
(D) attend

GO ON TO THE NEXT PAGE

120. The two eastbound lanes on the Napoleon's Gate Bridge that were closed ------- emergency repairs have reopened after nearly six hours.
(A) as a result
(B) in order to
(C) so that
(D) owing to

121. Your order will be processed and shipped within 3 business days ------- the date it is placed.
(A) when
(B) under
(C) than
(D) from

122. The road ------- has caused much inconvenience to travellers who have to find alternative routes.
(A) closure
(B) closed
(C) closes
(D) close

123. Synops Airlines will provide $180 to customers ------- flights were delayed more than three hours due to its system failures.
(A) when
(B) those
(C) whose
(D) their

124. Benjamin Frank's Coffee House offers a wide ------- of gift items, such as coffee cups, ornamental spoons and beautiful bowls.
(A) preference
(B) selection
(C) part
(D) compound

125. The users are expected to be ------- of any hazards and precautions regarding the chemicals that they use.
(A) alert
(B) aware
(C) present
(D) serious

126. Please ------- our web site for complete details of our services and price lists of all of our products.
(A) refer
(B) look
(C) notify
(D) consult

127. By the time he retires, Mrs. Maeva ------- for more than sixteen years as director of the company.
(A) will have served
(B) has served
(C) had served
(D) been served

128. To post your job opening on Valley Industry's website, ------- fill out an online application form and you will receive your receipt via e-mail.
(A) finally
(B) sparsely
(C) simply
(D) such

129. As principal administrative officer, Mr. Thomas has unlimited ------- to the performance evaluation files.
(A) access
(B) accessing
(C) accesses
(D) accessed

130. ------- impresses investors the most is that Muttoni Company has achieved international fame with its brand this year.
(A) What
(B) Neither
(C) When
(D) Nothing

PART 6

Directions: Read the texts that follow. A word, phrase, or sentence is missing in parts of each text. Four answer choices for each question are given below the text. Select the best answer to complete the text. Then mark the letter (A), (B), (C), or (D) on your answer sheet.

Questions 131-134 refer to the following notice.

Attention Staff: Underground Parking Lot Reopening

It has taken several months longer than ------- **131.** , but the Greenearth Paper company has finally started to reopen its underground parking lot. ------- **132.** means employees will no longer need to park their vehicles across the street at the abandoned mill. The parking lot will reopen in sections starting in the first week of June. ------- **133.** . Any employees ------- **134.** have difficulty with mobility will be given priority for the first section of parking spots. If you suffer from problems with mobility, contact the building manager to reserve a spot in the first section.

---

131. (A) planned
(B) planer
(C) planless
(D) planning

132. (A) What
(B) Those
(C) These
(D) That

133. (A) The old underground parking lot was so old that the renovation was necessary.
(B) The construction took longer than expected due to a delay in material supply.
(C) All employees must use an alternative parking lot until the parking lot reopens.
(D) By the end of July, the entire parking lot will be reopened and everyone can again park underground.

134. (A) whose
(B) they
(C) who
(D) which

GO ON TO THE NEXT PAGE

Questions 135-138 refer to the following e-mail.

From: Joshua Radnor <sales@buildersmaterial.com>

To: Taylor Moy <moy@diyconstruction.com>

Subject: Order #35987

Date: Thursday, April 19

Dear Mr. Moy,

We are processing your order, which we received on April 13. You indicated that you were interested in receiving the ceramic tiles ------- the end of the week. -------, the color you ordered
      135.   **136.**
will not be available from the manufacturer for another month. We apologize for the delay and ask for your understanding.

-------. They are slightly lighter in color, but we have plenty in stock. If you are interested, you
137.
can compare product colors on our website www.buildersmaterial.com or just visit our store.

For the moment, the cost of the ceramic tiles has been ------- from your order. You should
             138.
receive the in-stock items by tomorrow. We thank you for choosing Builders Material.

---

135. (A) from
(B) by
(C) of
(D) until

136. (A) Alternatively
(B) Subsequently
(C) Unfortunately
(D) Approximately

137. (A) Any defective tiles will be replaced with new ones.
(B) The cost of out-of-stock items will be refunded within 10 working days.
(C) Another retailer sells the same products in the area.
(D) We have the same style that you ordered in beige.

138. (A) promoted
(B) removed
(C) determined
(D) evolved

Questions 139-142 refer to the following letter.

Dear Mr. Capron,

This is to submit my resignation as an assistant photographer from the Colbert Weekly News, ------- March 2, as I seek to broaden my career. I am ------- you with one month's notice as
139. stipulated in my employment contract.

For some time, I have been considering ------- my own photography business. -------. The
141. **142.**
$40,000 grand prize I won has enabled me to start my own photography studio.

I will truly miss working at the Colbert Weekly News with all of you. I wish you and the company continued success.

Sincerely,

Jeffrey Sparshott

139. (A) outside
(B) effective
(C) afterward
(D) instead of

140. (A) writing
(B) providing
(C) showing
(D) prohibiting

141. (A) to start
(B) start
(C) starting
(D) started

142. (A) Finally, I decided to open my photography studio in May.
(B) Fortunately, the Wacom investment company has funded my own business.
(C) Three months ago, I won an award from the International Photographers Club for my landscape photography portfolio.
(D) As you know, our industry is increasingly competitive.

GO ON TO THE NEXT PAGE

To: Jim Patel <jpatel@Mckinney.com>

From: Julie Sarandon <jsarandon@Mckinney.com>

Date: Monday, March 1

Subject: Welcome

Dear Mr. Patel,

Welcome to Mckinney Electronics! We are glad to have you with us, and we, especially the Sales and Marketing Team, all look forward to working with you.

------- this is your first day with the company, we would like to have you join us in the main
143.
conference room to meet ------- officials and key people of Mckinney Electronics. -------. This
144. **145.**
meeting has been set for 10:00 A.M. today. After the short meeting, we will take you on a tour of our office facilities. The company president will then ------- welcome you at a lunch to be
146.
attended by other top managers.

We will see you later.

Julie Sarandon

---

143. (A) Even though
(B) Once
(C) As
(D) In order that

144. (A) the other
(B) another
(C) others
(D) the one

145. (A) The president called a special meeting to discuss Mckinney Electronics's strategy.
(B) This will help you get acquainted with the people who will be working with you in the coming days.
(C) The executives of Mckinney Electronics look forward to meeting you and celebrating your promotion.
(D) Considering your past experience, you are highly qualified for the position with Mckinney Electronics.

146. (A) formally
(B) periodically
(C) customarily
(D) solely

PART 5

Directions: A word or phrase is missing in each of the sentences below. Four answer choices are given below each sentence. Select the best answer to complete the sentence. Then mark the letter (A), (B), (C), or (D) on your answer sheet.

101. Mr. Smith told ------- that his company is currently supplying several kinds of construction materials for the new museum.
(A) I
(B) myself
(C) me
(D) mine

102. Riverdale Hotel is planning to ------- its parking space to reduce traffic congestion during the weekends.
(A) enlarge
(B) distract
(C) accomplish
(D) communicate

103. Najad's expertise of the local economy ------- by that of no other economist.
(A) to surpass
(B) is surpassed
(C) surpassable
(D) surpassing

104. Nowadays, rail transportation has been described as the most affordable and ------- means of transportation.
(A) correct
(B) reliable
(C) portable
(D) cooperative

105. To unlock the door, turn the dial clockwise slowly and ------- until the dial comes to a stop.
(A) nearly
(B) gently
(C) openly
(D) timely

106. At your -------, your appointment with Dr. Watson has been moved up to 6:30 P.M. on Friday, November 6.
(A) claim
(B) conflict
(C) paper
(D) request

107. Ruzzie Consulting has a main office in Paris and will ------- be opening a branch office in Nice.
(A) shortly
(B) almost
(C) initially
(D) equally

108. British and French translations of Mr. Choi's speech ------- marketing strategy should be available online on January 14.
(A) regarded
(B) regard
(C) regards
(D) regarding

GO ON TO THE NEXT PAGE

109. Please understand ------- we will not be able to process refunds or exchanges until the first week of February because it is so busy.
(A) where
(B) whom
(C) what
(D) that

110. The Neo Institute of Visual Arts will feature a variety of presentations by leaders of the ------- design companies.
(A) most prominent
(B) more prominently
(C) prominence
(D) prominently

111. BK's Personnel Training Academy always ------- constructive suggestions, which we assume are helpful to further improve the training programs.
(A) collaborates
(B) welcomes
(C) introduces
(D) correspond

112. The president decided to hire a consulting firm to help ------- potential business partners.
(A) investigated
(B) investigate
(C) investigator
(D) investigation

113. ESPY Sports TV will have full ------- of Judy Emilton's press conference tomorrow afternoon.
(A) occurrence
(B) response
(C) coverage
(D) announcement

114. ------- a few minor flaws, the construction of the building was smooth and efficient.
(A) As to
(B) Together
(C) Except that
(D) Aside from

115. In a TV interview, Chief Executive Officer Richard Hudson claimed that his ------- accomplishment was his success in negotiating the merger with Bixson Publishers.
(A) gratified
(B) most gratifying
(C) gratifyingly
(D) more gratified

116. According to the schedule, the new company ID will be distributed to all employees ------- the end of this month.
(A) on
(B) by
(C) of
(D) as

117. Despite the recent ------- in sales, the CEO of Cramax Electronics believes that his company will be profitable within a few months.
(A) conference
(B) overhead
(C) appraisal
(D) decline

118. ------- to our survey, Riverside residents are overwhelmingly in favor of adding walk lanes along the beach.
(A) Including
(B) Concerning
(C) Considering
(D) According

119. One ------- of today's sales meeting is to report the increased market share to the president.
(A) aim
(B) aims
(C) will aim
(D) aiming

120. You should notify the lecturer of your anticipated absences ------- alternate dates can be scheduled.
(A) despite
(B) ever since
(C) due to
(D) so that

121. Steve Jackson has been an authorized stockbroker for more than 25 years and also specializes in overseas -------.
(A) invested
(B) investments
(C) investor
(D) invests

122. All ------- of a confidential nature will be stored in locked filing cabinets that can be accessed only by designated personnel.
(A) effects
(B) positions
(C) repetitions
(D) documents

123. On account of his insight as a real estate analyst, Mr. Will is well ------- by his co-workers.
(A) respect
(B) respects
(C) respected
(D) respective

124. Using the survey data, Chef Frank Dols will ------- publish a new book, Famous French Food.
(A) soon
(B) lately
(C) well
(D) once

125. If you can prove that what a landlord is charging for rent is too high, you may be able to ------- the rent payment.
(A) negotiates
(B) negotiate
(C) negotiated
(D) negotiating

126. Southbank Park's plans to build a movie studio and a fancy hotel should bring ------- revenue to the city.
(A) increased
(B) designated
(C) renovated
(D) managed

127. Today's businesses have large volumes of critical data that must be protected and ------- at a moment's notice.
(A) constant
(B) useful
(C) competent
(D) accessible

128. The inventory system, ------- is used to keep track of items in stock, enables warehouse supervisors to order out of stock items immediately online.
(A) that
(B) who
(C) whom
(D) which

129. If you require ------- information concerning Mr. Brady's eligibility as a candidate for the senior managerial position, please contact our office without any hesitation.
(A) one
(B) many
(C) every
(D) more

130. As a director of sales and marketing, Mr. Richards has often travelled to Taiwan, ------- to Taipei.
(A) relatively
(B) primarily
(C) temporarily
(D) yet

GO ON TO THE NEXT PAGE

PART 6

Directions: Read the texts that follow. A word, phrase, or sentence is missing in parts of each text. Four answer choices for each question are given below the text. Select the best answer to complete the text. Then mark the letter (A), (B), (C), or (D) on your answer sheet.

Questions 131-134 refer to the following report.

Kelvin Hotels has successfully ------- from a local, family-owned hotel to a nationally known
131.
franchise of luxury business-class hotels. ------- the business started, its low rates and
132.
proximity to major interstates attracted many truck drivers and long-distance motorists. -------.
133.
Capital Hotels then refurbished all the rooms, built new hotels near major airports in the state,
and raised rates by about 50%. Since that time, about 60% of Kelvin Hotel's guests have been
from the corporate sector. The business is highly profitable and plans to expand to the Midwest
and Western areas of the country soon. Partnerships with travel agencies ------- this expansion.
134.

131. (A) used
(B) operated
(C) differed
(D) changed

132. (A) When
(B) Although
(C) However
(D) During

133. (A) However, after 8 consecutive years
of sagging revenues, the owners
decided to sell the business to
Capital Hotels Group Co.
(B) After talking with Boston Consulting
Group, Kelvin Hotel has recently
decided to upgrade its facility.
(C) All the staff of Kelvin Hotel were
extremely friendly and eager to make
customers comfortable.
(D) Kelvin Hotel became much more
popular to residents and tourists
alike.

134. (A) facilitates
(B) are facilitated
(C) will be facilitated
(D) have facilitated

Caldwell Motors has distributed a maintenance manual for its new Camry sedan. The Camry 3.2 liter model has been recalled ------- an issue related to its transmission system. In this latest
135.
model, the engine seems to speed up ------- when the car is shifted into neutral gear.
136.

Representatives of Caldwell point out that the problem is not hazardous and that no accidents or injuries have happened as a result of the malfunction, but they encourage owners to bring their cars to the nearest Caldwell service center. Caldwell technicians have been trained to fix the problem.

-------. Free rental vehicles will be provided while the cars are at the service center. Caldwell has
137.
issued an official apology to its customers. Owners of the affected cars will receive a written notice ------- the next month.
138.

135. (A) since
(B) due to
(C) as for
(D) among

136. (A) unnecessariness
(B) unnecessarily
(C) unnecessity
(D) unnecessary

137. (A) The manufacturer isn't responsible for technical flaws at all.
(B) Therefore, fixing the vehicle may require your expense.
(C) The manufacturer will cover all expenses associated with this recall.
(D) Unfortunately, the Caldwell service center in your area was closed only last year.

138. (A) between
(B) among
(C) along
(D) within

GO ON TO THE NEXT PAGE

Questions 139-142 refer to the following e-mail.

To: Nicole Cassidy

From: Murphey Harison

Date: April 6

Subject: Re: Recommendations

Nicole,

I'll be glad to assist you as much as I can. I'm assuming that you're intending to do a bit of research on London before you leave. When you get there, you should really try to go to a couple of places that are of cultural and historical importance. This will give you an ------- to **139.** have some interesting and pleasant conversations with your business colleagues.

-------. You should always keep this in mind because it is crucial that you are always on time for **140.** your appointments. ------- your negotiations start, be ready to ------- them with a generous spirit **141.** **142.** of give and take. Perhaps you should determine beforehand - with the help of your supervisor - exactly what sort of compromises you are prepared to make.

Have a wonderful trip. We'll see you at the next staff meeting.

---

139. (A) observation
(B) operation
(C) originality
(D) opportunity

140. (A) I enjoyed the holidays with my family in London.
(B) Please let me know if you have problems with traffic.
(C) London is such a wonderful city, and there are many amazing places to visit.
(D) I should warn you that traffic can sometimes be a great problem in London.

141. (A) whereas
(B) once
(C) provided
(D) however

142. (A) install
(B) repair
(C) conduct
(D) acquaint

Questions 143-146 refer to the following letter.

February 5, 2020

Ms. Mia Grathan

BMC Motors Incorporation

Oxford St., London, England

Dear Madam

Thank you very much for bringing this matter to our attention. The message ------- in your letter **143.** truly inspired us to do better. ------- the management and staff, I personally apologize for the **144.** incorrect information that was published on January 13 in Today's News. I assure you that we will publish a corrected article and apologize to you in print.

We hope this will ------- all your concerns regarding this matter and we will ensure this will not **145.** happen again in the future. -------. Just send us a copy of your advertisement and the specific **146.** date you intended to publish it.

Respectfully yours,

Tess Carter

Editor-in–Chief

Today's News

143. (A) was contained
(B) is to be contained
(C) contained
(D) to contain

144. (A) Instead
(B) Despite
(C) On behalf of
(D) Owing to

145. (A) approximate
(B) address
(C) streamline
(D) satisfy

146. (A) Also, you can get some discounts at our local shops when you present the coupon accompanied with this flyer.
(B) We recognized that your advertisement was eligible to be posted in Today's News.
(C) We specialize in designing advertisement at reasonable prices.
(D) At this time we would also like to offer you a complimentary advertising space of 1 column for your business needs.

최신 ② 10회분

토익 급상승
Part 5&6

정답 및 해설

101

------- to the swimming pool is exclusively for hotel guests and the pool is open during summertime.
(A) Accessing
(B) Accessed
(C) Access
(D) Accesses

수영장으로의 접근은 호텔 손님들에게 한 정되고, 수영장은 여름 동안에 개장한다.

해설 빈칸은 문장의 주어자리이다. Access는 불가산명사이므로 복수형태인 (D)는 오답이다. 그리고, 주어로 동명사가 올 수 있으므로 accessing을 고려할 경우, access는 타동사이므로 동명사가 되더라도 바로 뒤에 전치사가 올 수 없다. 그러므로, 명사인 (C) Access 가 정답이다.

어휘 access 접근 exclusively 오로지, 독점적으로

102

Air Brazil will ------- a new policy that requires two crew members to be in the cockpit at all times.
(A) implement
(B) acclaim
(C) convince
(D) renovate

Air Brazil은 항상 조종실에 두 명의 조종 사들이 있어야 한다고 요구하는 정책을 시 행할 것이다.

해설 빈칸은 a new policy(새로운 정책)를 목적어로 취하는 동사자리이다. a new policy와 의미가 가장 어울리는 동사는 (A) implement(시행하다)이다.

어휘 crew members 승무원 cockpit 조종석 at all times 항상 implement 이행하다, 시행하다, acclaim 격찬하다 convince 납득시키다, 설득하다 renovate 고치다, 수리하다

103

Vancouver's ------- has improved in the past couple of years following challenges largely based on the global economic crisis.
(A) economic
(B) economical
(C) economy
(D) economizes

밴쿠버 경제는 주로 글로벌 경제 위기에 근 거한 어려움을 겪은 후에 지난 2년 동안 개 선되었다.

해설 빈칸은 문장의 주어자리이다. 즉, 명사가 와야 하는 자리이므로, (C) economy(경제)가 정답이다

어휘 crisis 위기 in the past couple of years 지난 2년 동안 following ~후에 challenge 도전, 어려움 largely 주로 based on ~에 근거한 crisis 위기

104

Please note that in case of insufficient registered participants, the tour ------- and you will be fully refunded.
(A) to cancel
(B) has cancelled
(C) cancelling
(D) will be cancelled

등록된 참가자가 부족할 경우, 투어는 취소되며 귀하는 전액 환불받을 것이라는 점을 유의하십시오.

해설 빈칸은 the tour(주어) 뒤의 동사자리이다. cancel(취소하다)은 타동사인데, 빈칸 뒤에 목적어가 없으므로 수동태가 적합하다. 따라서 수동태 미래형태인 (D) will be cancelled가 정답이다.

어휘 insufficient 불충분한 note 유념하다, 유의하다 in case of ~의 경우에 register 등록하다 participant 참석자

105

PHLD's design team has created the most innovative and ------- tools in the Northern Irish market today.
(A) precision
(B) precise
(C) preciseness
(D) precisely

PHLD의 디자인 팀은 오늘날 North Irish 시장에서 가장 혁신적이고 정교한 도구를 만들어왔다.

해설 빈칸은 등위접속사 and로 연결되는 자리이다. and 앞에 형용사 innovative가 있으므로 빈칸도 형용사가 와야 한다. 그래서 정답은 (B) precise이다.

어휘 innovative 혁신적인, 획기적인 tool 도구 precise 정확한 precision 정확 preciseness 정확성

106

Mr. Richard will be spending three years as chief consultant of a global consulting firm after seventeen years of ------- motivational seminars for managers.
(A) participating
(B) leading
(C) instructing
(D) proving

Richard 씨는 매니저들을 위한 동기부여 세미나를 17년간 이끈 후에 국제적인 자문 회사의 최고 자문가로서 3년의 시간을 보냈다.

해설 빈칸은 전치사 of 다음의 동명사자리로 motivational seminars를 목적어로 가져야 한다. seminars와 의미상 어울리는 타동사는 lead(주재하다, 사회를 보다)이다. participate는 자동사로 전치사 in을 필요로 하고, 나머지 단어들은 의미상 어울리지 않는다.

어휘 motivational 동기 부여하는 spend 보내다 chief consultant 최고 전문가 firm 회사

107

The conference hosted by the Association of Language features several ------- speakers who are experts in the field of phonetics.
(A) notably
(B) notable
(C) notes
(D) noting

Association of Language에 의해서 주최된 회의는 음성학 분야에서의 전문가인 몇 명의 유명한 연설자를 특징으로 한다.

해설 명사 speakers(연설자) 앞의 빈칸은 형용사(notable)자리이다.

어휘 feature 특색, 특징 conference 회의 several 몇 명의 expert 전문가 phonetic 음성학 notable 주목할 만한

108

Hospice I.L.U.E. is a community-based registered charity that strives ------- the quality of life for people facing life-threatening illness or grief.
(A) to enhance
(B) enhanced
(C) enhances
(D) is enhancing

호스피스 I.L.U.E는 삶을 위협하는 질병이나 슬픔에 직면하는 사람을 위해 삶의 질을 개선하는 데 노력하는 지역사회에 기반을 둔 자선단체이다.

해설 strive는 '노력하다, 애쓰다'의 의미로 strive to V의 구조를 취하므로 정답은 (A) to enhance이다.

어휘 strive 분투하다 life-threatening 생명을 위협하는 charity 자선단체 illness 질병 grief (특히 누구의 죽음으로 인한) 비탄, 비통

109

Scott Gilchrist is highly respected ------- his colleagues for his devotion and willingness to share his knowledge.
(A) plus
(B) in
(C) to
(D) by

Scott Gilchrist 씨는 헌신과 지식을 기꺼이 공유하려는 마음 때문에 그의 동료들에 의해서 매우 존경받는다.

해설 빈칸은 수동태 뒤에 의미가 적절한 전치사가 와야 하는 위치이다. 의미상 '동료들에 의해 존경을 받으므로' 전치사 (D) by가 정답이다.

어휘 devotion 헌신 willingness 쾌히, 자진하여 respect 존경되는 colleague 동료 share 공유하다

110

These forms must be filled out completely before your ------- at Osaka International Airport customs desk.
(A) arrival
(B) priority
(C) attention
(D) account

이러한 양식들은 Osaka국제공항 관세데스크에 도착하기 전에 완벽하게 작성되어야 한다.

해설 빈칸은 의미가 적절한 명사가 들어갈 자리이다. before부터 끝까지 부분을 일단 해석해 보면 '오사카 국제공항 세관검사대에 당신의 ~전에'가 되므로, 장소에 어울리는 명사는 선택지 중 (A) arrival(도착)이다.

어휘 form 양식 filled out 작성하다 completely 완벽하게 priority 우선 사항 account 계좌 attention 주의

111

Due to the Thanksgiving holiday, though recycling items are normally collected on Tuesday, collection will be on Thursday -------.
(A) high
(B) alike
(C) instead
(D) seldom

재활용품은 보통 화요일에 수거되지만, 추수감사절로 인해 대신 목요일에 수거가 될 것이다.

해설 빈칸은 의미가 적절한 부사가 들어갈 자리이다. 앞부분의 내용에서 재활용품 수거가 보통 화요일이라 했지만, 추수감사절이 끼여 있는 기간이라, 일정이 변경된다는 내용이므로, 변화를 나타내는 의미인 (C) instead(대신에)가 정답이다.

어휘 due to ~ 때문에 recycling 재활용 collect 모으다 seldom 좀처럼 ~않는

112

We provide services in promoting any products of manufacturers, starting with an ------- of potential clients.
(A) analysis
(B) to analyze
(C) analyzed
(D) analyze

우리는 잠재 고객들의 분석에서부터 제조업체들의 생산품을 홍보하는 서비스를 제공한다.

해설 빈칸은 관사 뒤에 명사가 와야 하는 자리이다. 그래서 정답은 (A) analysis이다.

어휘 potential 잠재적인 manufacturer 제조자, 제조사 product 상품 client 고객 analysis 분석

113

It is a ------- for all Public High schools to conduct at least two annual evaluations.
(A) speculation
(B) acquisition
(C) requirement
(D) training

모든 공립고등학교는 적어도 두 번의 연례 평가를 수행하는 것이 필요조건이다.

해설 빈칸에는 의미가 적절한 명사가 와야 한다. 전체적인 내용을 보면 '모든 공립고등학교는 적어도 두 번의 연례평가를 하는 것은 ~ 이다'이므로 의무사항의 뉘앙스를 갖는 (C) requirement(필수사항)가 정답이다.

어휘 conduct 조사하다, 지휘하다 evaluation 평가 at least 적어도 annual 연간

114

Spring-hill Inn, which has a magnificent ocean view, is located ------- across the street from a white sandy beach.
(A) direct
(B) directly
(C) directive
(D) directness

장대한 해안광경을 가진 Spring-hill Inn은 하얀 모래사장으로부터 길 바로 건너편에 위치되어 있다.

해설 빈칸은 be p.p와 전치사 사이이므로 부사자리이다. 정답은 (B) directly이며, directly across는 '~바로 맞은편에'라는 의미이다.

어휘 magnificent 감명 깊은, 훌륭한 across 건너편 directly 바로 directive 지시

115

For optimal performance and appearance, C&C sliding doors must be installed ------- great care.
(A) with
(B) for
(C) during
(D) in

최적의 성능과 외형을 위해서, C&C 미닫이 문은 매우 조심해서 설치되어야 한다.

해설 빈칸은 뒤의 명사 care와 연결되는 전치사자리이다. <전치사 + 명사>가 부사의 의미가 되는 경우로 with care = carefully라고 알아두면 쉽게 정답을 찾을 수 있다.

어휘 appearance 외모, 겉모습 optimal 최선의 sliding door 옆으로 여는 문 great care 세심한 주의

116

This weekend the assistant chef, Mr. John Smith, will supervise the dinner service in Ms. Mayer's -------.
(A) absence
(B) absences
(C) absent
(D) absently

이번 주말에 보조 요리사인 John Smith 씨는 Mayer 씨의 부재 시에 저녁식사 서비스를 감독할 것이다.

해설 빈칸은 소유격 뒤에 명사가 와야 하는 자리이다. 단수형태인 absence와 복수형태인 absences가 있지만 in one's absence는 항상 단수형태를 사용하므로 정답은 (A) absence이다.

어휘 supervise 감독하다, 지휘하다 assistant chef 보조 요리사 absence 부재 absent 결석한

117

RASP National Transportation ------- passengers with a long-distance bus service to and from Melbourne, Brisbane and Sydney.
(A) provides
(B) collects
(C) commutes
(D) accommodates

RASP National Transportation은 승객들에게 Melbourne, Brisbane과 Sydney를 왕복하는 장거리 버스 서비스를 제공한다.

해설 빈칸은 passengers를 목적어로 가지며, 그 뒤의 전치사 with와 어울리는 동사자리이다. provide가 사람목적어를 취할 때에는 전치사 with가 온다.

어휘 passenger 승객 long-distance 장거리 provide 제공하다 collect 모으다 commute 통근하다 accommodate 수용하다

118

------- Sankai Electronics' stock price has increased recently, the company's board of directors is worried about the slowdown in the appliance industry.
(A) As soon as
(B) So that
(C) Although
(D) Despite

Sankai Electronics의 주가가 최근에 올랐음에도 불구하고, 회사의 이사회는 전기기기 산업의 둔화에 대해서 걱정했다.

해설 빈칸은 두 문장을 연결하는 접속사자리이다. 두 문장의 내용을 보면 '주가가 최근에 올랐다'와 '이사회는 걱정한다'이다. 주가가 오르면 좋아해야 하는데, 걱정을 한다고 하니, '주가가 올랐음에도 불구하고'의 의미인 although가 정답이다.

어휘 stock 주식 appliance 가전제품, 가정용 기기 board of directors 이사회 be worried about ~에 대해 걱정하다 slowdown 둔화

119

With around sixty thousand visitors coming every month, La Défance is a ------- busy tourist spot during the holiday season.
(A) particularly
(B) formerly
(C) generously
(D) popularly

La Défance는 매달 대략 6만 명의 관광객이 방문하는 곳으로 휴가시즌 동안 특히 바쁜 관광명소이다.

해설 빈칸은 뒤의 busy tourist spot(바쁜 관광지)을 수식하는 부사자리이다. '여름휴가 기간 동안에 특히 바쁘다'의 의미이므로 (A) particularly가 정답이다.

어휘 visitor 관광객 particularly 특히 formerly 이전에 generously 기꺼이 popularly 일반적으로

120

The latest poll shows that a ------- of voters are in favor of the presidential candidate from the Democrat Party.
(A) rate
(B) majority
(C) point
(D) summary

가장 최근의 여론조사는 유권자 대부분이 민주당의 대선후보에 우호적이라는 것을 보여준다.

해설 빈칸은 관사 a와 전치사 of 사이에 의미를 적절하게 이어주는 명사자리이다. a majority of는 '대다수의', a summary of는 '~의 요약'으로 투표자들과 의미가 적절한 표현은 a majority of이다.

어휘 in favor of ~에 지지하여, ~에 우호적인 latest 최근의 poll 여론조사 voter 투표자 presidential candidate 대선후보 a majority of 대다수의

121

Many specialists ------- that the merger of the two stationery companies will be completed within the next month.
(A) predict
(B) predicting
(C) predicts
(D) predictable

많은 전문가들은 다음 달 안에 두 개의 문구회사 합병이 마무리될 것으로 예상한다.

해설 주어(specialists) 뒤의 빈칸은 동사자리이다. 주어가 복수이므로 동사는 단수형태인 (A) predict가 정답이다.

어휘 merger 합병 stationery 문구류 specialist 전문가 predict 예상하다 within ~내로 predictable 예측할 수 있는

122

Flight 927 to St. Anthony took off one hour ------- than scheduled on account of heavy snow in the New Orleans area.
(A) later
(B) lately
(C) late
(D) latest

St. Anthony로 가는 927 비행기는 New Orleans 지역의 폭설 때문에 예정보다 1시간 늦게 이륙했다.

해설 비교급을 나타내는 than이 나온다. 선택지 중에서 비교급 형태인 (A) later를 정답으로 쉽게 고를 수 있다.

어휘 take off 이륙하다 take something off (옷 등을) 벗다 on account of ~때문에 heavy snow 폭설 lately 최근에

123

CFPB Loan Services has conditionally approved your loan application, though we are still waiting for ------- of forms mentioned previously.
(A) receiving
(B) recipient
(C) receipt
(D) to receive

비록 우리가 여전히 이 편지에 언급된 양식의 수령을 미리 기다리긴 하지만, CFPB Loan Services는 귀하의 대출 신청서를 조건부로 승인했다.

해설 전치사 for 뒤에 오는 적절한 형태를 묻고 있다. 우선 동명사 형태인 receiving을 살펴보자. receive는 '~을 받다'라는 타동사이므로 동명사가 되더라도 바로 뒤에 목적어를 취해야 하므로 전치사 of와 어울리지 않는다. recipient는 '수령인'이라는 의미로 의미상 부적절하고 사람명사이므로 단수일 경우 관사가 필요하다, (C) receipt는 '영수증'이라는 의미를 가지기도 하지만, 동사 receive의 명사 형태로 '수령, 받음'이라는 의미로 해석도 적절하게 되는 정답이다.

어휘 loan 대출 previously 이전에, 미리 conditionally 조건부로 approve 승인하다 application 지원서 receipt 수령, 영수증

124

Bear in mind that the results of official tests are only valid for a limited ------- of time.
(A) value
(B) amount
(C) setting
(D) venue

공식적인 테스트 결과가 단지 제한된 시간 동안만 유효하다는 것을 명심하세요.

해설 빈칸은 limited와 의미가 연결되는 명사자리이다. 그리고 뒤에 of time(시간의)이 나오므로 양을 나타내는 (B) amount가 정답이다. a limited amount of time는 '한정된 시간'의 의미로 통째로 암기하자.

어휘 valid 유효한 bear in mind ~을 명심하다 result 결과 official test 공식적인 시험 value 가치 amount 양 venue 장소

125

U&M has ------- its decision on a cleanup plan for the sediments of the Luice River.
(A) finalized
(B) consumed
(C) hosted
(D) designed

U&M은 Luice 강의 침전물에 대한 청소 계획의 결정을 마무리지었다.

해설 빈칸은 뒤의 its decision을 목적어로 취하는 타동사자리이다. 문맥상 '결정을 마무리 짓다'의 의미인 (A) finalized가 정답이다.
어휘 sediment 침전물 finalize 마무리 짓다 consume 소비하다 cleanup 청소

126

This two-day career fair is an excellent opportunity for ILS students to meet with ------- from more than 100 companies.
(A) recruit
(B) recruitments
(C) recruiting
(D) recruiters

이틀 동안의 취업박람회는 ILS학생들이 100개 이상의 회사로부터 온 채용담당자들을 만날 좋은 기회이다.

해설 전치사 뒤의 빈칸은 명사자리이다. 빈칸 앞의 meet with(~와 만나다)를 통해 전치사 with 뒤에는 사람명사가 와야 한다. 사람을 나타내는 recruit(신입사원)와 recruiters(채용 담당자) 중에서 문맥상 ILS학생들이 만날 사람이 적절하므로 (D) recruiters가 정답이다.
어휘 career fair 취업 박람회 recruiter 채용담당자 recruit 모집하다 recruiting 구인활동

127

------- of the sales representatives is evaluated monthly on the basis of the number of products sold during the past month.
(A) Their own
(B) The others
(C) Each one
(D) All

판매직원 각자는 지난 달 동안에 팔린 제품들의 수를 기반으로 매달 평가된다.

해설 빈칸은 of 이하와 연결이 자연스러운 어휘가 들어갈 자리이다. 우선, their own of, the others of는 영어에 없는 형태이다. <Each one of the + 복수명사>, <all of the + 복수명사> 중에서 정답을 골라보자. <each one of the + 복수명사>는 뒤에 단수동사를 취하며, <all of the + 복수명사>는 뒤에 복수동사를 취한다. 따라서 정답은 (C) Each one(각각)이다.
어휘 on the basis of ~을 기반으로, ~에 근거하여 evaluate 평가하다 during ~동안의

128

Wellington Point is a nature park of ------- meadowlands and forests, located in Moreton Bay within easy reach of city residents.
(A) vast
(B) ethical
(C) final
(D) economic

Wellington Point는 도시 거주민들이 쉽게 접근할 수 있는 Moreton Bay에 위치하는 방대한 목초지와 숲이 있는 자연공원이다.

> 해설 빈칸 뒤의 meadowlands and forests(목초지와 숲)와 의미상 어울리는 형용사어휘를 고르는 문제이다. '아주 넓다'는 뜻을 지닌 (A) vast(광대한, 광활한)가 정답이다. ethical(윤리적인), final(마지막의), economic(경제적인).

> 어휘 meadowland 목초지 forest 숲 located in ~ 위치된

129

Hundreds of emails and web-forms arrive daily from customers and must be appropriately responded to ------- strict time limits.
(A) past
(B) throughout
(C) near
(D) within

수백 개의 이메일과 웹 양식은 고객들에게 매일 도착하고 엄격히 제한된 시간 내에 적절하게 응답되어야 합니다.

> 해설 빈칸은 뒤의 strict time limits(엄격히 제한된 시간)와 잘 어울리는 전치사가 들어갈 자리이다. 그래서 시간의 범위를 나타내는 전치사 (D) within(~ 내에)이 정답이다.

> 어휘 appropriately 적당하게, 알맞게 arrive 도착하다 strict 엄격한 limit 제한

130

------- is allowed to enter the company building after 7:30 P.M. unless accompanied by security personnel.
(A) No one
(B) One another
(C) Whoever
(D) Somebody

만약 보안직원과 동행하지 않는다면, 오후 7시 30분 이후에는 어떤 사람도 회사 건물에 들어올 수 없습니다.

> 해설 빈칸에는 문맥상 적합한 주어가 들어가야 한다. unless 이하는 '경비원에 의해 동행되지 않는다면'이고 앞 문장은 그 경우를 제외하고는 '빌딩 안으로 들어오는 것을 허락하지 않는다'는 의미이다. 따라서 부정의 의미를 나타내는 no one(어느 누구도 ~ 않다)이 정답이다.

> 어휘 accompany 동반하다, 동행하다 be allowed to 허용되다 unless ~하지 않는 한 security personnel 보안직원

PART 6

Questions 131-134 refer to the following notice.

Attention Associates!

The Capebile Group's continuing lecture series on policy design and implementation is adding a new voice. Ms. Berna Hopper, the former house speaker and head of the budget committee, will present her views on the future of American growth.

Coming from years of experience as a senator and having sat on many powerful committees, Ms. Hopper is a welcome ------- to our series. -------.
131.
132.

The talk will be given ------- September 18th at 3:30 in the main
133.
auditorium. As this is sure to be a very popular talk, please make sure to sign up for it in advance ------- admittance.
134.

동료 여러분 주목하세요!

Capebile Group의 정책 설계와 시행에 대한 계속적인 강의 시리즈에 새로운 의견을 덧붙입니다. 이전 의회 대변인이자 예산위원회 의장이었던 Berna Hopper 씨가 미국 성장의 미래에 대한 그녀의 견해를 발표할 것입니다.

의원으로서 수년간의 경험에서 나온 그리고 많은 힘 있는 위원회에 있었던 Hopper 씨는 우리 강연 시리즈에 아주 반가운 추가(새로운 인물)입니다. 그녀는 경제에 성장을 유발하는 투자자 신뢰와 정부 정책 사이의 관계를 논의할 것입니다.

강연은 대강당에서 9월 18일 3시 30분에 있을 것입니다. 아주 인기 있는 강연이 될 것이 확실하기 때문에, 입장을 확보하기 위해서 반드시 미리 신청하시기 바랍니다.

어휘 continuing 계속되는 policy 정책 implementation 이행, 실행 voice 의견, 강연자 budget committee 예산 위원회 view 견해 senator 상원의원 addition 추가, 충원 make sure 확실히 ~하다 sign up for 신청하다 in advance 미리 admittance 입장

131
(A) case
(B) addition
(C) instance
(D) attendee

해설 첫 단락을 보면 강연 시리즈에 새로운 연설자 Hopper 씨가 '충원'되었음을 알 수 있다. 따라서 정답은 (B) addition(추가, 충원)이다.

132
(A) She will discuss the relationship between investor confidence and governmental policies.
(B) It had an impact on our policy formulation.
(C) She used to design innovative systems over the last 10 years.
(D) She regularly participated in the seminar held by The Federal Government.

해설 문장삽입문제는 위치에 따라, 주제 문장, 앞 문장과의 관계, 뒤 문장과의 관계로 크게 나눌 수 있다. 본 문제는 앞 문장과의 관계를 따져서 해석이 적절한 문장을 선택하자. 앞 문장에서 새로운 강연자가 추가되었음을 언급했다. 그 말을 이어받아서 강연자의 강연 내용을 언급하는 (A)가 가장 적절하다.

(A) 그녀는 투자자 신뢰와 정부 정책 사이의 관계를 논의할 것이다.
(B) 그것은 우리의 정책 형성에 영향을 미쳤다.
(C) 그녀는 지난 10년간 혁신적인 시스템을 고안했었다.
(D) 그녀는 연방정부에 의해 열리는 세미나에 정기적으로 참석했었다.

133
(A) as
(B) in
(C) on
(D) to

해설 빈칸 다음에 9월 18일과 어울리는 전치사를 고르는 문제이다. 기본적으로 시간 전치사는 하루를 표현하면 전치사 on, 하루보다 큰 개념(2019년)은 전치사 in, 하루보다 작은 표현(3시)은 전치사 at을 쓴다. 9월 18일은 하루를 표현하므로 (C) on이 정답이다.

134
(A) ensures
(B) ensured
(C) ensuring
(D) to ensure

해설 빈칸 앞의 문장이 완벽하므로 빈칸은 부사자리임을 알 수 있다. 동사형태를 to부정사로 바꾸면 부사적 용법(~하기 위해서)이 가능하므로 정답은 (D) to ensure이다.

ACTUAL TEST 01 | ACTUAL TEST 02 | ACTUAL TEST 03 | ACTUAL TEST 04 | ACTUAL TEST 05

Questions 135-138 refer to the following e-mail.

To: ron.portwell@ymail.com
From: gian@greatgraphics.com
Subject: For your job application
Date: January 2, 2020

Dear Mr. Portwell,

We have reviewed your letter of application and résumé, and we want to set up an interview for the position you have applied for. Based on your letter, you are seeking an immediate full-time job as graphic designer. -------, we would like to offer you an
    135.
apprenticeship for three months, from January 15 to April 14.
-------.
136.

Sometimes applicants who have successfully undergone their apprenticeship are offered ------- positions upon completion,
    137.
and they are encouraged to take advantage of this opportunity.

If you wish ------- an apprenticeship, please reply to this e-mail
    138.
as soon as you can.

Gian Smith, Manager
Great Graphics Company

수신: ron.portwell@ymail.com
발신: gian@greatgraphics.com
제목: 당신의 지원서에 대해
날짜: 2020년 1월 2일

Portwell 씨께,

우리는 당신의 지원서와 이력서를 검토했고, 당신이 지원한 자리에 대해 면접을 보기를 원합니다. 편지에 의하면 당신은 그래픽 디자이너로서 즉시 정규직을 찾고 있습니다. 그러나 우리는 당신에게 1월 15일부터 4월 14일까지 3개월 동안의 수습기간을 제안하고자 합니다. 이 기간 동안 당신은 기술을 향상시키고, 그래픽 디자인 분야에서 실질적인 경험을 얻을 수 있을 것입니다.

때때로, 수습기간을 성공적으로 마친 지원자들에게는 정규직이 제공되며, 지원자들에게 이 기회를 잡도록 권장하고 있습니다.

만일 수습직을 원한다면, 가능한 한 빨리 이 이메일에 답장을 주기를 바랍니다.

Gian Smith, 매니저
Great Graphics Company

어휘 review 검토하다 résumé 이력서 based on ~을 기초로 해서 apprenticeship 견습직 undergo 겪다 upon completion 완료 시에 take advantage of ~을 이용하다

135
(A) As a result
(B) In addition
(C) However
(D) Rather than

해설 알맞은 접속부사를 선택하는 문제이다. 빈칸 앞의 내용은 '당신은 정규직을 구하고 있다'이고 빈칸 뒤 내용은 '우리는 당신에게 수습직을 제안한다'는 역접의 내용이므로 (C) However(그러나)가 정답이다.

136
(A) During this period, you will be able to enhance your skills and obtain practical experience in the graphic design field.
(B) You demonstrated your qualifications as a designer during the interview.
(C) If you accept this offer, your career as a chief designer is set to begin next month.
(D) You need to submit some samples of your work to be eligible for this.

[해설] 빈칸 앞 문장과의 관계를 확인하자. 빈칸 앞 내용이 수습직을 제안한다는 내용이다. 그 말을 바로 이어 받아서 수습직에서 할 일과 장점에 대해 설명하는 (A)가 가장 적절하다.

(A) 이 기간 동안 당신은 기술을 향상시키고, 그래픽 디자인 분야에서 실질적인 경험을 얻을 수 있을 것입니다.
(B) 당신이 인터뷰하는 동안 디자이너로서 자격요건을 입증하기 때문입니다.
(C) 만일 당신이 이 제안을 수락한다면, 수석 디자이너로서 당신의 일은 다음 달에 시작할 것입니다.
(D) 당신은 이것에 자격을 갖추기 위해 당신의 작품 견본을 제출할 필요가 있습니다.

137
(A) persistent
(B) durable
(C) sturdy
(D) permanent

[해설] 빈칸 다음에 명사 position(직책)과 어울리는 형용사를 고르는 문제이다. '영구직, 정규직'을 의미하는 permanent position이 적절하므로 (D)가 정답이다.

138
(A) pursued
(B) pursuing
(C) to pursue
(D) pursues

[해설] 빈칸은 동사 wish의 목적어자리이다. 동사형태를 to부정사 또는 동명사로 바꾸면 명사적 용법이 가능하다. 하지만 wish는 to부정사만을 목적어로 취하므로 (C) to pursue가 정답이다.

Questions 139-142 refer to the following announcement.

Nominations for Student Volunteers -------. Faculty members, staff and students can all nominate **139.** ------- students by completing the necessary form and **140.** submitting it to the Registrar's Office. The form must include the activities that the nominee has undertaken as a volunteer. The Awards Committee ------- all the nominations in January. **141.** The candidates will be ranked ------- the services that they **142.** performed at school and in the community. An awards ceremony will be held in February during the school festival. The deadline for nominations is December 25. Guidelines and forms for nominations are now available at the Registrar's Office and on the school website at www.southvillhigh.org.	학생자원봉사 후보지명 SouthVill 고등학교는 '올해의 뛰어난 자원봉사학생'에 대한 후보자 지명을 받고 있다. 교수진, 직원 그리고 학생들은 필요한 서류를 작성해서 등록사무실에 제출함으로써 자격 있는 학생들을 후보 지명할 수 있다. 양식서는 후보 지명자가 자원봉사자로서 했던 활동들을 포함해야 한다. 시상위원회는 1월에 모든 후보 지명을 검토할 것이다. 후보자들은 그들이 학교와 지역사회에서 했던 봉사에 근거해서 순위가 매겨 질 것이다. 시상식은 2월 학교 축제 동안 열릴 것이다. 후보 지명의 마감일은 12월 25일이다. 후보 지명에 대한 안내 사항과양식들은 등록사무실과 학교 홈페이지(www.southvillhigh.org)에서 이용 가능하다.

어휘 faculty 교원, 교직원 nominate 후보 지명하다 qualified 자격 있는 nominee 후보지명자 undertake 떠맡다 rank 순위 매기다 based on ~에 근거로 해서

139
(A) South Vill High School held the Annual Festival last week.
(B) We are seeking qualified faculty members to join our school.
(C) South Vill High School is accepting nominations for Outstanding Student.
(D) We are in need of volunteers who will be responsible for setting up the booths.

해설 본 문제와 같이 문장 맨 앞의 문장삽입문제는 지문의 주제를 표현한다. 뒤쪽 문맥을 살펴보면 학교에서 학생들에게 시상식을 하는데 후보 추천을 받는다는 내용이므로 (C)가 가장 적절하다.

(A) 고등학교는 지난주 연례 축제를 했다
(B) 우리는 학교에 들어올 자격 있는 교직원을 찾고 있다
(C) SouthVill 고등학교는 '올해의 뛰어난 자원봉사학생'에 대한 후보자 지명을 받고 있다.
(D) 우리는 부스를 설치하는 데 책임을 맡을 자원 봉사자를 필요로 한다.

140

(A) graduate
(B) qualified
(C) licensed
(D) numerical

해설 빈칸은 문맥을 이해하고 명사 student를 수식하는 적절한 형용사어휘를 선택하는 문제이다. 명사 student와의 관계만 고려하면 오답을 찾기 쉽다. 앞 문장에서 Outstanding Student Volunteers of the Year(올해의 뛰어난 자원봉사학생)를 언급했으므로 상에 맞는 '자격 있는 학생'이 적절하다. 따라서 정답은 (B) qualified이다.

141

(A) reviewing
(B) reviewed
(C) will review
(D) to be reviewed

해설 빈칸은 동사자리이며, 문맥상 후보지명 마감일이 12월 25일이고, 1월에 후보지명을 검토할 예정이므로 미래시제인 (C) will review가 정답이다.

142

(A) since
(B) due to
(C) for
(D) based on

해설 빈칸 앞 rank(순위 매기다)와 어울려서 service(봉사)를 목적어로 수반하는 전치사를 선택하는 문제이다. '수행했던 봉사에 근거해서 순위를 매기다'가 적절하므로 (D) based on이 정답이다.

Questions 143-146 refer to the following letter.

Mr. Smith
Chapter Chairperson

This is in reference to the memorandum which prescribes the deadline for the submission of monetary claims, dated January 9, 2020, and issued by Brandon Moore, our Finance Manager.

-------. All claims submitted after the deadline will not be
143.
accepted by the accounting division.

Please be ------- that February 2, 2020 the accounting division
144.
received a form for the payment of expenses for the fuel consumption of Frederick Merck, the company driver, by attaching the receipt issued by Afrilco Gasoline Station for the period of December 16-31, 2019. -------, you are asked to justify
145.
the delay of the submission of the form to head office ------- 5
146.
days from receipt of this letter.

Yours truly,

Christopher Perez
Overall Accountant

Smith 씨
지부장

이것은 우리의 재정담당 관리자인 Brandon Moore 씨에 의해 발행된 2020년 1월 9일자 자금청구서 제출에 대한 마감일을 규정하는 기록에 관한 것입니다.

메모에 적힌 대로, 모든 자금 청구에 대한 마감일은 2020년 1월 25일입니다. 마감기일 뒤에 제출된 모든 청구들은 회계부서에서 승인되지 않을 것입니다.

2020년 2월 2일 회계부서는 2019년 12월 16일부터 31일의 기간 동안 Afrilco 주유소에 의해 발행된 영수증을 첨부함으로써 회사 운전사 Frederick Merck의 연료 사용에 대한 비용 지불에 대한 서류를 받았습니다. 그 결과, 당신은 이 편지를 받은 5일 이내에 본사로 양식서의 제출 지연을 해명하도록 요청됩니다.

진심을 담아

Christopher Perez
종합 회계원

어휘 in reference to ~에 관련하여 prescribe 규정하다 submission 제출 monetary claim 자금 청구서 issue 발행하다 accounting 회계 expense 비용 consumption 소비 justify 해명하다

143

(A) He can extend the deadline as long as you report that it is not possible to complete the project.
(B) As stated in the memo, the due date for all monetary claims was on January 25, 2020.
(C) There was a change to the procedure in processing the claims.
(D) Please note that our company has a financial aid system for employees who have difficulty with finance.

해설 빈칸은 두 번째 단락을 시작하는 부분이므로 빈칸 뒤 내용과 어울리는 문장을 선택한다. 빈칸 다음 내용이 '마감일 이후에는 청구를 받지 않겠다'고 명시하므로 빈칸에서는 마감일에 대한 정의를 내리는 내용이 적절하다. 그러므로 (B)가 정답이다.

(A) 그는 당신이 프로젝트를 완수하는 것이 불가능하다고 보고한다면 마감기일을 연장할 것입니다.
(B) 메모에 적힌 대로, 모든 자금 청구에 대한 마감일은 2020년 1월 25일입니다.
(C) 청구를 처리하는 데 절차에 변경이 있었습니다.
(D) 우리 회사는 재정에 어려움이 있는 직원들을 위한 재정지원시스템이 있다는 것을 알아두길 바랍니다.

144

(A) noticed
(B) ensured
(C) informed
(D) said

해설 수동태에 알맞은 동사어휘를 선택하는 문제이다. 명령문은 주어 you가 생략된다. 그러므로 주어 you를 목적어로 가질 수 있는 동사가 필요하다. 사람목적어를 취하는 (C) informed가 정답이다. Please be informed that(~을 알아 두십시오) 형태를 기억하자.

145

(A) Instead
(B) On the other hand
(C) Nevertheless
(D) As a result

해설 앞뒤 문맥 사이에서 적절하게 내용을 연결시키는 접속부사자리이다. 빈칸 앞 내용은 '마감일이 지나서 청구서를 제출했다'는 내용이고 빈칸 뒤 내용은 '청구서 제출이 늦은 이유를 설명하라'이므로 인과관계를 연결하는 (D) As a result가 정답이다.

146

(A) until
(B) into
(C) within
(D) during

해설 빈칸 뒤 5 days를 수반하는 전치사 어휘문제이다. 기간명사 5 days를 수반하는 것은 (C) within이다. (A) until은 시점명사를 수반하므로 탈락되고 (D) during 뒤에는 일반명사(the vacation, the meeting 등)가 와야 한다.

ACTUAL TEST 01 ACTUAL TEST 02 ACTUAL TEST 03 ACTUAL TEST 04 ACTUAL TEST 05

PART 5

101

As Mr. Lim used Luxe software, he recovered the data that he had ------- erased from his computer.
(A) accidental
(B) accidentally
(C) accidents
(D) accident

Lim 씨는 Luxe software를 사용해서 컴퓨터에서 우연히 지웠던 데이터를 복구했다.

해설 빈칸은 동사 앞에 어울리는 품사가 와야 하는 자리이다. 동사는 부사가 수식하므로 정답은 (B) accidentally(우발적으로, 우연히)이다.

어휘 use 사용하다 recover 복구하다 accidentally 우연히 erase 지우다 accident 사고 accidental 우연한

102

Kaplani Corporation received the ------- approval of its business loan application by National Australian Bank.
(A) prompt
(B) promptness
(C) promptly
(D) prompts

Kaplani Corporation은 National Australian Bank로부터 사업 대출신청서의 즉각적인 승인을 받았다.

해설 빈칸은 뒤의 명사(approval)와 어울리는 형용사자리이다. 선택지 중에 형용사는 (A) prompt(즉각적인, 신속한)이다.

어휘 receive 받다 approval 승인 loan application 대출 신청서 prompt 즉각적인 promptly 지체 없이

103

The Norwich Theme Park construction plan has been ------- reviewed, and an analytical report of it has been posted at www.bonheurcity.go.com.
(A) consecutively
(B) exclusively
(C) approximately
(D) extensively

Norwich테마파크 건설 계획은 광범위하게 검토되었고, 건설 계획의 분석보고서는 www.bonheurcity.go.com에 게시되어 있다.

해설 빈칸은 동사 review(검토하다)와 의미가 적절한 부사(extensively 광범위하게, 폭넓게)자리이다. has been extensively reviewed 광범위하게 검토되어 왔다.

어휘 analytical 분석적 construction 건설 review 검토하다 post 게시하다 consecutively 연속하여 exclusively 오로지, 오직 approximately 거의 extensively 널리

104

Jacob Lim will stay on the executive committee for the ------- of his term and will serve as Vice President until August 14.
(A) remaining
(B) remainder
(C) remain
(D) remained

Jacob Lim 씨는 잔여 임기 동안 집행위원회에 남을 것이고, 8월 14일까지 부사장으로서 역할을 할 것이다.

해설 빈칸은 관사 the 뒤에 의미가 어울리는 명사가 올 자리이다. remainder는 '나머지, 여분'의 의미이고, remain은 보통 동사로 쓰이지만 명사로는 '유적, 잔재'의 의미도 있다. 빈칸 뒤의 of his term(그의 임기의)과의 의미연결을 볼 때 (B) remainder가 정답이다.

어휘 executive committee 집행 위원회 stay 머무르다 serve as ~역할을 하다 remain 계속 ~이다

105

The upgraded software package recently ------- in our laboratory has been used to improve daily operations.
(A) installed
(B) been installed
(C) installing
(D) to install

최근 우리 실험실에 설치된 업그레이드 된 소프트웨어 패키지는 일상적인 작업을 개선시키기 위해 사용되고 있다.

해설 빈칸은 명사 package를 수식하는 형용사자리이다. install(~을 설치하다)은 타동사가 앞의 명사를 수식하는데, 뒤에 목적어가 없으므로 '~된'의 의미인 (A) installed가 정답이다.

어휘 laboratory 실험실 recently 최근에 improve 개선하다 operation 작업 install 설치하다

106

The accounting firm of Nimbin and Byron Bay has ------- in tax returns and auditing for over 50 years.
(A) signed
(B) specialized
(C) maintained
(D) offered

Nimbin and Byron Bay의 회계사무소는 50년 이상 동안 세금환급과 회계 감사를 전문으로 해왔다.

해설 전치사 in과 어울리는 동사어휘를 고르는 문제이다. sign(서명하다), maintain(유지 보수하다), offer(제공하다)는 모두 타동사로 오답이다. specialize in은 '~을 전문으로 하다'라는 뜻의 토익 빈출어휘이다.

어휘 auditing 회계 감사 accounting firm 회계사무소 tax 세금 specialize 전공하다, 전문으로하다 maintain 유지하다 offer 제의하다

ACTUAL TEST 01 ACTUAL TEST 02 ACTUAL TEST 03 ACTUAL TEST 04 ACTUAL TEST 05

107

Despite ------- competition, in recent years all the VAMOS subsidiaries have continued to achieve steady growth in the British market.
(A) short
(B) strong
(C) positive
(D) perfect

치열한 경쟁에도 불구하고, 최근에 모든 VAMOS 자회사는 영국 시장에서 꾸준한 성장을 계속 이뤄왔다.

해설 빈칸은 명사 competition(경쟁)을 적절하게 수식해주는 형용사자리이다. 의미상 어울리는 형용사는 선택지 중 (B) strong이다. strong competition 치열한 경쟁

어휘 in recent years 최근에, 근래에 subsidiary 계열사, 자회사 steady 꾸준히 achieve 성취하다, 이루다 growth 성장 positive 긍정적인

108

It is important to consume generous amounts of vegetables since they contain antioxidants that will make your skin -------.
(A) healthiness
(B) more health
(C) healthier
(D) health

채소는 피부를 좀 더 건강하게 만들어주는 항산화제를 포함하고 있기 때문에, 넉넉한 양의 채소를 섭취하는 것이 중요하다.

해설 빈칸은 앞의 동사 make와 연결되어 <make + 목적어 + 형용사>의 구조가 되어야 한다. 따라서 형용사 형태인 healthy의 비교급인 (C) healthier가 정답이다.

어휘 antioxidant 산화 방지제 consume 소비하다 generous 후한, 넉넉한 vegetable 채소 contain ~이 들어 있다

109

All items purchased online before 5 P.M. will be delivered ------- two business days to addresses across Switzerland.
(A) since
(B) besides
(C) between
(D) within

오후 5시 전에 온라인으로 구매된 모든 물건들은 스위스 전역의 주소로 영업일 2일 내에 배달될 것입니다.

해설 빈칸은 뒤의 two business days(2영업일)와 어울리는 전치사자리이다. 기간의 단어와 의미가 어울리는 전치사는 (D) within(~이내)이다. since가 전치사로 '~이래로'라고 쓰이는 경우에는 시점을 나타내는 단어와 어울린다(within + 시점/기간명사).

어휘 purchase 구입하다 deliver 배달 besides ~ 외에 between ~ 사이에 within ~ 내에

110

Perth City Council has started receiving ------- for the Perth Volunteer of the Year award.
(A) nominates
(B) nominate
(C) nominated
(D) nominations

Perth 시의회는 올해의 Perth 자원봉사자상을 위해 추천을 받기 시작했다.

해설 빈칸은 동명사(receiving)의 목적어자리이므로 명사인 (D) nominations(후보 지명)가 정답이다. receiving은 본동사 start의 목적어(동명사)이지만 동명사가 되더라도 동사의 성질은 그대로 유지하므로 빈칸은 receive의 목적어자리가 되는 것이다.

어휘 council 시의회 start 시작하다 receive 받다 nominate 지명하다, 추천하다

111

------- has been recorded about the products made by Luxy Textile Company in the mid-twentieth century.
(A) Little
(B) Few
(C) Who
(D) Anyone

20세기 중반에 Luxy Textile 사에 의해 만들어진 제품에 관한 기록이 거의 없다.

해설 빈칸은 주어자리이다. few는 복수로 취급하므로 동사 has와 어울리지 않는다. who는 관계대명사로 쓰이면 선행사가 필요하고, 의문사로 쓰였다면 의문문의 형태로 물음표로 끝나는 문장이 되어야 하므로 이것 역시 오답이다. anyone을 주어로 넣고 해석을 해 보면 '누군가가 제품에 대해 기록되었다'라는 엉뚱한 의미로 해석된다. little은 셀 수 없는 의미를 나타내면서 부정의 의미로 쓰인다. 해석은 '제품에 관한 기록이 거의 없다'처럼 의미 전달 역시 자연스럽다.

어휘 record 기록하다 product 상품

112

Dr. Jason's ------- comes from his 35 years of working in the pharmaceutical and biochemical industry.
(A) indication
(B) expense
(C) impression
(D) expertise

Jason 박사의 전문지식은 제약과 생화학 업계에서 일한 35년 경력에서 나온 것이다.

해설 소유격(Dr. Jason's) 다음의 빈칸은 명사자리이다. 문맥상 Jason 박사의 ~은 35년간의 경력에서 온 것이라는 의미이므로 (D) expertise(전문지식)가 가장 자연스럽다.

어휘 pharmaceutical industry 제약업 biochemical industry 생화학 산업 indication 조짐 expense 돈, 비용 impression 인상 expertise 전문지식

113

Notice of your ------- to take a vacation must be given to the company no less than 4 days prior to your vacation.
(A) policy
(B) intention
(C) proposal
(D) direction

휴가 계획에 관한 통지는 회사에 휴가 가기 4일 전에 미리 알려져야 한다.

해설 빈칸을 제외한 부분의 해석을 보면 '휴가를 가기 위한 당신의 ~에 관한 통지는 회사에 주어져야 한다'이다. ~에 해당되는 적절한 의미의 단어는 (B) intention(의도, 계획)이다. policy(정책), proposal(제안서), direction(지시, 길 안내)은 어울리지 않는다.

어휘 어휘 vacation 방학, 휴가 no less than 적어도 policy 정책 intention 의도, 계획 proposal 제안 direction 방향

114

Although the requisition for the processing equipment was sent four days ago, we have ------- to receive confirmation of its approval.
(A) still
(B) nor
(C) yet
(D) even

비록 처리장비 요청이 4일 전에 보내졌음에도 우리는 아직 승인 확인을 받지 못했다.

해설 have와 to 사이에 어울리는 단어를 고르는 문제이다. have yet to(아직 ~ 않다, 여전히 ~해야 한다)를 알고 있다면 쉽게 해결할 수 있다.

어휘 requisition 요청 processing equipment 처리장비 confirmation 확인 approval 승인

115

The construction of a new bus terminal in Neo Town, that was set to start this year, -------.
(A) has been postponed
(B) postpones
(C) will have postponed
(D) is postponing

올해 착수하기로 했던 Neo Town의 새로운 버스 터미널 건설이 연기되었다.

해설 빈칸은 앞의 주어 construction과 연결되는 postpone의 적절한 동사형태를 고르는 문제이다. postpone은 '~을 연기시키다'라는 타동사이므로 목적어가 필요한데, 빈칸 뒤에 목적어가 없으므로 수동태가 적절하다. 선택지 중에서 수동태는 (A) has been postponed(연기되어 왔다)이다.

어휘 set to 시작(착수)하다. construction 건설 postpone 연기하다, 미루다

102

116

Highly ------- musicians can easily be hired from universities or orchestras when they need to fill the vacant positions.
(A) qualified
(B) potential
(C) apparent
(D) enclosed

매우 자질이 있는 음악가들은 대학교나 오케스트라에서 공석을 채울 필요가 있을 때, 쉽게 채용될 수 있다.

해설 부사 highly(매우)와 명사 musicians(음악가들) 사이의 빈칸은 형용사자리이다. 빈출표현인 highly qualified(매우 자질 있는)를 암기해두자.

어휘 vacant 비어 있는, 공석의 musician 음악가 hire 고용하다 university 대학 orchestra 관현악단 qualified 자격을 갖춘 potential 잠재적인 apparent 분명한 enclosed 동봉된

117

Representatives from Maxtopia Publishing ------- a welcome reception in the IBS Building next Friday at 6:30 P.M..
(A) will be hosting
(B) will have hosted
(C) hosted
(D) will be hosted

Maxtopia Publishing의 담당자는 IBS빌딩에서 다음 주 금요일 오후 6시 30분에 환영회를 주최할 것이다.

해설 빈칸은 동사자리이다. 빈칸 뒤에 a welcome reception(환영회)이라는 목적어(명사)가 있으므로 수동형인 will be hosted는 오답이다. 그리고 뒤에 next Friday(다음 금요일)라는 미래표현이 보이므로 미래진행형인 (A) will be hosting이 정답이다. will have hosted는 미래완료의 형태로 미래 시점까지 계속 행위를 이어갈 때 쓰는 표현이다. 본 문장은 단순히 다음 금요일에 있을 사건을 말하는 내용으로 미래완료의 느낌과는 거리가 있다.

어휘 representative 대표 welcome reception 환영회 host 주최하다, 열다

118

Although Raymond plays a trivial role in the opera, his passionate song leaves a ------- impression on audiences.
(A) lasted
(B) lasting
(C) lastly
(D) lasts

Raymond 씨가 오페라에서 사소한 역할을 맡을지라도, 그의 열정적인 노래는 청중들에게 지속적인 인상을 남긴다.

해설 명사(impression) 앞의 빈칸은 형용사자리이다. 동사 last(지속하다)의 형용사형인 (B) lasting(지속적인)이 정답이다.

어휘 trivial 사소한, 하찮은 although ~에도 불구하고 role 역할 passionate 열정적인 impression 인상 audience 청중 lasting 지속적인

119

A plumber from Horrin Maintenance will arrive at the Q&G Building at 9:00 A.M. tomorrow to ------- the water pipe problem.
(A) invite
(B) commend
(C) assess
(D) proceed

Horrin Maintenance 사의 배관공이 배수관 문제를 평가하기 위하여 내일 오전 9시에 Q&G 빌딩에 도착할 것이다.

해설 빈칸은 명사 the water pipe problem(수도관 문제)를 목적어로 취하는 타동사자리이다. 문맥상 적절한 선택지는 (C) assess(평가하다)이다. invite는 '초대하다, 권유하다'의 의미로 사람목적어를 가지며, commend는 '칭찬하다'로 의미가 어색하고, proceed(나가가다, 진행하다)는 자동사이다.

어휘 plumber 배관공 arrive 도착하다 assess 평가하다 invite 초대하다 commend 칭찬하다 proceed 진행하다

120

All products are ------- inspected and tested before shipment from the factory.
(A) largely
(B) thoroughly
(C) highly
(D) steeply

모든 상품은 공장으로부터 배송 전에 철저하게 점검되고 검사된다.

해설 빈칸은 동사 inspect(검사하다)와 의미상 어울리는 부사가 올 자리이다. largely는 '주로'의 의미로, largely due to는 '주로 ~ 때문에', largely determine는 '주로 결정하다' 등으로 쓰이고, highly(매우)는 highly recommend(매우 권장하다)로 자주 출제된다. steeply는 '가파르게'의 의미이다. inspect와 잘 어울리는 부사는 (B) thoroughly(철저하게)이다. thoroughly inspect 철저히 점검하다

어휘 inspect 점검하다 test 시험하다 shipment 배송 factory 공장 largely 주로 thoroughly 철저히 highly 매우 steeply 가파르게

121

Author Andrew Rixson, who has sold over 10 million copies of Au nom de la rose, is busy working on the sixth ------- of the series.
(A) installation
(B) instalment
(C) installer
(D) install

천만 부가 넘게 팔렸던 「Au nom de la rose」의 저자인 Andrew Rixson은 6번째 시리즈물을 준비하느라 바쁘다.

해설 installation은 '설치', instalment는 '할부, 분납, 연재물의 한 회분'의 의미인데, 문장에서 10-million copies(천만 부), series(시리즈)와 어울리는 명사는 (B) instalment(연재물의 한 회분)이다. the sixth instalment of the series 시리즈 중 6번째 편

어휘 sell 팔다 series 시리즈, 연속물 installation 설치 instalment 할부, 분할(의 1회분)

122

A one hour guided tour is available for groups of 15 or more and the price is $ 28.00 ------- person.
(A) with
(B) per
(C) by
(D) despite

한 시간 가이드투어는 15명 또는 그 이상의 그룹이 이용 가능하고 가격은 1인당 28 달러이다.

해설 빈칸은 뒤의 person과 적절하게 연결되는 전치사자리이다. 문맥상 '가격은 28달러이다'이므로 '한 명당 얼마이다'라는 의미가 적절하다. 단위를 나타내는 전치사 (B) per(~당, ~마다)가 정답이다.

어휘 available 이용 가능한 price 가격 per ~당, ~마다 despite ~에도 불구하고

123

The Shown Pen Inc., is known for its tractors and other farm machines, but ------- of us are familiar with modern farm equipment today than ever before.
(A) fewest
(B) fewer
(C) few
(D) a few

Show Pen 사는 트랙터와 다른 농장 기계로 유명하지만 지금은 예전에 비해 현대 농기구에 친숙한 사람이 훨씬 적다.

해설 빈칸은 선택지의 few 중에서 적절한 형태를 고르는 문제이다. 뒷부분을 살펴보면 than이 보이므로, than 앞쪽에 비교 형태가 등장해야 한다. 빈칸을 제외한 나머지 부분에서 비교급이 보이지 않으므로 빈칸에는 비교급이 와야 한다. 그래서 정답은 (B) fewer이다.

어휘 be known for ~로 알려져 있다 tractor 트랙터 farm 농장 be familiar with ~와 친숙한 equipment 기계, 장비

124

The College Office will start its process for reviewing each of the applications ------- the deadline for submitting applications has passed.
(A) now that
(B) how
(C) neither
(D) whether

지원서 제출 기한이 지났기 때문에 College Office는 각각의 지원서를 검토하기 위한 절차를 시작할 것이다.

해설 빈칸은 앞뒤 문장을 연결해주는 접속사자리이다. 앞 문장은 ~start its process(진행을 시작하다)이고, 뒤 문장은 ~the deadline has passed(마감일이 지났다)이므로 두 문장을 자연스럽게 연결해주는 접속사는 (A) now that(~이니까)이다. 즉, '마감일이 지났기 때문에 검토를 시작할 것이다'라는 의미가 된다.

어휘 start 시작하다 process 절차, 과정 review 검토하다 application 지원서, 신청서 deadline 마감일 submit 제출하다

ACTUAL TEST 01 ACTUAL TEST 02 ACTUAL TEST 03 ACTUAL TEST 04 ACTUAL TEST 05

105

125

Our experienced team can work together to put a quality finish on any house in a ------- short time.
(A) surprise
(B) surprised
(C) surprisingly
(D) surprising

우리의 숙련된 팀은 어떠한 집이라도 놀랍게도 짧은 시간에 양질의 마감처리를 위해 함께 일할 수 있다.

해설 빈칸은 형용사(short) 앞의 빈칸은 부사자리이다. 문맥상 어울리는 부사는 (C) surprisingly(놀랍게, 대단히)이다.

어휘 experienced 숙련된 quality 양질의, 양질 surprisingly 놀랍게

126

Viva Net today announced that the company will not ------- its agreement with the Cable Network Epix next month.
(A) proceed
(B) attract
(C) avoid
(D) renew

Viva Net은 회사가 다음달에 Cable Network Epix와 합의서를 갱신하지 않는다는 것을 오늘 발표했다.

해설 빈칸은 뒤의 its agreement(협정)를 목적어로 취하는 동사자리이다. 자동사인 proceed는 우선 탈락되고, attract(매혹시키다), avoid(피하다)는 의미연결이 어색하다. 의미상 renew its agreement(협정을 갱신하다)가 자연스럽다.

어휘 announce 발표하다 agreement 협정 renew 갱신하다 attract 매혹시키다 avoid 피하다

127

Northern Construction Inc. has received several awards ------- its efforts to promote energy efficiency.
(A) off
(B) away
(C) for
(D) across

Northen Construction 사는 에너지 효율성을 촉진시키는 노력 때문에 상을 몇 개 받았다.

해설 빈칸은 뒤의 its efforts(그것의 노력)와 의미가 연결되는 전치사자리이다. '~에 대해서, ~때문에'의 의미를 지닌 전치사 (C) for가 정답이다.

어휘 effort to 노력하다, 애를 쓰다 receive 받다 several 여러 개의 award 상 promote 촉진하다 efficiency 효율성

128

Four copy machines that ------- to copying manuals are being set up in the marketing department.
(A) dedicate
(B) dedication
(C) had dedicated
(D) will be dedicated

매뉴얼을 복사하는 데에만 사용될 4대의 복사기가 마케팅 부서에 설치되고 있다.

해설 동사 dedicate의 적절한 형태를 묻고 있다. be dedicated to(~에 헌신하다, 전념하다)표현을 기억해두면 쉽게 해결할 수 있는 문제이다.

어휘 set up 설치하다 department 부서

129

After all, advancement within the company is ------- decided by the individual employee's achievements and performance.
(A) deeply
(B) largely
(C) continually
(D) formerly

결국, 회사 내의 승진은 주로 직원 각자의 업적과 성과에 의해서 결정된다.

해설 be동사(is)와 과거분사(decided) 사이의 빈칸은 부사자리이다. 빈칸에 들어갈 적절한 부사는 largely(주로)이다. deeply(매우)는 deeply appreciate 매우 감사하다, deeply apologize 매우 미안하다 등으로 자주 쓰인다. continually 계속해서 formerly 이전에

어휘 advancement 발전, 진보 decide 결정하다 individual 각각의 achievement 성취 performance 성과

130

All four parties agree to the terms of the contract and sign the document in support of each -------.
(A) another
(B) the other
(C) others
(D) other

모든 네 그룹이 계약서의 조건에 동의하고 서로를 지지해서 문서에 서명했다.

해설 빈칸은 앞의 each와 어울리는 단어가 들어갈 자리이다. 선택지 중에서 (D) other만이 연결 가능한 형태이다. each other 서로 서로

어휘 in support of ~을 지지하여, ~를 옹호하여 party 일행 agree to ~에 동의하다 contract 계약서 document 문서 another 또 하나의 the other (둘 중의) 다른 하나 other (그 밖의) 다른

PART 6

Questions 131-134 refer to the following letter.

Dear Mr. Sardina

For the past two years, we ------- you a monthly newsletter, The
            131.
Motor Dealer, containing information about many companies

and services ------- to clients.
             132.

To show our ------- to loyal customers like you, we would like
            133.
to send you two tickets for an evening pottery exhibit at the

Pillsbury Capitol. I am sure you will love it because famous

pottery makers from around the country will display their artwork

for a week. -------. The tickets will be valid only on the stamped
           134.
date, so we hope you can make time to visit this unique display.

The exhibit is entitled "The Andrei." and we hope you will enjoy

it.

Sincerely Yours,

Jayden
Customer Service Manager

Sardina 씨께

지난 2년간, 우리는 당신에게 많은 회사들과 고객들에게 제공되는 서비스에 대한 정보를 담고 있는 월간지 The Motor Dealer를 보냈습니다.

당신과 같은 단골 고객들에게 감사를 표하기 위해서, Pillsbury Capitol에서 열리는 야간 도자기 전시회 표를 두 장 보내고자 합니다. 전국의 유명한 도자기 제조자들이 일주일간 그들의 작품을 전시할 것이기 때문에, 당신이 좋아할 것이라고 확신합니다. 사실, 몇몇은 그들의 재능에 대해 국제적인 상을 수상했습니다. 표는 단지 표시된 날짜에만 유효할 것입니다. 그래서, 우리는 이 독특한 전시회를 방문할 시간을 내어 주시기를 바랍니다. 전시회 명칭은 The Andrei이고, 즐거운 관람이 되길 바랍니다.

진심을 담아

Jayden
고객 서비스 관리자

어휘 contain 포함하다 gratitutde 감사 loyal customers 단골 고객 like ~처럼 pottery 도자기 around the country 전 세계에 valid 유효한 stamped date 표시된 날짜 be entitled 제목이 붙어져 있다, 자격 있다

131
(A) have sent
(B) are sent
(C) will send
(D) are to send

해설 문장 앞에 for the past two years(지난 2년 동안)을 보면 지난 2년간 월간지를 보내고 있다는 계속적 용법이므로 현재완료 시제인 (A) have sent가 정답이다. for(during, over, in) the past (last) + 기간명사는 현재완료시제와 어울린다는 것을 알아두자.

132
(A) offer
(B) will be offered
(C) offering
(D) offered

[해설] 이 문장의 본동사는 143번 (A) have sent이다. 빈칸 앞을 보면 마침표 또는 접속사가 없으므로 빈칸은 본동사가 올 수 없다. 그러므로 (A), (B)는 탈락된다. 따라서 빈칸은 선행사 information을 수식하는 분사자리이며, 정보는 제공되는 수동의 의미이므로 (D) offered가 정답이다.

133
(A) gratitude
(B) attitude
(C) recognition
(D) regret

[해설] 문맥상 어울리는 명사 어휘를 선택하는 문제이다. 지난 2년간 정기구독자였다는 것을 보답하는 내용이므로 (A) gratitude가 정답이다.

134
(A) Some of them are subject to a small fee.
(B) It attracted more visitors than the previous year.
(C) You need to hurry because the number of the visitors is limited to 500.
(D) In fact, some of them even received international awards due to their talents.

[해설] 빈칸 앞뒤 문맥을 살펴보면 구독자에 대한 보답으로 도자기 전시회 티켓을 제공하고 있다. 빈칸은 그 전시회의 내용을 소개하는 (D)가 적절하다.

(A) 몇몇은 약간의 비용을 조건으로 합니다.
(B) 전년도보다 더 많은 방문객을 유치했습니다.
(C) 방문자 수가 500명으로 제한되어 있기 때문에 서둘러야 합니다.
(D) 사실, 몇몇은 그들의 재능에 대해 국제적인 상을 수상했습니다.

From: Sam Smith

Sent: Wednesday, April 3

To: Office staff

Subject: Chair Replacements

Hello, staff

This email is to let ------- know that we will finally be replacing
135.
the worn out office chairs we have been using for years. -------.
136.
Please note that we do not have the ------- to replace every
137.
chair in the office, so please do not request a new one if you are
still comfortable with your present one.

Requests can be made by ------- the form on the company
138.
website. New chairs will be purchased next month and will
replace the old chairs no later than May 14. If you have any
questions or special requests, please contact me.

Emily Hunts

Office Furniture Appropriation Officer, Extension 2382

발신: Sam Smith

날짜: 4월 3일 수요일

수신: 사무실 직원

제목: 의자 교체

안녕하세요, 직원 여러분

이 이메일은 우리가 수년간 사용해온 오래된 사무실 의자들을 결국 교체할 것임을 당신에게 알려 주기 위한 것입니다. 만일 의자를 교체할 필요가 있다면, 늦어도 4월 30일까지 요청서를 제출하시기 바랍니다. 사무실의 모든 의자를 교체할 예산을 가지고 있지 않다는 점을 알아두길 바랍니다. 그래서, 만일 현재 사용하는 의자가 편하다면 새것을 요청하지 않길 바랍니다.

회사 홈페이지에서 양식을 작성함으로써 요청은 이루어집니다. 새 의자들은 다음 달에 구매될 것이고, 늦어도 5월 14일까지 이전 의자들을 대체할 것입니다. 만일 질문이나 특별한 요청 사항이 있다면, 연락 바랍니다.

Emily Hunts
사무실 가구 담당 직원, 내선번호 2382

어휘 replace 교체하다 worn out 낡은 budget 예산 comfortable 편안한 extension 내선번호

135
(A) you
(B) your
(C) your own
(D) yours

해설 빈칸은 사용동사 let 다음에 목적어자리이다. '당신에게 알려주다'가 적절하므로 목적격 대명사 (A) you가 정답이다.

136

(A) The accounting department assigned us funds to be given to outstanding employees.
(B) Office chairs were made by a unique local artisan.
(C) If you feel your chair is in need of a change, please submit a request by no later than April 30.
(D) You need to fill out the form to be considered qualified for the position.

> **해설** 빈칸 앞 문장과 어울리는 문장을 선택하는 문제이다. 앞 문장을 살펴보면 '낡은 의자를 교체할 것이다'라고 언급했으므로 '필요하다면 요청서를 제출하라'는 (C)가 가장 적절하다.

(A) 회계부서는 훌륭한 직원들에게 주는 자금을 우리에게 할당했습니다.
(B) 사무실 의자는 독특한 지방 예술가에 의해 제작되었습니다.
(C) 만일 의자를 교체할 필요가 있다면, 늦어도 4월 30일까지 요청서를 제출하시기 바랍니다.
(D) 당신은 그 자리에 자격이 있다고 고려되기 위해서는 양식서를 작성할 필요가 있습니다.

137

(A) charge
(B) cost
(C) budget
(D) expense

> **해설** 알맞은 명사 어휘를 선택하는 문제이다. 이메일을 쓰는 회사의 입장으로 보면 사내 의자를 교체하려면 '예산'이 필요하므로 (C) budget(예산)이 정답이다.

138

(A) complete
(B) completed
(C) completing
(D) completion

> **해설** 빈칸 앞에 전치사 by와 빈칸 다음에 목적어 the form 사이에 적절한 품사는 동명사이다. 따라서 (C) completing이 정답이다.

Questions 139-142 refer to the following e-mail.

To: calone@teleworm.us
From: jenkins@dayrep.com
Subject: Career Application
Date: February 9

Dear Mr. Calone,

Having read over your application and accompanying letter explaining your interest in joining ------- firm, we would be very
139.
interested in speaking to you in person.

We see you hope to join our company as a manager. Normally, we would not entertain such requests. -------, after reviewing
140.
your background experience, we remain open-minded.

The competition between our rivals has become intense -------,
141.
and somebody with your skill set could be very useful in helping us hold on to our market share. We hope to speak to you by no later than Wednesday, February 11th. We realize that you are located in Seattle and our headquarters are in Chicago. -------.
142.
She will provide you with information on the soonest available airplane ticket, which we will of course pay for.

We look forward to seeing you.

수신: calone@teleworm.us
발신: jenkins@dayrep.com
제목: 지원서
날짜: 2월 9일

Calone 씨께

귀하의 지원서와 당사에 입사하려는 관심을 설명하는 편지를 읽은 후에 저희는 귀하와 만나서 직접 이야기를 나누고 싶습니다.

귀하가 매니저로서 우리 회사에 입사하기를 바란다는 것을 알고 있습니다. 통상적으로는 그러한 요청을 고려하지 않습니다. 하지만 귀하의 경력을 검토한 뒤에, 편견이 사라졌습니다.

최근에 경쟁자들 사이에서 경쟁이 날로 심해지고 있으며, 귀하와 같은 기술을 갖춘 사람이 시장 점유율을 유지하는 데 무척 많은 도움이 될 것입니다. 저희는 늦어도 2월 11일 수요일 이전에 이야기를 나누고 싶습니다. 귀하는 시애틀에 있고, 본사는 시카고에 있다는 것을 알고 있습니다. 제 비서인 Emma 씨에게 555-0134로 연락을 주세요. 비서는 저희가 당연히 지불할 가장 빠른 항공권에 대한 정보를 귀하에게 줄 것입니다.

당신을 조만간 뵙기를 희망합니다.

어휘 application 지원서 accompany 동반하다 in person 직접 entertain 받아들이다 competition 경쟁 rival 경쟁자 market share 시장 점유율 no later than 늦어도 ~까지 of course 물론

139
(A) our
(B) ours
(C) us
(D) ourselves

해설 인칭대명사를 고르는 문제이다. 빈칸 다음에 firm(회사) 명사가 있으므로 소유격 대명사 (A) our가 정답이다.

140
(A) However
(B) Thus
(C) Therefore
(D) Afterwards

해설 빈칸은 앞 문장과 뒤 문장의 의미를 연결해주는 접속부사자리이다. 앞 문장은 '통상적으로 이런 요청을 받지 않는다'이고 뒤 문장은 '우리는 편견이 없어졌다'는 역접의 내용이므로 (A) However가 정답이다.

141
(A) promptly
(B) shortly
(C) lately
(D) currently

해설 알맞은 부사어휘를 선택하는 문제이다. (A) promptly는 의미상 부적절하며 (B) shortly는 미래시제와 어울린다. 그리고 (D) currently는 현재시제와 어울리기 때문에 탈락된다. 현재완료시제 또는 과거시제와 어울리는 (C) lately가 정답이다.

142
(A) Our headquarters are very conveniently located near the subway station.
(B) Please contact my secretary, Mrs.Emma, at 555-0134.
(C) In case of emergency, you can contact me directly not my assistant, Mrs. Emma.
(D) We will assist you with the travel costs.

해설 뒤 문장에서 '그녀가 당신에게 정보를 제공할 것이다'이므로 그녀에 대한 연락처를 알려주는 (B)가 가장 적절하다.

(A) 본사는 지하철 역 근처에 아주 편리하게 위치하고 있습니다.
(B) 제 비서인 Emma 씨에게 555-0134로 연락을 주세요.
(C) 비상시, 비서인 Emma가 아니라 나에게 직접 연락할 수 있습니다.
(D) 우리는 당신에게 여행 경비를 지원할 것입니다.

Questions 143-146 refer to the following letter.

Dear Sir,	귀하께,
Our office officially received your letter last Tuesday, September 26. We appreciate your noble intention for holding this kind of program.	우리 사무실은 9월 26일 지난 화요일 귀하의 편지를 공식적으로 받았습니다. 우리는 이러한 종류의 프로그램을 개최하는 것에 대한 귀하의 숭고한 의도에 감사드립니다.
However, the ------- you requested for your medical services is not available on that date because there are already activities that ------- there. We appeal to your management if you could possibly postpone your medical project to the next day, or decide to change venues. -------.	그러나 의료 봉사에 대해 요청한 장소는 예정된 활동이 이미 있기 때문에 그날에는 이용 불가능합니다. 우리는 의료 프로젝트를 그다음 날로 연기할 수 있는지 또는 장소를 바꾸기로 결정할 수 있는지 귀하의 운영진에 요청합니다. 이 방법으로, 귀하의 활동을 계속 주관할 수 있을 것입니다.
143. **144.** **145.**	
We deeply apologize for this inconvenience. We are ------- of having your radio station serve as our partner in upholding our commitment to help other people.	불편을 끼쳐드려 진심으로 죄송합니다. 다른 사람들을 도우려는 약속을 지켜주는 우리 파트너로서의 역할을 해주는 귀하 라디오 방송국에 대해 감사드립니다.
146.	
Thank you very much.	감사합니다.
Sincerely yours,	진심을 담아
James Carter City Representative	James Carter 시 대표

어휘 officially 공식적으로 appreciate 감사하다 noble 고귀한, 숭고한 intention 의도 appeal 호소하다 venue 장소 be appreciative of ~에 감사하다 uphold 받치다

143
(A) vehicle
(B) time
(C) place
(D) equipment

해설 본 문제는 문맥상 적절한 명사 어휘를 선택하는 문제이다. 하단에 decide to change venues(장소를 바꾸기로 결정하다)를 확인하면 (C) place가 정답임을 알 수 있다.

144
(A) schedule
(B) scheduled
(C) has been scheduled
(D) are scheduled

해설 빈칸 앞 that은 주격 관계대명사로 선행사 activities를 수식한다. 일단 선행사가 복수 형태이므로 (C)는 탈락된다. 문맥상 일정이 이미 예정되었다는 의미이므로 수동태(are scheduled)가 적절하다.

145
(A) We are so sorry to refuse your participation this time.
(B) We consider your proposal very useful for producing our new radio program.
(C) There will be no exception to the participants.
(D) This way, you can still continue to host your activities.

해설 빈칸 앞 내용과 어울리는 문장을 선택하는 문제이다. 앞 내용을 살펴보면 '장소가 이용가능하지 않으므로 날짜를 연기하든지 장소를 바꿀 결정을 하다'는 내용이므로 그런 노력을 통해서 '활동을 계속할 수 있다'는 (D)가 가장 적합하다.

(A) 우리는 이번에 귀하의 참여를 거부하게 되어 매우 죄송합니다.
(B) 우리는 새로운 라디오 프로그램을 제작하는데 귀하의 제안서가 아주 유용하다고 생각합니다.
(C) 참가자들에 대한 예외는 없을 것입니다.
(D) 이 방법으로, 귀하의 활동을 계속 주관할 수 있을 것입니다.

146
(A) appreciating
(B) appreciated
(C) appreciative
(D) appreciation

해설 빈칸은 be동사 다음에 주격보어자리이다. 주격 보어자리는 형용사가 어울리므로 (C) appreciative가 정답이다. be appreciative of(~에 감사하다)를 외워두자.

PART 5

101

A list of restaurant owners that participated in this year's slow food festival ------- on the desk next to the cabinet.
(A) will be finding
(B) can be found
(C) are finding
(D) can find

올해 슬로푸드 축제에 참석했던 레스토랑 주인들의 명부는 캐비닛 옆에 있는 책상 위에서 발견될 수 있다.

해설 빈칸은 문장을 구성하기 위한 동사가 올 자리이다. find(~을 찾다)는 타동사이며, 빈칸 뒤에 목적어가 없으므로 수동형태인 (B) can be found가 정답이다.

어휘 participate 참석하다 restaurant 식당 find 발견하다

102

All customers are requested to express their meal ------- by marking their selection on the menu.
(A) prefers
(B) preferable
(C) preferences
(D) preferential

모든 손님들은 메뉴판에 선택을 표시함으로써 선호 식사를 표현하도록 요청된다.

해설 빈칸은 동사 express의 목적어자리이면서 their meal과의 연결도 자연스러워야 한다. meal preference를 복합명사로 '선호 식사'라고 챙겨두면 쉽게 정답 확인이 가능하다.

어휘 customer 손님 request 요청하다 express 표현하다 selection 선택, 선호

103

As snow was expected, the organizers ------- the customer dinner to the reception hall.
(A) have been moved
(B) will be moved
(C) moved
(D) were moved

눈이 예상되었기 때문에, 주최자들은 고객 만찬을 연회 홀로 옮겼다.

해설 빈칸은 형태가 적절한 동사가 들어갈 자리이다. 빈칸 뒤에 목적어(the customer dinner)가 있으므로 능동형태의 동사인 (C) moved가 정답이다.

어휘 expect 예상하다 organizer 주최자 customer 고객 indoors 실내에서 reception hall 연회 홀

104

If it has been longer than 7 business days and your order ------- has not arrived, please contact customer service via email.
(A) yet
(B) already
(C) still
(D) nearly

만약 7영업일보다 더 걸리고 주문이 여전히 도착하지 않았다면, 고객서비스부서에 이메일로 연락하세요.

해설 빈칸은 문맥상, 위치상 부사자리이다. 빈칸 뒤에 has not이 보이고, '아직'이라는 의미로 연결되어야 전체 해석이 자연스럽다. 정답은 (C) still이다. yet도 의미상 가능은 하지만, yet은 not 뒤에 위치해야 한다. 즉, still ~ not, not ~ yet의 형태로 둘 다 '~ 않다'라는 의미이다.

어휘 via ~을 통해서 arrive 도착하다 contact 연락하다

105

MARU Convention Center has the latest audio and visual equipment ------- all of its conference rooms.
(A) into
(B) on
(C) before
(D) in

MARU Convention Center는 모든 회의실에 최신식의 오디오와 시각장비를 갖추고 있다.

해설 빈칸은 장소를 나타내는 전치사자리이다. conference rooms와 어울리는 전치사는 (D) in이다.

어휘 latest 최신의 visual equipment 시각장비 conference room 회의실

106

Eloise Peter's design for the community center was ------- regarded by all members of the planning committee.
(A) higher
(B) high
(C) highest
(D) highly

커뮤니티 센터를 위한 Eloise Peter의 디자인은 계획 위원회의 모든 멤버들에 의해서 매우 높게 평가되었다.

해설 빈칸은 동사 regard를 수식하는 부사자리이다. regard와 의미상 잘 어울리는 부사는 highly이다. highly regard는 '매우 존경하다'로 기억해두자. high(높이)도 부사이긴 하지만 의미상 적절하지 않다.

어휘 regard 존경하다 committee 위원회 highly 매우

ACTUAL TEST 01 ACTUAL TEST 02 ACTUAL TEST 03 ACTUAL TEST 04 ACTUAL TEST 05

107

All River Side apartments are ------- with an environment-friendly heating and cooling system.
(A) equip
(B) equipping
(C) equipped
(D) equipment

모든 River Side 아파트는 환경 친화적인 난방과 냉방 시스템이 갖추어져 있다.

해설 be동사 are와 전치사 with 사이에 들어갈 적절한 형태의 단어를 찾도록 하자. 빈출어휘인 be equipped with(~을 갖추다)를 잘 챙겨두자.

어휘 environment-friendly 환경 친화적 heating 난방 cooling 냉방 equipment 장비

108

The ------- of the new task force team is to find more efficient methods to improve employee productivity.
(A) mission
(B) attitude
(C) benefit
(D) reason

새로운 대책위원회 팀의 임무는 직원 생산성을 개선시킬 더 효율적인 방법을 찾는 것이다.

해설 빈칸은 주어자리이며 의미가 적절한 명사가 들어갈 자리이다. 빈칸 뒤의 of the task force team(대책위원회 팀)과 잘 어울리는 명사는 mission(임무)이다. attitude 태도 benefit 혜택, 이득 reason 이유

어휘 productivity 생산성 task force team 대책위원회 팀 efficient 효율적인 improve 개선하다

109

Each management workshop is limited to 20 participants and is accepted on a first-come, first-served -------.
(A) view
(B) focus
(C) custom
(D) basis

각 경영 워크숍은 20명의 참석자로 제한이 되고 선착순으로 받는다.

해설 빈칸은 적절한 의미의 명사가 들어갈 자리이다. 묶음표현인 on a first come, first served basis(선착순으로)를 알고 있다면 쉽게 풀 수 있는 문제이다.

어휘 first-come, first-served 선착순 limited 제한된 participant 참가자 accept 받아들이다

110

Due to ------- decisions made by the brilliant CEO Eddie Max, Myer Flex has raised its yearly sales to 3 million dollars.
(A) **strategic**
(B) contented
(C) voted
(D) unanimous

훌륭한 CEO인 Eddie Max에 의한 전략적인 결정 때문에, Myer Flex는 연간 매출을 300만 달러로 올렸다.

해설 빈칸은 명사인 decision(결정)을 수식하는 형용사자리이다. decision과 어울리는 형용사는 strategic(전략적인), unanimous(만장일치의) 정도가 있다. 뛰어난 최고경영자인 Eddie Max에 의한 결정이라는 의미이므로, 혼자 한 결정으로 만장일치라는 의미와는 어울리지 않는다. 따라서 정답은 (A) strategic이다.

어휘 decision 결정 brilliant 훌륭한 raise 올리다 strategic 전략적인 contented 만족해하는 voted 투표를 통해 선발된 unanimous 만장일치의

111

Luis Nam's presentation was so impressive ------- the transit committee swiftly approved his plan.
(A) which
(B) **that**
(C) what
(D) during

Luice Nam의 발표는 너무 인상적이어서 수송위원회는 그의 계획을 신속히 승인했다.

해설 빈칸은 뒤의 문장을 연결해주는 접속사자리이다. 빈칸 앞쪽에 so가 등장하므로 <so + 형용사 [부사] + that; 너무 ~해서 that 이하하다>구문을 떠올릴 수 있다.

어휘 presentation 발표 impressive 인상적인 transit 수송 swiftly 신속히 approve 승인하다

112

Terry Johns visited the Taiwan factory only ------- before he returned to his company's headquarters.
(A) exactly
(B) easily
(C) **briefly**
(D) widely

Terry Johns는 회사 본사로 돌아오기 전에 짧게 타이완 공장을 방문했다.

해설 빈칸은 의미가 적절한 부사가 들어갈 자리이다. 빈칸 앞의 문장에서 동사 visit(방문하다)와 의미연결이 적절한 부사는 (C) briefly(짧게)이다.

어휘 factory 공장 return 돌아오다 headquarter 본사 exactly 정확히 easily 쉽게 briefly 잠시 widely 널리

ACTUAL TEST 01 ACTUAL TEST 02 ACTUAL TEST 03 ACTUAL TEST 04 ACTUAL TEST 05

113

As one of its policies, the management of Bruce Art Museum reminds all of its visitors to refrain ------- using their camera while they are inside the establishment.
(A) from
(B) with
(C) through
(D) between

정책들 중 하나로서, Bruce Art Museum의 경영진은 모든 방문자들에게 건물 안에 있는 동안 카메라 사용을 자제할 것을 상기시킨다.

해설 빈칸은 앞의 동사인 refrain과 연결되는 전치사가 들어갈 자리이다. refrain은 자동사로 from과 어울린다.(refrain from -ing ~하기를 자제하다, 삼가다)

어휘 refrain 삼가다 policy 증권 refrain 삼가다 establishment 기관

114

For commercial vehicles, tires designed for winter conditions are a must as they ensure that bad weather will not ------- deliveries.
(A) interfere with
(B) depend on
(C) fall behind
(D) correspond to

영업용 차량을 위해서, 겨울철 조건에 맞게 고안된 타이어는 악천후 날씨에도 배달을 방해하지 않을 것을 보장하기 때문에 필수조건이다.

해설 빈칸은 문장에서 의미가 적절한 동사가 들어갈 자리이다. 빈칸이 있는 문장의 주어가 bad weather(악천후)이고, 빈칸 뒤에 deliveries(배달)가 있으므로 이 표현들과 어울리는 동사는 (A) interfere with(방해하다)이다.

어휘 ensure 반드시 ~하게 하다, 보장하다 vehicle 차량 designed 고안된 ensure 보장하다 delivery 배달 interfere with ~을 방해하다 depend on ~에 의존하다 fall behind ~에 뒤지다 correspond to ~에 일치하다

115

In order to have a fun and rewarding trip, it is important that you dress appropriately and have the proper -------.
(A) equipping
(B) equipment
(C) equipped
(D) equip

재미있고 보람 있는 여행을 하기 위해서는 옷을 알맞게 입고 제대로 된 장비를 가져가는 것이 중요하다.

해설 빈칸은 앞의 형용사 뒤에 어울리는 품사가 들어갈 자리이다. 형용사는 명사를 수식하므로 빈칸은 명사인 (B) equipment가 들어갈 자리이다.

어휘 appropriately 적당하게, 알맞게 in order to ~위하여 rewarding 보람 있는 dress 입다 appropriately 알맞게 proper 적절한

116

Most meteorologists say that increasing temperatures make it ------- for sea levels to rise as much as 10cm in some areas.
(A) possible
(B) durable
(C) perfect
(D) allowable

대부분의 기상학자는 증가하는 기온이 몇 몇 지역에서 해수면을 10cm 정도 상승시 킨다고 말한다.

해설 이 문제는 <make + 목적어 + 형용사>의 구조이다. 목적어인 it은 의미가 없는 가목적어이므로, 진짜 목적어 의미가 있는 빈칸 뒤의 부분을 해석해 보면 '해수면을 상승시키는 것'이 된다. 이를 자연스럽게 연결하는 형용사는 (A) possible(가능한)이다.

어휘 meteorologist 기상학자 increase 증가하다 temperature 온도 possible 가능한 durable 내구성이 있는 perfect 완벽한 allowable 허용되는

117

Remodelling of Sunrise Gallery will ------- begin as soon as a construction company is chosen.
(A) lately
(B) previously
(C) probably
(D) almost

Sunrise Gallery의 재건축은 아마도 건설 회사가 선택되자마자 시작할 것이다.

해설 빈칸은 의미가 적절한 부사가 들어갈 자리이다. 선택지 중에서 (A) lately(최근에)는 현재완료시제와 어울리고, (B) previously(이전에)는 과거시제와 어울리는 오답들이다. (D) almost(거의)라는 의미도 해석이 어색해지는 오답이다. 문맥상 (C) probably(아마)가 가장 적절하다.

어휘 remodelling 재건축 as soon as ~하자마자 construction 건설

118

Although laptops ------- desktops for the past several years, desktops certainly still dominate the modern office workstations.
(A) have been outselling
(B) are outsold
(C) will be outselling
(D) would have been outsold

비록 노트북이 지난 몇 년 동안 더 많이 팔렸을지라도, 여전히 데스크톱이 확실하게 현대적인 사무실 작업 공간에 우세하다.

해설 빈칸은 문장과 어울리는 형태의 동사가 들어갈 자리이다. 시제를 나타내는 단서인 for the past several years(지난 몇 년간)와 어울리는 시제는 현재완료이다. 선택지 중에서 현재완료진행은 (A) have been outselling이다.

어휘 certainly 확실하게 dominate 우세하다 modern 현대의 outsell ~보다 더 많이 팔다

119

As City Councilman, Rick continues to oversee many important city building projects including the ------- opened aquatic centre and central park.
(A) recently
(B) unanimously
(C) directly
(D) typically

시 의원으로서, Rick 씨는 최근에 개장한 아쿠아틱센터와 센트럴파크를 포함한 많은 중요한 도시 건축 프로젝트의 감독을 계속하고 있다.

해설 빈칸은 의미가 적절한 부사가 들어갈 자리이다. 빈칸 뒤의 opened(개장한)와 의미가 적절한 부사는 (A) recently(최근에)이다. recently opened 최근에 개장한

어휘 continue 계속하다 oversee 감독하다 including 포함하여 aquatic centre 수족센터 recently 최근에 unanimously 만장일치로 directly 직접적으로 typically 전형적으로

120

LINC Consulting Office staff members are prohibited from parking their cars in the restricted area ------- prior approval.
(A) due to
(B) as opposed to
(C) except
(D) without

LINC Consulting Office 직원들은 사전 승인 없이는 제한구역에서 자동차 주차가 금지됩니다.

해설 빈칸은 뒤의 prior approval(사전승인)과 어울리는 전치사가 들어갈 자리이다. 빈칸 앞부분을 보면 are prohibited(금지되다)를 통해 '사전 승인 없이는 주차가 금지된다'의 의미가 자연스럽다. 따라서 (D) without(~ 없이)이 정답이다.

어휘 restricted area 금지구역, 제한구역 prohibit 금지하다 prior approval 사전 승인 due to ~ 때문에 as opposed to ~와는 대조적으로 except ~ 제외하고 without ~ 없이

121

The CEO of Kanasaki Bicycle rides ------- bicycle to work three or four times a week from the west side of Australia.
(A) him
(B) he
(C) his
(D) himself

Kanasaki Bicycle의 CEO는 호주 서쪽으로부터 일주일에 서너 번 자전거를 타고 출근한다.

해설 대명사의 격을 묻고 있다. 명사 앞에는 소유격(his)이 온다.

어휘 ride 타다 bicycle 자전거

122

The coupon holders should note that these are non-transferable coupons, which can only be used by the owner, ------- must provide identification when redeemed.

(A) who
(B) which
(C) whom
(D) whose

쿠폰 소지자는 반드시 이 쿠폰이 단지 소유자에 의해서만 사용되는 양도 불가능한 것이고 소유주는 교환될 때 반드시 신분증을 제공해야 한다는 점을 유의해야 한다.

해설 관계대명사의 종류와 격을 묻는 문제이다. 빈칸 앞의 선행사가 사람(the owner)이고, 빈칸 뒤에 바로 동사(must provide)가 등장하므로 사람 주격을 나타내는 관계대명사 (A) who가 정답이다.

어휘 non-transferable 양도할 수 없는 provide ~을 제공하다 identification 신분증 redeem 쿠폰을 사용하다

123

Nokis Mobile has launched a new application that ------- its customers to a get a discount on their bills if they are willing to view advertisements on their mobile phones.
(A) allowed
(B) was allowed
(C) will allow
(D) allow

Nokis Mobile는 만약 고객들이 기꺼이 그들의 휴대폰에서 광고를 본다면, 고객들의 청구서에서 할인을 받을 수 있도록 허락하는 새로운 앱을 출시했다.

해설 빈칸은 주격 관계대명사 that 뒤에 어울리는 동사가 들어갈 자리이다. 선행사인 a new application에 동사의 수를 맞추어야 하므로, 복수동사인 allow는 오답이다. 빈칸 뒤에 its customers라는 목적어가 있으므로, 수동형인 was allowed도 오답이다. 앞 문장의 시제는 현재완료(has launched 출시했다)이므로 과거시제인 allowed도 어울리지 않는다.

어휘 launch 시작하다 application 앱 customer 고객 discount 할인 bill 계산서, 청구서 be willing to 기꺼이 ~하다 view 보다 advertisement 광고

124

Employees at Brady Plum Inc. should complete sixteen training sessions so as to gain ------- to the company's database.
(A) access
(B) advance
(C) approach
(D) routine

Brady Plum 사의 직원들은 회사 데이터베이스로의 접근을 위해 16개의 훈련과정을 마쳐야 한다.

해설 빈칸은 gain의 목적어(명사)자리이다. 빈칸 뒤의 to the company's database(회사의 데이터베이스에)를 통해 의미상 '접근'이라는 단어가 어울린다. 선택지 중에서 access와 approach가 '접근'이라는 의미가 있다. access는 셀 수 없는 명사(불가산명사)이고 approach는 셀 수 있는 명사(가산명사)이므로 관사 없이 사용 가능한 불가산명사인 (A) access가 정답이다.

어휘 so as to ~(목적) 위하여 complete 완료하다 access 접근 advance 발전, 진전 approach 다가가다 routine 일상

125

Star Bike is a nation-wide distributor selling high quality, yet ------- bicycling products.
(A) unaware
(B) inexpensive
(C) undecided
(D) incomplete

Star Bike는 고품질이지만 적절한 자전거 용품을 파는 전국적인 유통업체이다.

해설 빈칸은 앞의 high quality, yet(고품질이지만)과 어울리는 형용사자리이다. 왜냐하면 yet은 등위접속사로 앞뒤를 같은 품사로 연결해야 하기 때문이다. 문맥상 의미가 적절한 형용사는 (B) inexpensive(비싸지 않은)이며, high quality, yet inexpensive는 '고품질이지만 비싸지 않은'이라는 의미로 연결이 매끄럽다.

어휘 nation-wide 전국적인 distributor 배급업자 sell 팔다 product 상품 unaware ~알지 못하는 inexpensive 비싸지 않은 undecided 결정하지 못한 incomplete 불완전한

126

KP Package Design and its staff are ------- researching new technologies and ways to improve existing ones.
(A) continual
(B) continue
(C) continues
(D) continually

KP Package Design 사와 직원은 새로운 기술과 기존의 기술을 향상시킬 방법을 계속해서 찾고 있다.

해설 빈칸은 동사 앞에 어울리는 품사가 들어갈 자리이다. 동사를 수식하는 품사는 부사이므로 정답은 (D) continually(계속해서)이다.

어휘 existing 기존의, 현재 사용되는 continually 지속적으로 researching 찾다 improve 개선하다 existing 기존의

127

Ms. Peche believes that she is the most ------- person to lead the research project because she has twelve years of prior experience.
(A) qualifying
(B) qualified
(C) qualification
(D) qualifiable

Peche 씨는 그녀가 연구 프로젝트를 이끌기 위해서 12년의 경험이 있기 때문에 가장 자격이 있다고 믿는다.

해설 빈칸은 명사 앞에 어울리는 품사가 들어갈 자리이다. 명사 앞은 형용사자리이므로 qualifying, qualified, qualifiable이 위치상 적절하다. 빈칸 뒤의 person과 의미연결이 적절한 선택지는 (B) qualified(자격을 갖춘)이다.

어휘 qualified 자격을 갖춘 lead 이끌다 research 연구 qualification 자격

128

This product has been successful in the Asian market but should be changed to ------- the European market.
(A) call out
(B) demand
(C) update
(D) appeal to

이 상품은 아시아 시장에서는 성공적이었으나, 유럽 시장에서 매력을 끌기 위해서는 바뀌어야 한다.

해설) 빈칸은 뒤의 the European market과 의미연결이 적절한 동사가 들어갈 자리이다. 선택지 중 (D) appeal to가 '매혹시키다'의 의미로 가장 적절하다.

어휘) successful 성공적 change 바꾸다 call out ~를 부르다 demand 요구하다 update 갱신하다 appeal to 매혹시키다

129

Preliminary data from Jason Travel Research indicates ------- in Massachusetts has been steadily regaining popularity since September 2019.
(A) tourism
(B) toured
(C) tours
(D) tourists

Jason Travel Research의 기초자료는 Massachusetts의 관광산업이 2019년 9월 이래로 꾸준하게 인기를 회복하고 있다는 것을 나타내고 있다.

해설) 빈칸은 적절한 의미의 주어(명사)가 들어갈 자리이다. 빈칸 뒤의 동사 has been을 보면 주어가 단수이므로 선택지 중 tourism(관광산업)이 정답이다.

어휘) preliminary ~예비의 indicate 나타내다 steadily 꾸준하게 regaining 회복 popularity 인기 tourism 관광산업

130

Many travel agencies are increasing their ------- because the airline companies are limiting commission to their vendors.
(A) rating
(B) to rate
(C) rated
(D) rates

많은 여행사들은 항공사들이 거래처들에 대한 수수료를 제한하기 때문에 그들의 요금을 인상한다.

해설) 소유격대명사 다음의 빈칸은 명사자리이다. 선택지 중 명사인 rating은 '등급, 평가'이고, rates는 '속도, 요금, 비율'의 의미로 문맥상 (D) rates가 정답이다.

어휘) vendor 행상인, 공급업체 travel agency 여행사 increase 증가하다 commission 수수료

PART 6

Questions 131-134 refer to the following article.

-------.
131.

------- a Ph.D. in petroleum extraction, Mr. Smith began working
132.
in the industry with some of the biggest companies more than
a decade ago. He established ------- by discovering new, highly
133.
profitable methods of oil extraction in deposits long considered
depleted.

------- he has joined Collin Minerals, he can again use his unique
134.
methods to tap North America's vast energy reserves, which
until now have remained locked deep beneath the earth.

Simon Smith 씨는 석유 에너지 시장에 선구적인 회사인 Collin Minerals의 탐사대장으로 임명되었다.

석유 추출분야에 박사학위를 받은 후에, Smith 씨는 10여 년 전부터 몇몇 대기업들과 그 산업분야의 일을 시작했다. 그는 오랫동안 고갈되었다고 여겨졌던 매장지에서 원유추출의 새롭고 매우 수익성이 있는 방법들을 발견하여 명성을 떨쳤다.

그가 Collin Minerals사에 입사했기 때문에, 현재까지 지구 깊은 아래에 있는 북미의 아주 광대한 에너지 보유량을 개발하도록 그의 독창적인 방법을 다시 사용할 수 있다.

어휘 petroleum 석유 extraction 추출 decade 10년 establish 설립하다 discover 발견하다 highly 매우 methods 방법 depleted 고갈된 deposits 침전물 unique 독특한 beneath ~ 아래

131 　**(A) Simon Smith has been appointed head of exploration of Collin Minerals, a pioneering firm in oil energy markets.**
　(B) Collin Minerals announced Simon Smith's decision to resign.
　(C) Collin Minerals has expanded into oil energy markets in Europe.
　(D) There were a lot of challenges in pioneering oil markets.

해설 문장 맨 앞에 문장삽입문제는 지문의 주제를 나타낸다. 뒤의 내용이 Simon Smith의 이력에 대한 설명이므로 (A)가 가장 적절하다.

(A) Simon Smith 씨는 석유 에너지 시장에 선구적인 회사인 Collin Minerals의 탐사대장으로 임명되었다.
(B) Collin Minerals는 사임하려는 Simon Smith의 결정을 발표했다.
(C) Collin Minerals는 유럽 석유 에너지 시작으로 확장했다.
(D) 석유 시장을 개척하는 데 많은 어려움들이 있었다.

132
(A) To complete
(B) Completed
(C) Having been completed
(D) Having completed

해설 빈칸은 완료형태 분사구문자리이다. Having p.p의 경우 '~한 후에'로 해석되며 능동의 형태이므로 뒤에 목적어를 취할 수 있다. 그러므로 (D)가 정답이다.

133
(A) he
(B) his
(C) his own
(D) himself

해설 빈칸은 타동사 established의 목적어자리이다. 재귀대명사의 경우 주어와 목적어가 동일할 때 목적어자리에 올 수 있다. 해석을 해보면 '그는 자기 자신을 확고히 하다'는 표현이 적절하므로 (D) himself가 정답이다.

134
(A) So that
(B) Since
(C) By the time
(D) Although

해설 빈칸 다음에 두 문장을 연결시키는 알맞은 접속사를 선택하는 문제이다. 앞 문장(그가 Collin Minerals사에 입사하다)이 원인이 되고, 뒤 문장(그의 독창적인 방법을 사용하다)이 결과가 되므로 (B) Since가 정답이다.

Harriot Hanson

2043 Terra Cotta Street

Fairmount, MN 58030

USA

We ------- received your email in which you expressed interest in
135.
becoming a member of our exciting sales team. We are always

looking for talented and eager people to join our workforce and

would be ------- to look over your application.
136.

All sales representative applicants are asked to mail us their

resumes and cover letter ------- why they wish to join our team.
137.
We will contact you to schedule an interview shortly thereafter.

-------. Please take a sufficient amount of time to prepare for the
138.
interview.

Sincerely,

Jessie Swanton

Sales Department Manager

Qframe Inc.

Harriot Hanson
2043 Terra Cotta Street
Fairmount, MN 58030
미국

우리는 재미있는 판매 팀의 일원이 되는 데 관심을 보인 당신의 이메일을 최근에 받았습니다. 우리 팀에 합류할 재능 있고 열심히 일하는 사람들을 항상 찾고 있으며 당신의 지원서를 기꺼이 검토했습니다.

모든 판매담당 지원자들은 이력서와 왜 우리 팀에 들어오려고 하는지를 기술한 자기소개서를 우편으로 보내도록 요청됩니다. 우리는 그 후에 곧 면접 일정을 잡기 위해 연락할 것입니다. 당신이 판매부서에 가져올 기술이 무엇인지를 알고 싶습니다. 면접을 준비하도록 충분한 시간을 갖기 바랍니다.

진심을 담아

Jessie Swanton
영업부 부장
Qframe Inc.

어휘 recently 최근에 express 표현하다 talented 재능 있는 eager 열렬한, 의욕이 있는 workforce 인력 representative 대표, 직원 cover letter 자기소개서 shortly thereafter 직후에 sufficient 충분한

135
(A) kindly
(B) closely
(C) recently
(D) regretfully

해설 빈칸은 동사 received를 수식하는 부사자리이다. received와 의미가 잘 연결되고 과거시제와 현재완료시제와 어울리는 부사는 (C) recently이다.

136
(A) pleased
(B) pleasing
(C) pleasant
(D) please

해설 be동사 뒤에 알맞은 품사 형태를 선택하는 문제이다. be동사 뒤는 주격 보어로 형용사나, 수동이나 진행을 나타내는 p.p / v-ing 형태가 적절하다. 그러나 이 문제는 be pleased to V (기꺼이 ~하다)형태를 외우면 간단하게 해결된다. 따라서 (A) pleased가 정답이다.

137
(A) updating
(B) planning
(C) notifying
(D) explaining

해설 빈칸은 선행사인 '이력서와 자기소개서'를 수식하는 분사자리이다. 정답은 빈칸 다음에 명사절(why S+V)과 어울리는 (D) explaining(설명하는)이다. 참고로 (C) notifying은 사람 목적어를 취하므로 탈락된다.

138
(A) We already knew about previous careers.
(B) You are scheduled to start your work on September 9.
(C) We would like to know what skills you can bring to our sales department.
(D) Interview strategies will be addressed in those sessions.

해설 빈칸 앞뒤 문장을 살펴보면 모두 면접에 관한 내용이다. 편지의 발신자인 면접관 입장에서 생각을 해본다면, 면접에서 지원자의 장점이나 비전에 관해서 듣고 싶어 할 것이다. 따라서 (C)가 가장 적절하다.

(A) 우리는 이미 이전 경력을 알고 있습니다.
(B) 당신은 9월 9일에 근무를 시작할 예정입니다.
(C) 당신이 판매부서에 가져올 기술이 무엇인지를 알고 싶습니다.
(D) 면접 전략들이 그 모임에서 다루어 질 것입니다.

Questions 139-142 refer to the following memo.

As our new office space ------- customers the ability to see our
        139.
floor, management has determined that the employee dress
code should be revised to reflect the professionalism we wish to
convey.

-------, starting immediately, all employees will be required to
140.
wear business attire when in the office. For men, that means a
suit and a tie. Women must wear a skirt and blouse.

Casual Fridays are now cancelled. Furthermore, tags with your
name and title must be worn at all -------. -------.
                141. **142.**

우리의 새로운 사무실 공간을 고객들이 볼 수 있기 때문에, 경영진은 직원 복장규정이 우리가 전달되기 바라는 전문성을 반영하도록 수정되어야 한다고 결정했습니다.

따라서, 지금부터, 모든 직원들은 사무실에 있을 때 정장을 착용하도록 요구됩니다. 남성들에게, 그것은 정장과 넥타이를 의미합니다. 여성들은 치마와 블라우스를 입어야 합니다.

이제 캐주얼 프라이데이는 취소되었습니다. 더욱이, 이름과 직책이 있는 명찰이 항상 착용되어야 합니다. 이것들은 당신의 감독관에 의해 제공될 것입니다.

어휘 ability 능력 determine 알아내다 reflect 반영하다 professionalism 전문성 convey 전달하다 starting immediately 지금부터 furthermore 더욱이

139
(A) giving
(B) given
(C) has been given
(D) will give

해설 알맞은 동사시제를 선택하는 문제이다. 고객들이 현장을 보는 것은 아직 일어난 상황이 아니기 때문에 미래시제 (D)가 정답이다.

140
(A) Therefore
(B) Instead
(C) On the other hand
(D) Moreover

해설 빈칸은 앞 단락과 뒤 문장을 의미상 연결시켜주는 접속부사자리이다. 앞 문장 내용이 뒤 문장의 원인이 되므로 (A) therefore가 정답이다.

141
(A) time
(B) times
(C) timing
(D) timed

해설 빈칸은 at all과 어울리는 명사자리이다. at all times(항상)을 외워두면 간단히 풀 수 있다. 참고로 at any time(언제든지)도 함께 외워두자.

142
(A) From now on, you should present your name tag to the security guard to enter the facilities.
(B) These will be provided by your supervisor.
(C) Also, some of the safety regulations will be revised by next week.
(D) Your personnel information should be updated accordingly.

해설 빈칸 앞 문장과 어울리는 문장을 선택하자. 앞 문장에서 직원들에게 tags(명찰들)를 꼭 착용하도록 당부 했다. 따라서 그 tags(these)를 제공해 주겠다는 내용인 (B)가 가장 적절하다.

(A) 지금부터, 시설에 들어가기 위해 보안직원에게 명찰을 보여 주어야 합니다.
(B) 이것들은 당신의 감독관에 의해 제공될 것입니다.
(C) 또한, 몇몇 안전규정들은 다음 주까지 수정될 것입니다.
(D) 당신의 인사정보는 그에 따라서 업데이트 될 것입니다.

Questions 143-146 refer to the following article.

According to some records, the average oil production at major oil companies went down from the expected 6.5 to 3.29 million barrels of oil per day. -------. **143.** As a result, prices have increased tremendously, ------- **144.** in a global economic crisis. -------, **145.** car companies are cautiously ------- **146.** about the future. Despite the change in oil prices worldwide, car manufacturers are not directly affected by it because many car owners nowadays are driving energy efficient vehicles.	몇몇 기록에 따르면, 주요 정유사의 평균 석유생산은 일일 예상치 6.5백만 배럴에서 3.29백만 배럴로 떨어졌다. 따라서 석유의 공급이 국제적인 수요를 충족시키는 데 충분하지 않다. 그 결과, 세계적인 경제 위기를 초래하면서, 유가는 엄청나게 상승했다. 그럼에도 불구하고, 자동차 회사들은 미래에 대해 조심스럽게 낙관한다. 전 세계에 유가 변동에도 불구하고, 요즘 많은 자동차 소유주들이 연료 효율적인 자동차를 운전하기 때문에 자동차 제조사들은 그것에 의해 직접적으로 영향을 받지는 않는다.

어휘 according to ~에 따르면 record 기록 as a result 결과로서 tremendously 엄청나게 result in ~을 야기하다 cautiously 조심스럽게 directly 직접 affect 영향을 미치다

143
(A) This is because of the increasing number of the travellers who use airplanes.
(B) However, many experts expect that their production rate will be accelerated.
(C) Oil is a useful resource in operating airplanes.
(D) Therefore, the supply of oil is insufficient to meet international demand.

해설 빈칸 앞뒤 문장의 문맥을 살펴보고 문장을 선택하자. 앞 문장은 '생산량이 하락했다'는 근본적인 원인을 얘기한다. 뒤 문장은 '석유값이 올랐다'는 결과를 말하고 있으므로 빈칸은 원인과 결과 사이에서 인과 관계를 보충·설명하는 (D)가 정답이다.

(A) 이것은 항공기를 이용하는 점점 많은 여행객들 때문이다.
(B) 그러나, 많은 전문가들은 그들의 생산율이 빨라질 것이라고 예상한다.
(C) 석유는 항공기를 운행하는데 유용한 자원이다.
(D) 따라서, 석유의 공급이 국제적인 수요를 충족시키는 데 충분하지 않다.

144
(A) resulted
(B) resulting
(C) results
(D) have resulted

해설 빈칸 앞은 완전한 문장이다. 그러므로 빈칸이 동사가 될 순 없다. 분사구문형태의 문장으로 보면 result는 자동사이므로 result in의 형태로 사용된다. 따라서 능동 형태인 (B) resulting이 정답이다. S + V, v-ing~(S가 V했다, V하면서~) 형태를 기억하자.

145

(A) **Nevertheless**
(B) In addition
(C) After that
(D) To this end

해설 빈칸 앞 내용은 석유 생산량으로 인한 경제의 부정적인 얘기를 하고 있다. 하지만 빈칸 뒤 내용을 보면 기업들은 낙관적이라는 얘기를 한다. 따라서 정답은 (A) Nevertheless(그럼에도 불구하고)이다.

146

(A) confident
(B) **optimistic**
(C) frustrated
(D) confused

해설 빈칸으로 인해 145번의 정답이 바뀔 수 있으니 문장을 끝까지 해석하기 바란다. 빈칸 뒤의 내용을 살펴보면 car manufacturers are not directly affected(자동차 제조업자들은 영향을 직접적으로 받지 않는다)고 언급하므로 석유 생산과 상관없이 자동차 업계는 '낙관적임'을 알 수 있다. 따라서 (B) optimistic(낙관적인)이 정답이다.

PART 5

101

Since 2019, Mr. Leon has ------- as the Vice President, and is the person most responsible for all aspects of marketing.
(A) served
(B) regarded
(C) involved
(D) implemented

2019년 이래로, Leon 씨는 부사장으로서 역할을 했고 마케팅의 모든 분야에서 가장 책임이 있는 사람이다.

해설 문맥상 의미가 적절한 동사어휘를 고르는 문제이다. 빈칸 뒤의 as와 어울리는 자동사는 serve이다. 빈출표현인 serve as는 '~로써 역할을 하다'라는 의미이다.

어휘 aspect 측면 responsible 책임지고 있는 serve as ~로써 역할을 하다 regard ~로 여기다 involved 관련된 implement 시행하다

102

------- Nexus Corporation is the smallest construction company in the province, it is the most successful.
(A) Until
(B) So
(C) How
(D) While

Nexus 사는 이 지역에서 가장 작은 건설회사이긴 하지만 가장 성공했다.

해설 완전한 문장이 두 개 나오고 빈칸 다음에 주어와 동사가 나오면 빈칸은 접속사자리이다. 문장 첫 부분에 쓸 수 없는 So, 그리고 접속사가 아닌 How가 우선 오답이다. 그리고, 앞 문장의 the smallest company(가장 작은 회사)와 뒤 문장의 the most successful(가장 성공적인)을 통해 '가장 작은 회사이지만 가장 성공적'이라는 의미가 적절하므로 (D) While(~이긴 하지만, ~에도 불구하고)이 정답이다.

어휘 province (행정 단위인) 주 construction 건설

103

The ------- of Ray's restaurant and Sohee's Cafe has led to a higher number of visitors to shops in the area.
(A) popularize
(B) popularly
(C) popularity
(D) popular

Ray레스토랑과 Sohee Cafe의 인기가 이 지역에 있는 매장으로 더 많은 방문자들을 이끌었다.

해설 빈칸은 관사 뒤에 어울리는 품사가 들어갈 자리이다. 관사 뒤는 명사가 와야 하므로 정답은 (C) popularity(인기)이다.

어휘 lead to ~로 이끌다 visitor 방문자 popular 인기 있는 popularity 인기

104

The president of Jake Motors has ------- that the company has improved worker productivity significantly while reducing operating costs.
(A) applied
(B) joined
(C) notified
(D) announced

Jake Motors의 사장은 회사가 운영비를 줄이는 동안 직원 생산성을 상당히 개선했다고 발표했다.

해설 빈칸은 뒤의 that절을 받을 수 있는 동사가 들어갈 자리이다. that절을 목적어로 취하는 announce가 정답이다. notify도 that절을 받기는 하지만, notify와 that절 사이에 사람목적어가 와야 한다. 즉 <notify + 사람 + that절>의 구조가 되어야 한다.

어휘 productivity 생산성 significantly 상당히 improve 향상시키다 reduce 감소시키다 operation 운영 apply 신청하다 announce 발표하다

105

Heal Literature Monthly's new advertising campaign has resulted in a ------- 45 percent increase in the number of subscribers over the last five months.
(A) rigid
(B) receptive
(C) remarkable
(D) perpetual

Heal Literature Monthly의 새로운 광고 캠페인으로 인해 지난 5개월 동안 구독자 수가 45% 현저히 증가했다.

해설 빈칸은 뒤의 increase(증가)와 의미가 어울리는 형용사자리이다. 선택지 중 remarkable(현저한, 두드러진)이 의미 연결이 매끄럽다. rigid 엄격한, receptive 수용적인 perpetual 끊임없이 계속되는

어휘 result in something (결과적으로) ~을 낳다 subscriber 구독자 remarkable 두드러진

106

Those who have been let go of are reminded to go to the personnel office ------- their last day of work to return all hotel property.
(A) into
(B) from
(C) before
(D) around

은퇴하는 사람들은 모든 호텔 소유물을 반납하기 위하여 근무 마지막 날 이전에 인사부로 가도록 상기된다.

해설 their last day of work(근무 마지막 날)와 의미연결이 어울리는 전치사는 (C) before(전에)이다.

어휘 property 재산 remind 상기시키다 return 반납하다

135

107

Please contact the company's security manager when preparations ------- for the installation of the new central cooling system.
(A) be made
(B) made
(C) have been made
(D) will make

새로운 중앙 냉방시스템의 설치를 위해 준비가 되었을 때 회사 보안매니저에게 연락해주십시오.

해설 빈칸은 형태가 적절한 동사가 들어갈 자리이다. make는 preparation과 짝을 이루어 make preparations(준비를 하다)로 쓰인다. 본문에서는 preparations가 주어이므로 수동태 형태임을 알 수 있다. 따라서 be made와 have been made가 정답 후보이다. 빈칸은 동사자리이므로 동사원형인 be made는 탈락되고 정답은 (C) have been made가 된다.

어휘 preparation 준비 contact 연락하다 installation 설치

108

Ms. Eloise watches all our gauges ------- so that she can ensure accurate humidity records.
(A) personalize
(B) personable
(C) personally
(D) personal

Eloise 씨는 정확한 습도 기록을 확실히 하기 위해 모든 측정기를 직접 살펴본다.

해설 이 문장은 완전한 문장으로 동사는 watches이고 목적어는 all our gauges이다. 완전한 문장에 추가로 들어갈 수 있는 품사는 부사이다.(personally 직접, 몸소) 문맥상 '모든 측정기를 본인이 직접 살펴본다'는 의미가 적절하다. (A) personalize (동사) 개인에게 맞추다, 표시하다 (B) personable (형용사) 매력적인 (C) personally (부사) 개인적으로 (D) personal (형용사) 개인의

어휘 ensure 반드시 ~하게 하다. accurate 정확한 humidity 습도 gauge 측정기 personally 직접 personal 개인의

109

With just two weeks remaining before South Bank's annual festival, the organizing committee has ------- to decide the parade route.
(A) already
(B) yet
(C) finally
(D) never

South Bank의 연례 축제 전까지 단지 2주가 남았지만, 조직위원회는 아직 퍼레이드 경로를 결정하지 않았다.

해설 빈칸은 앞의 has와 뒤의 to 사이에 들어갈 적절한 형태의 부사를 묻고 있다. have yet to를 '아직 ~않다' 또는 '여전히 ~해야 한다'로 알아두면 쉽게 해결 가능한 문제이다.

어휘 remain 남다 organizing committee 조직위원회 decide 결정하다 route 길, 노선

110

------- the firm's work schedule is now posted on its website, we will no longer distribute paper copies.
(A) Besides
(B) Regardless of
(C) In the event of
(D) Since

회사의 근무 일정이 웹 사이트에 지금 게시되기 때문에, 우리는 더 이상 유인물을 배포하지 않을 것이다.

해설 이 문제 역시 빈칸 다음에 주어와 동사가 연결되므로 빈칸은 접속사자리이다. 선택지 중에서 접속사는 since(~ 때문에)뿐이다. besides(~ 외에)는 전치사, regardless of(~에 상관없이), in the event of(만약 ~하면)는 부사구이다.

어휘 distribute 분배하다 schedule 일정 post 게시하다

111

The new software program can ------- organizations to share information more quickly and efficiently.
(A) refuse
(B) acquire
(C) except
(D) enable

새로운 소프트웨어 프로그램은 여러 기관들이 정보를 더욱 더 빠르고 효율적으로 공유하도록 한다.

해설 빈칸은 의미가 적절한 동사어휘를 찾는 문제이다. 목적어인 organizations 뒤에 to share(to부정사)가 등장한다. 이러한 문장 구조에 어울리는 동사는 enable이다. enable은 <enable + 목적어 + to부정사; 목적어가 ~하는 것을 가능하게 하다>의 구조로 쓰인다.

어휘 organization 기관, 조직 quickly 빠르게 efficiently 효율적으로 refuse 거절하다 acquire 습득하다 except ~제외하고 enable ~을 할 수 있게 하다

112

Customers at our Hamilton branch know that our warehouse always has products ------- want in stock.
(A) them
(B) their
(C) themselves
(D) they

Hamilton 지사의 고객들은 우리의 창고에 그들이 원하는 제품이 항상 비축되어 있다는 것을 알고 있다.

해설 빈칸은 동사 want 앞에 어울리는 대명사자리이다. 동사 앞은 주어이므로 주격인 they가 정답이다.

어휘 branch 지사 warehouse 창고 product 상품 in stock 재고

113

Aside from some minor setbacks with the design team, the first edition of the book is ------- to be printed.
(A) readiness
(B) readily
(C) ready
(D) readies

디자인팀의 사소한 차질을 제외하고, 책의 초판은 인쇄될 준비가 되었다.

해설 이 문제는 be ready to(~할 준비가 되어 있다)를 알고 있다면 쉽게 해결할 수 있다. be동사 뒤에는 명사나 형용사가 올 수 있는데, 명사가 오면 주어와 동격이 된다. 이 문제는 주어와 상태를 나타내는 형용사가 정답이다.

어휘 aside form ~을 제외하고 setback 차질 edition 판

114

------- company regulations, female employees who will go on maternity leave must obtain their supervisor's permission two weeks in advance.
(A) In accordance with
(B) On behalf of
(C) As soon as
(D) Prior to

회사 규정에 따라 출산 휴가를 갈 여성 직원들은 2주 전에 반드시 그들의 상관의 허가를 얻어야 합니다.

해설 빈칸 뒤의 company regulations와 의미가 어울리는 전치사가 들어갈 자리이다. 선택지 중 '회사 규정'과 의미가 어울리는 단어는 (A) in accordance with(~에 따라)이다.

어휘 maternity leave 출산 휴가 female 여성의 in advance 미리 in accordance with ~에 따라 on behalf of ~을 대신하여 as soon as ~하자마자 prior to ~ 전에

115

------- the product that was delivered not be the correct one, please send it back to us in the original packaging or bring it to a retail outlet for exchange.
(A) If
(B) Should
(C) Had
(D) Whether

만약 배달된 상품이 정확한 것이 아니라면 원래의 포장에 넣어서 다시 보내주시거나, 교환을 위해서 소매점에 다시 가져와 주십시오.

해설 빈칸은 두 문장을 이끄는 접속사자리인 것 같지만 앞 문장의 that부터 delivered까지를 괄호치고 나면 not be가 나오므로, be동사원형과 연결된다는 것을 알 수 있다. 때문에 선택지 중에서 조동사인 should만 동사원형과 연결이 가능하다. should가 문장의 맨 앞으로 간 이유는 <If + 주어 + should 동사원형>의 형태에서 If가 생략되면서, should가 자리를 옮기기 때문이다.

어휘 product 상품 deliver 배달하다 correct 옳은 send 보내다 bring 가져오다 retail 소매 exchange 교환

116

The price of coffee beans doubled, and coffee chains increased ------- prices accordingly to cover the costs.
(A) their
(B) themselves
(C) them
(D) they

커피콩의 가격이 두 배가 되었고, 커피 가맹점은 비용을 충족하기 위해서 그에 따라서 가격을 올렸다.

해설 빈칸 뒤에 명사가 나온다. 명사 앞에 올 수 있는 대명사의 격은 소유격이다.

어휘 accordingly 부응해서, 그에 맞춰 bean 콩 increase 증가하다 price 가격 cover 충족하다 cost 비용

117

------- editing content for Limited Publishers, Showna Kim is a correspondent for the Weekly Head newspaper.
(A) Together
(B) Moreover
(C) Otherwise
(D) In addition to

Showna Kim 씨는 Limited Publishers의 내용 편집뿐 아니라, Weekly Head의 특파원이다.

해설 해설 빈칸은 동명사 editing(편집하는 것)과 연결이 적합한 품사가 들어갈 자리이다. 동명사는 전치사 뒤에 올 수 있으므로, 빈칸은 전치사자리이다. 선택지 중에서 전치사인 (D) In addition to(~뿐만 아니라)가 정답이다. 나머지 선택지는 모두 부사이다. (A) Together 함께 (B) Moreover 게다가 (C) Otherwise 그렇지 않으면.

어휘 correspondent 기자, 특파원 content 내용 otherwise 그렇지 않으면

118

According to National Gas Agency, the gap between demand and supply will ------- decrease and then the price is likely to rise.
(A) recently
(B) soon
(C) extremely
(D) lately

National Gas Agency에 따르면, 수요와 공급의 차이는 곧 줄어들 것이고 그 후에 유가는 아마도 상승할 것이다.

해설 빈칸은 동사(decrease)와 의미가 자연스럽게 연결되는 부사가 들어갈 자리이다. 문장의 시제가 미래이므로, 현재완료와 어울리는 recently, lately는 오답이다. 정답은 미래시제와 어울리는 (B) soon이다.

어휘 according to ~에 따라 gap 차이 demand 수요 supply 공급 decrease 감소하다 price 가격 be likely to ~할 것 같다

119

According to our policies, requests for changes to the membership account must be submitted ------- writing within 30 days.
(A) on
(B) through
(C) in
(D) at

우리의 정책에 따르면, 멤버십 변경을 위한 요청서는 30일 내로 서면으로 제출되어야 한다.

해설 빈칸은 writing과 어울리는 전치사자리이다. 빈출표현인 in writing(서면으로)을 알고 있다면 쉽게 풀 수 있는 문제이다.

어휘 policy 정책 request 제안 change 변경, 변화 submit 보내다 within ~ 내에

120

If you plan to visit the civic center downtown, taking one of the public transportation systems such as the bus or subway is much more ------- than driving as parking is very expensive.
(A) economics
(B) economical
(C) economy
(D) economically

만약 당신이 시내에 있는 시민회관을 방문할 계획이라면, 주차비용이 무척 비싸기 때문에 버스나 지하철과 같은 대중교통을 이용하는 것이 직접 운전하는 것보다 훨씬 경제적이다.

해설 빈칸 앞의 more는 비교급을 나타내고, 그 앞의 much는 비교급 강조부사이다. 그 앞의 is를 통해 빈칸은 형용사자리임을 알 수 있다. 선택지 중 형용사는 (B) economical(경제적인)이다.

어휘 civic center 시민회관 take 타다 transportation 대중교통 such as ~와 같은 economical 경제적인 expensive 비싼

121

Mr. Eddie Retuna will have to complete all remaining work in the project -------, because her supervisor, Ms. Watson, is going on vacation next week.
(A) herself
(B) her
(C) she
(D) hers

Eddie Retuna 씨는 상사인 Watson 씨가 다음 주에 휴가를 가기 때문에 프로젝트의 잔무를 그녀가 직접 끝마쳐야 한다.

해설 빈칸은 문장의 형태에 어울리는 대명사가 들어갈 자리이다. 빈칸이 없어도 문장의 구성에는 전혀 문제가 없으므로, 강조를 하는 형태인 재귀대명사가 들어가야 한다.

어휘 remaining 남은, 남아 있는 complete 완료하다 supervisor 상사 vacation 휴가, 방학

122

It is important that you make ------- records of all transactions and make sure that they are kept safe and in an orderly manner.
(A) accurate
(B) distant
(C) caring
(D) refunded

당신이 모든 거래의 정확한 기록을 하는 것과 그 거래가 질서 정연하고 안전하게 유지됨을 보장하는 것은 중요하다.

해설 빈칸은 명사인 records(기록)를 수식하는 형용사자리이다. 선택지 중 (A) accurate(정확한)가 의미상 적절하다.

어휘 transaction 거래, 매매 important 중요한 record 기록

123

Deposits received after 5:30 P.M. on business days ------- credited to your account on the next business day.
(A) being
(B) will be
(C) was
(D) to be

영업일 오후 5시 30분 이후에 받은 보증금은 다음 영업일에 당신의 계좌에 입금될 것입니다.

해설 빈칸 앞의 received부터 days 부분을 지우면 주어인 Deposits가 남는다. 즉 주어와 연결이 자연스러운 동사형태를 고르는 문제이다. 동사형태가 아닌 being과 to be는 바로 오답이다. 그리고 주어가 복수이므로 was도 탈락이다. 남은 선택지인 (B) will be가 자동으로 정답이 된다.

어휘 receive 받다 business day 영업일 account 계좌

124

Please note that this document serves only as a guideline and Northern Service should ------- be contacted for full details and an accurate quotation.
(A) than
(B) exactly
(C) always
(D) evenly

이 문서는 단지 지침서로서만 역할을 한다는 점을 명심하시고, Northen Service는 항상 전체 세부사항과 정확한 견적서를 위해서 연락이 취해져야 합니다.

해설 동사와 의미연결이 적절한 부사를 고르는 문제이다. 선택지 중에 should be contacted(연락이 되어야 한다)와 자연스럽게 연결되는 부사는 (C) always이다.

어휘 quotation 견적 document 문서 serve as ~의 역할을 하다 detail 세부사항 accurate 정확한 evenly 고르게

125

Tickets to Shark's concert sold so fast that the concert hall was moved from C.P Theater to Metro Concert Hall to ------- a larger audience.
(A) conduct
(B) accommodate
(C) develop
(D) broadcast

Sharks의 콘서트 티켓은 너무 빨리 팔렸기 때문에 콘서트홀은 더 많은 청중을 수용하기 위해서 C.P Theater에서 Metro Concert Hall로 옮겨졌다.

해설 목적어인 a larger audience(더 많은 청중)와 의미상 잘 어울리는 동사는 accommodate(수용하다)이다.

어휘 audience 청중 conduct 수행하다, 지휘하다 accommodate 수용하다 develop 개발하다 broadcast 방송하다

126

Computer technology has made it possible for businesses to process information more ------- and at a faster rate.
(A) efficiency
(B) efficient
(C) efficiencies
(D) efficiently

컴퓨터 기술은 회사가 정보를 더 효율적이고 더 빠른 속도로 처리하는 것을 가능하게 했다.

해설 동사와 목적어가 모두 앞에 왔으므로, 빈칸은 부사(efficiently 효율적으로)자리이다.

어휘 technology 기술 possible 가능한 process 과정 efficiently 효율적으로

127

Tippi Hedren Arts is ------- to have such tremendous talent as instructors.
(A) fortunate
(B) obvious
(C) encouraging
(D) skilled

Tippi Hedren Arts는 엄청난 재능을 갖춘 강사들이 있어서 운이 좋습니다.

해설 빈칸은 be동사와 to부정사 사이에 어울리는 형용사가 들어갈 자리이다. 선택지 중 정답인 fortunate는 be fortunate to(다행히 ~하다)로 쓰인다.

어휘 tremendous 엄청난, 굉장한 talent 재능, 인재 fortunate 운 좋은 obvious 명백한 skilled 숙련된

128

Food that is produced ------- is one of the best choices for the environment and requires less transportation.
(A) locally
(B) locals
(C) locality
(D) local

지역에서 생산되는 음식은 환경을 위한 최고의 선택 중 하나이고 운송비가 더 적게 들 것이다.

해설 수동태(is produced) 뒤에 빈칸이 있고 그 뒤에 be동사가 등장하므로 빈칸은 부사(locally 지역적으로)자리이다.

어휘 choice 선택 environment 환경 require 요구하다 transportation 운송

129

The overseas manager will approve issuance of a company cellular phone for any foreign sales ------- who signs up for one.
(A) representative
(B) representatively
(C) representation
(D) represent

해외 매니저는 휴대폰을 신청하는 어떤 해외 영업직원들에게도 회사 휴대폰의 발급을 승인할 것이다.

해설 sales와 자연스럽게 연결되는 어휘를 고르는 문제이다. 복합명사인 sales representative를 기억해두면 쉽게 해결할 수 있다.

어휘 issuance 배급, 배포, 발행 approve 찬성하다 issuance 배급 sign up 신청하다 representative 담당 직원

130

A project plan is currently being prepared for a 13-kilometer ------- of the new road from Leichard to Stich.
(A) stretch
(B) proximity
(C) journey
(D) duration

Leichard에서 Stich까지 가는 13km의 쭉 뻗은 새로운 도로를 위한 프로젝트 계획이 현재 준비되고 있다.

해설 빈칸은 앞의 13-kilometer라는 거리와 어울리는 명사가 들어갈 자리이다. 선택지 중 길이나 범위와 잘 어울리는 단어는 (A) stretch(길이, 범위)이다.

어휘 currently 현재 prepare 준비하다 road 길 stretch 늘이다 proximity 가까움 duration 지속기간

Questions 131-134 refer to the following e-mail.

To: All staff

From: Emily Reynold

Date: Wednesday, December 26

Subject: Printer supplies and printer repair

I am writing this e-mail to inform you that the deadline for ------- **131.** supplies for the printer in your office, such as paper, ink, and toner cartridges, is on Friday, December 29.

In addition, please take note ------- for printers requiring repair, **132.** you have to fill out a form and submit it to the maintenance department. -------. ------- cannot be processed without **133.** **134.** receiving the documentation you need to complete.

After submitting the document, you will receive a call, and a service technician will visit your office, either to repair your machine or replace the unit if needed. If you have any questions, please contact me during office hours.

수신: 전 직원

발신: Emily Reynold

날짜: 12월 26일 수요일

제목: 프린터 비품과 프린터 수리

저는 종이, 잉크, 카트리지와 같은 사무실 프린터 비품을 주문의 마감일이 12월 29일, 금요일이라는 것을 알리기 위해 이메일을 쓰고 있습니다.

뿐만 아니라, 수리를 필요로 하는 프린터들은 서식을 작성해서 유지보수부서로 제출해야 합니다. 회사 홈페이지를 통해 서식을 다운로드하거나 직접 받아갈 수도 있습니다. 작성해야 할 필요가 있는 서류를 받지 않고서는 요청은 처리되지 않을 것입니다.

서류 제출 후에 여러분은 전화를 받고, 서비스기사가 사무실을 방문하거나 필요하면 기기를 교체하거나 수리를 할 것입니다. 질문이 있으면 근무 시간 중에 저에게 연락하시기 바랍니다.

어휘 inform 알리다 deadline 마감기한 supplies 비품 in addition 게다가 take note 알아 두십시오 maintenance 유지보수 process 처리하다 clarification 설명

131
(A) order
(B) ordered
(C) ordering
(D) orders

해설 빈칸은 전치사 다음에 목적어 역할을 하며 빈칸 다음에 명사 supplies를 목적어로 취할 수 있는 동명사(ordering)자리이다. 참고로 빈칸을 명사 supplies를 수식하는 형용사로 판단하여 (B) ordered를 선택할 수 있겠지만 해석(주문된 제품을 위한 마감기한)상 적절하지 않다

132
(A) that
(B) them
(C) with
(D) when

해설 빈칸은 동사 take note(주목하다) 다음에 위치하여 뒤 문장을 받는 명사절 접속사자리이다. 선택지 중 명사절 접속사는 (A), (D) 가 있지만 해석상 (A)가 적절하다. take note that S + V(주어가 동사하는 것을 주목하다)를 기억하자.

133
(A) Without it, your requests for the reimbursement will be denied.
(B) It was distributed to anyone who attended that session.
(C) It is necessary to explain why you are requesting those printers to be purchased.
(D) You can download the form through our company website, or you can get one from me personally.

해설 빈칸 앞뒤 문장을 살펴보고 문맥상 적절한 문장을 선택하자. 앞 문장은 '양식을 작성해야 한다.' 뒤 문장은 '그 서류 없이는 처리되 지 않는다'고 언급하므로 빈칸은 form(양식)을 수령할 수 있는 방법을 설명하는 (D)가 가장 적절하다.

(A) 그것 없이, 상환에 대한 당신의 요청은 거절될 것입니다.
(B) 그것은 모임에 참석한 누구에게나 나누어졌습니다.
(C) 당신이 그러한 프린터가 주문되도록 요청하는 이유를 설명할 필요가 있습니다.
(D) 회사 홈페이지를 통해 서식을 다운로드하거나 직접 받아갈 수도 있습니다.

134
(A) Requests
(B) Proposals
(C) Substitutes
(D) Materials

해설 문장의 주어자리에 들어가는 명사를 선택하는 문제이며 앞부분의 문맥을 살펴보면서 정답을 선택해야 한다. 빈칸은 필요한 부품 에 대해 회사에 주문을 하도록 '요청'하는 의미이므로 (A) Requests(요청서)가 정답이다.

ACTUAL TEST 01 ACTUAL TEST 02 ACTUAL TEST 03 ACTUAL TEST 04 ACTUAL TEST 05

Questions 135-138 refer to the following letter.

Dear Mr. Anderson, I would like to verify my bill at your resort. I was charged more than I expected. When I checked my credit card bill the other day, I noticed that an item was charged to my bill twice. This could be my boat ride on September 8, which cost $ 50.00 per hour ride. The amount indicated on my bill was $ 870, but when I checked it again, my total ------- $ 820. I paid for my ride **135.** in cash to a woman named Amanda Baeck. She even gave me a receipt. For some reason, I think one of your hotel employees charged it again to my credit card. -------. **136.** -------, I would like to ask that you make the necessary ------- to **137.** **138.** my billing to reflect the correct amount of my bill. Thank you. Yours truly, Robert Henry	Anderson 씨께 당신의 리조트에 계산서를 확인하고 싶습니다. 내가 예상했던 것보다 더 많이 부과되었습니다. 얼마 전에 신용카드 계산서를 확인했는데 계산서에 한 항목이 두 번 청구되었다는 것을 알아차렸습니다. 이것은 9월 8일 보트 타기인데, 시간당 50달러였습니다. 계산서상의 총액은 870달러였으며, 내가 다시 확인했을 때, 총액은 820달러여야 했습니다. 나는 Amanda Baeck이라는 이름의 여성에게 현금으로 보트 타기 요금을 지불했습니다. 그녀는 심지어 영수증도 줬습니다. 어떤 이유에선지 직원 중 한 명이 내 신용카드에 그것을 다시 청구한 것 같습니다. 따라서 나는 당신의 청구시스템을 관리하는 방식에 만족하지 못합니다. 이것으로 비추어 봐서, 청구서에 정확한 금액을 반영하기 위해 필요한 수정을 해주기를 요청합니다. 감사합니다. 진심을 담아, Robert Henry

어휘 verify 확인하다 bill 청구서 charge 청구하다 notice 알아차리다 twice 두 번 amount 금액 in cash 현금으로 receipt 영수증 in view of 이것에 비추어 보아 adjustment 조정 reflect 반영하다 correct 정확한

135

(A) should have been
(B) must be
(C) will be
(D) could have been

해설 빈칸에는 주어 total(총액)과 어울리는 동사가 들어가야 한다. 동사의 시제를 고르는 문제가 아니라 해석을 통해 문맥이 적절하게 연결되는 동사를 고르는 문제이다. 지문 내용은 부정확한 청구에 대한 불만을 표시하며 본인의 주장을 펼치고 있으므로 (A) should have p.p(~했었어야 했는데)가 가장 적절하다. 참고로 (D) could have p.p는 '했을 수도 있었을 텐데'로 해석하며 결국은 '못했음을 아쉬워한다'는 의미이다.

136
(A) **I was not, therefore, satisfied with the way you manage your billing system.**
(B) Here is my suggestion to improve your customer service.
(C) They must have been well trained by the experts.
(D) So, I want it to be all cancelled with my previous orders.

해설 앞 문맥과 어울리는 문장을 선택하는 문제이다. 앞 문장에서 '과다 청구에 대한 불만을 표시하다'는 내용이 담겨 있으므로 불만을 토로하는 (A)가 가장 적절하다.

(A) 따라서, 나는 당신이 청구시스템을 관리하는 방식에 만족하지 못합니다.
(B) 당신의 고객 서비스를 향상시키기 위한 나의 제안은 이것입니다.
(C) 그들은 전문가들에 의해 잘 훈련되었음이 틀림없습니다
(D) 그래서, 나는 그것이 내 이전 주문들과 함께 모두 취소되기를 바랍니다.

137
(A) Even so
(B) Instead
(C) **In view of this**
(D) In case

해설 빈칸은 앞 문장과 뒤 문장을 연결시켜주는 부사자리이다. 앞 문맥에서 잘못된 청구 사항에 대한 불만을 얘기하며 '영수증을 주었다'는 근거까지 제시하였으므로 (C) in view of this(이것에 비추어 보아)가 적절하다.

138
(A) charge
(B) **adjustment**
(C) access
(D) replacement

해설 빈칸 뒤의 to reflect the correct amount(정확한 금액을 반영하기 위해)와 의미가 잘 어울리는 선택지는 (B) adjustment(수정)이다.

Intersil Corp.

Marketing Manager

-------. The ideal candidate must be able to assist the marketing
　　139.
team in ------- promoting the company's products to potential
　　　140.
customers.

Qualified applicants must possess a bachelor's degree in
marketing or a related field. Marketing related graduate study
is preferred. At least five years of work experience, excellent
market analysis skills, superior communication skills, and the
ability to handle a variety of assignments ------- are required for
　　　　　　　　　　　　　　　　　　　　141.
the position.

Intersil Corp. only accepts online applications. Interested
candidates can ------- their résumé and salary expectations to
　　　　　　　142.
Andea Bucket mkelly@Intersil.com before October 30.

Intersil Corp.
마케팅 관리자

Intersil Corp.은 마케팅 관리자 자리에 대한 지원서를 받고 있습니다. 이상적인 지원자는 잠재적인 고객들에게 회사의 제품을 효율적으로 홍보하는 마케팅팀을 도울 수 있어야 합니다.

자격을 갖춘 지원자들은 마케팅이나 관련 분야에서 학사 학위를 소지하여야 합니다. 적어도 5년의 경험, 뛰어난 시장 분석 기술, 우수한 의사소통 기술, 그리고 다양한 업무를 동시에 처리할 능력이 요구됩니다.

Intersil Corp.는 오직 온라인 지원서만 허용합니다. 관심 있는 지원자들은 이력서와 기대 급여를 Andea Bucket에게 이메일로 10월 30일까지 보낼 수 있습니다.

어휘 ideal 이상적인 promote 홍보하다 potential customers 잠재고객 possess 보유하다 bachelor's degree 학사 학위 field 분야 handle 처리하다 a variety of 다양한

139 (A) We are pleased to offer you a marketing manager position in Intersil Corp.
(B) Intersil Corp. is planning to open a second branch in Texas.
(C) Intersil Corp. is accepting applications for the position of marketing manager.
(D) Intersil Corp. appreciate you applying for the Marketing Manager position.

해설 빈칸은 문장 맨 앞에 적절한 문장이 들어갈 자리이다. 지문의 첫 문장은 주제를 나타낸다. 뒤 문맥을 살펴보면 직업 공지임을 알 수 있으므로 이 글을 쓰는 의도를 나타내는 (C)가 가장 적절하다.

(A) 우리는 당신에게 기꺼이 Intersil Corp.에 마케팅 관리자직을 제공합니다.
(B) Intersil Corp.은 텍사스에 두 번째 지사를 열 계획입니다.
(C) Intersil Corp.은 마케팅 관리자직의 지원서를 받고 있습니다.
(D) Intersil Corp.은 당신이 마케팅 관리자직에 지원한 것에 감사합니다.

140

(A) effective
(B) effectively
(C) effectiveness
(D) effect

해설 동명사 promoting을 수식하는 적절한 품사를 선택하는 문제이다. 동명사 수식은 부사가 하므로 (B) effectively가 정답이다. 참고로 V ing 형태는 동명사, 형용사가 동일하지만 둘 다 부사가 수식한다는 점을 기억하자.

141

(A) simultaneously
(B) potentially
(C) inconclusively
(D) patiently

해설 빈칸은 문장 뒤에서 동사 handle를 수식하는 부사자리이다. '다양한 업무를 동시에 처리하는 능력'이 가장 적절하므로 (A) simultaneously가 정답이다.

142

(A) place
(B) forward
(C) renew
(D) calculate

해설 목적어 heir résumé and salary expectations(그들의 이력서와 기대 급여)를 취하는 동사 어휘문제이다. 단순히 목적어와의 관계만 생각하면 어려울 수 있지만 뒤에 전치사 to(~에게)까지 확인하면 '전송하다'의 의미인 (B) forward가 정답이다. 추가로 동의어인 send, direct도 외워두자.

Questions 143-146 refer to the following article.

For many years, Oklahoma City has been the capital of theatrical plays. This might be because many students choose a theatrical course or other related majors in college. A few years after graduating, these people are now ------- their achievements in
143.
the field of entertainment.

Truly, the quality of shows has gradually increased over the years, with plays ------- than ever with audiences. In fact,
144.
famous plays such as Ms. Taylor's The Crusade and Mr. Joshua's The Korean Way have received several awards and constructive reviews from international critics. -------. For
145.
instance, Ms. Juana Wood directed a show that lost $ 100,000.

-------, many stage directors still become rich and famous
146.
because of their talent in directing.

여러 해 동안, Oklahoma City는 연극의 중심지였다. 이것은 많은 학생들이 연극학이나 다른 관련 전공을 대학에서 택했기 때문일 수도 있다. 졸업 몇 년 뒤에, 이런 사람들은 현재 연예 분야에서 그들의 성과에 대해 인정을 받고 있다. 정말, 공연의 질은 관중들에게 더욱 인기 있는 연극들로 수년간 점차 향상되었다.

실제로, Taylor 씨의 The Crusade와 Joshua 씨의 The Korean Way와 같은 유명한 연극들은 몇몇 상을 수상하고 해외 비평가로 좋은 평을 받았다. 그러나 몇몇 공연은 많은 비평가들로부터 부정적인 의견을 받았다. 예를 들면, Juana Wood 씨는 십만 달러를 손해 본 공연을 감독했다.

그것에도 불구하고, 많은 감독들은 감독 역할에 그들의 재능으로 여전히 부유하고 유명하다.

어휘 capital 수도, 중심지 theatrical 연극의 course 수업 major 전공 constructive 건설적인 critic 비평가 for instance 예를 들면 direct 감독하다 rich 부유한

143
(A) **recognized for**
(B) transferred to
(C) promoted to
(D) criticized by

해설 문맥상 어울리는 동사 어휘를 고르는 문제이다. '연예 분야에서 그들의 성과에 대해 인정을 받고 있다'가 적절하므로 (A) recognized for이 정답이다.

144
(A) popular
(B) **more popular**
(C) more popularities
(D) more popularly

해설 빈칸은 than을 확인하면 비교급 형태가 필요함을 알 수 있다. 따라서 (A)는 탈락된다. 그리고 앞에 명사 plays(연극)을 수식하는 형용사자리이므로 (B) more popular가 정답이다.

145
(A) They are renowned for critically acclaimed novels.
(B) In addition to them, there are a lot of creative and reputable directors.
(C) However, a few shows received negative opinions from many critics.
(D) After graduating, many people have decided to begin their careers as stage directors.

해설 빈칸 앞 내용은 '좋은 평가를 받았다'이고 빈칸 뒤 내용은 '제작한 쇼가 손해를 봤다'는 내용이다. 앞뒤 내용이 서로 상반되므로 빈칸이 부정적인 내용을 암시한다면 적절하겠다. 따라서 (C)가 가장 적절하다.

(A) 그들은 격찬을 받는 소설로 유명하다.
(B) 그들뿐만 아니라, 많은 창의적이고 명성 있는 감독들이 있다.
(C) 그러나, 몇몇 공연은 많은 비평가들로부터 부정적인 의견을 받았다.
(D) 졸업 뒤에, 많은 사람들은 감독으로 그들의 일을 시작하기로 결정했다.

146
(A) In spite of that
(B) Whereas
(C) As far as
(D) In other words

해설 빈칸은 앞 문단과 뒤 문장을 자연스럽게 연결하는 자리이다. 하지만 (B), (C)는 접속사이므로 탈락된다. 앞 문단에 마지막 내용이 연극에서의 부정적인 면을 언급했다면 뒤 문장은 '아직도 부유하고 유명하다'는 긍정적인 면을 언급하고 있다.

101

Before stepping out of the office, Mr. Morbos ------- his budget proposal for the next fiscal year on his supervisor's desk.
(A) waited
(B) remained
(C) left
(D) offered

사무실에서 나가기 전에 Morbos 씨는 상사의 책상 위에 다음 회계연도의 예산제안서를 놔두었다.

해설 목적어 his budget proposal과 on his supervisor's desk와 의미연결이 자연스러운 동사어휘를 고르는 문제이다. waited와 remained는 자동사로 바로 오답이고, offered는 his budget proposal(그의 예산 제안서)을 목적어로 취할 수 있지만 on his supervisor's desk(그의 상사의 책상에)와는 의미연결이 되지 않는다. left(두다)는 leave의 과거형으로 '그의 예산 제안서를 그의 상사의 책상에 두다'라는 의미로 연결이 매끄럽다.

어휘 fiscal year 회계 연도 step out 나가다 budget proposal 예산제안서 leave 두다 offer 제공하다

102

Following are the various suggestions that ------- by survey respondents.
(A) had been indicating
(B) were indicated
(C) has indicated
(D) are indicating

설문조사 응답자에 의해서 표시된 다양한 제안들은 다음에 있다.

해설 빈칸은 주격 관계대명사 that 뒤에 어울리는 동사형태가 들어갈 자리이다. indicate는 '~을 나타내다'라는 타동사인데, 빈칸 뒤에 목적어가 없으므로 수동형태가 들어가야 한다. 그래서 정답은 (B) were indicated이다.

어휘 various 다양한 suggestion 제안 survey 설문 respondent 응답자 indicate 나타나다

103

While the headquarters is -------, most work at Wide Steel Corporate should be conducted at the Wony Office Building.
(A) to renovate
(B) renovation
(C) being renovated
(D) renovate

본사가 개조되는 동안, Wide Steel Corporate의 대부분의 업무는 Wony Office Building에서 처리되어야 한다.

해설 빈칸은 be동사 is 뒤에 어울리는 형태가 들어갈 자리이다. be동사 뒤의 들어갈 수 있는 동사형태는 -ing(능동형), -ed(수동형)가 있다. 사물주어일 경우 능동형을 쓰기 때문에 정답은 (C) being renovated이다.

어휘 headquarter 본부 conduct 수행하다, 시행하다 renovate 개조하다

104

The regulations revised by the manager of the marketing department list all the ------- which employees should observe in case of emergency.
(A) guidelines
(B) facilities
(C) functions
(D) inquiries

마케팅부서의 매니저에 의해 수정된 규정들은 비상시에 직원들이 준수해야 하는 모든 지침들을 나열하고 있다.

해설 빈칸은 관계대명사 which 앞에 의미가 어울리는 명사가 들어가야 한다. 관계대명사 문장은 형용사절로 선행사를 수식하므로, which 이하는 빈칸을 수식해주는 역할을 한다. 문맥상 '비상시에 직원들이 준수해야 하는 지침들(guidelines)'이다.

어휘 regulation 규정 emergency 비상

105

In some cases, we may need to cancel items from your order if they are discontinued and we have ------- in stock.
(A) none
(B) most
(C) finally
(D) even

어떤 경우에는, 만약 상품이 생산 중단이 되거나 재고가 없다면 주문으로부터 상품을 취소할 수 있습니다.

해설 빈칸은 have의 목적어가 들어갈 자리이다. 선택지 중에서 목적어가 될 수 있는 단어는 대명사 (A) none밖에 없다. most는 형용사, finally, even은 부사이다.

어휘 cancel 취소하다 discontinue 중단하다 in stock 재고

106

When leaving for a vacation, give your coworkers ------- instructions about how to take care of the sales calls in your absence.
(A) clear
(B) blank
(C) entire
(D) repetitive

휴가를 떠날 때, 직장 동료에게 당신의 부재 시에 영업 전화를 처리하는 방법에 대해 명확한 지시를 해주세요.

해설 빈칸은 instructions(지시, 설명)와 의미가 어울리는 형용사자리이다. 선택지 중 (A) clear(명확한, 분명한)가 의미연결이 적절하다. clear instructions 명확한 지시

어휘 absence 결석 instruction 지시, 설명 take care of ~을 처리하다, 다루다 blank 빈 entire 전체의 repetitive 반복적인

153

107

The recent increase in interest rates has made it more difficult for consumers to ------- home loans.
(A) implement
(B) cement
(C) obtain
(D) review

최근의 이자율 증가는 소비자들이 주택 대출을 받는 것을 더 어렵게 만들었다.

해설 빈칸은 뒤의 home loans(주택대출)를 목적어로 취하는 동사자리이다. loan(대출)과 어울리는 동사는 (C) obtain(얻다)이다. obtain home loans 주택 대출을 받다

어휘 recent 최근의 increase 증가 interest rate 이율 implement 시행하다 cement 접합시키다 obtain 얻다 review 검토하다

108

------ buying products online is convenient, most consumers continue to value the experience of shopping in store.
(A) Rather
(B) Regarding
(C) Except
(D) Although

온라인에서 물건을 구입하는 게 편리하긴 하지만, 대부분의 고객들은 상점에서 쇼핑하는 것을 가치 있다고 여긴다.

해설 빈칸 다음에 주어와 동사로 연결되고 두 개의 문장이 등장하므로 빈칸은 접속사자리이다. 선택지 중에서 접속사는 (D) Although 뿐이다. 정답을 고르기가 비교적 쉬운 문제이다.

어휘 convenient 편리한 value 가치 experience 경험 rather 꽤 regarding ~에 관하여 except ~를 제외하고

109

Place the copies of the receipt on Mr. John's desk when ------- are done copying them.
(A) yours
(B) your own
(C) you
(D) yourself

당신이 영수증을 복사하는 끝냈을 때, 영수증의 사본을 John 씨의 책상 위에 놔주세요.

해설 빈칸은 접속사 when 뒤에 어울리는 주어자리이다. 주어로는 주격인 (C) you가 정답이다.

어휘 receipt 영수증

110

On account of recent price increases, nonessential purchases of all office supplies ------- until further notice.
(A) will be deferred
(B) have deferred
(C) have been deferring
(D) are deferring

최근의 가격 상승 때문에, 모든 사무용품의 불필요한 구매는 추가공지가 있을 때까지 연기될 것이다.

해설 동사 defer의 적절한 형태를 묻고 있다. defer(연기시키다)는 타동사인데 뒤에 목적어가 없으므로 수동태가 적절하다. 따라서 정답은 (A) will be deferred이다.

어휘 nonessential 비본질적인, 꼭 필요하지 않은 increase 증가 purchase 구입, 구매 notice 공지 defer 연기하다

111

Transport England has released new safety guidelines ------- the use of drone aircraft, which people use for recreation.
(A) either
(B) for
(C) and
(D) so

Transport England는 사람들이 레크레이션용으로 이용하는 드론의 사용에 관한 새로운 안전지침을 발표했다.

해설 빈칸은 앞의 명사인 guidelines와 뒤의 use를 연결하는 적절한 어휘를 고르는 문제이다. 뒤 부분은 the use of drone aircraft(드론 항공기의 이용)이고, 앞은 new safety guidelines(새로운 안전지침)이므로 '사용에 관한 지침'으로 연결됨이 매끄럽다. 정답은 전치사 (B) for(~에 대한)가 적절하다.

어휘 release 출시하다 recreation 오락

112

The project team members have come up with a slight ------- to an existing solar technology to make it even more efficient.
(A) modification
(B) modifying
(C) to modify
(D) modified

프로젝트 팀원들은 현존하는 태양열 기술을 더 효과적으로 만들기 위해 약간의 수정사항을 고안해냈다.

해설 빈칸은 앞의 형용사 slight 뒤에 형태가 어울리는 단어가 들어갈 자리이다. 형용사 뒤의 빈칸은 명사자리이므로 정답은 (A) modification(수정사항)이다.

어휘 come up with 찾아내다 slight 약간의 existing 기존의 efficient 효율적 modification 수정사항

113

In accordance with company regulations, hospitality expenses are not considered ------- for reimbursement.
(A) considerable
(B) useful
(C) complete
(D) appropriate

회사 규정에 따르면, 접대비는 상환이 적절하다고 간주되지 않습니다.

해설 문맥상 의미가 적절한 형용사를 고르는 문제이다. consider는 능동형일 때 <consider + 목적어 + 형용사>의 구조이며 수동으로 바뀌면 <be considered + 형용사>의 형태가 된다. 빈칸 뒤의 for reimbursement(상환에 대해)를 통해 의미가 가장 적절한 형용사는 (D) appropriate(적절한)임을 알 수 있다.(appropriate for ~에 적합한)

어휘 in accordance with ~에 따라 regulation 규정 hospitality 접대 expense 비용 reimbursement 배상, 상환 appropriate 적절한 considerable 상당한

114

Unfortunately, the stadium is located on a red train line and not ------- enough to a grand station.
(A) closer
(B) closed
(C) close
(D) closest

불행하게도, 경기장은 red train노선에 있고 Grand 역에 충분히 가깝지 않다.

해설 and 뒤의 not이 앞에 있는 is와 연결된다고 보면 빈칸은 형용사자리이다. 문맥상 의미가 적절한 형용사는 (C) close이다. closer와 closest도 형용사의 비교급, 최상급 형태이지만, 문장에서 비교, 최상의 의미가 전혀 없기 때문에 오답이다. closed는 '폐쇄된, 닫힌'의 의미이다.

어휘 unfortunately 불행하게도 located ~에 위치한

115

The Department offers support to children who have a disability, through a ------- of programs targeted to meet their specific needs.
(A) deposit
(B) range
(C) manner
(D) kind

부서는 그들의 특별한 요구를 맞추기 위해 목표로 된 다양한 프로그램을 통하여 장애를 가진 학생들에게 지원을 제공한다.

해설 빈칸은 관사 a와 전치사 of 사이에 의미가 적절한 단어가 올 자리이다. 전체적인 내용으로 '다양한 ~'의 의미인 a range of가 적합하다.

어휘 disability 장애 meet 충족하다 needs 필요 deposit 보증금 a range of 다양한

116

Dessert may be added as an option for an additional ------- to the set menu prices.
(A) money
(B) information
(C) charge
(D) interest

디저트는 세트메뉴 가격에 추가 비용으로 선택사항에 추가될 수 있다.

해설 빈칸은 의미가 적절한 명사가 들어갈 자리이다. 빈칸 앞부분의 해석은 '디저트는 선택사항으로 추가될 수 있다'이고 뒤이어 '추가적인'이라는 표현이 나오므로 '추가적인 비용'의 의미로 (C) charge가 정답이 된다. money는 셀 수 없는 명사(불가산명사)로 관사 an과 어울리지 않는 오답이다. 또한 interest가 돈의 개념을 나타낼 때 '이자'라는 뜻으로 쓰인다.

어휘 additional 추가적인 information 정보 charge 비용

117

Joe has been a key contributor to our company's growth and we would like to thank him publicly for his years of service and for ------- dedication.
(A) himself
(B) he
(C) him
(D) his

Joe 씨는 우리 회사의 성장에 주요한 기여를 해왔고 우리는 그의 헌신과 7년의 근무에 대하여 공개적으로 감사를 드립니다.

해설 빈칸은 명사 앞에 어울리는 대명사의 격은 소유격(his)이다.

어휘 dedication 헌신 contributor 헌신자 growth 성장 publicly 공공연하게

118

The Texas Redevelopment Authority recently approved Journey Development's proposal ------- a parking lot in South Texas into a vibrant residential and commercial complex.
(A) transformation
(B) is transforming
(C) have transformed
(D) to transform

Texas Redevelopment Authority는 남쪽 Texas에 있는 주차장을 활기찬 주상복합단지로 바꾸기 위해 최근에 Journey Development의 제안서를 승인했다.

해설 빈칸은 적절한 형태의 동사가 들어갈 자리이다. 빈칸 앞에는 이미 <주어 + 동사 + 목적어>가 갖추어져 있고, 뒤에는 다시 목적어가 될 수 있는 명사(a parking lot)가 있으므로, 이 두 가지를 동시에 충족시킬 수 있는 형태는 to부정사인 (D) to transform밖에 없다.

어휘 vibrant 활기찬 approve 승인하다 proposal 제안 residential 거주하기 좋은, 주택지의 transformation 변화

119

Please keep in mind that all product orders are ------- to cancellation unless payment is received at least seventy two hours prior to the shipping date.
(A) subject
(B) eligible
(C) reluctant
(D) likely

만약 배송일에 앞서 적어도 72시간 이내에 지불이 되지 않는다면 모든 제품 주문은 취소된다는 것을 명심해주십시오.

해설 선택지 중 (A) subject가 '~을 조건으로 하는, ~하기 쉬운'의 의미로 연결이 적절하다. eligible은 be eligible for(~할 자격이 있는), reluctant는 be reluctant to(~하기를 꺼리는), likely는 be likely to(~할 것 같은)의 의미로 쓰인다.

어휘 cancellation 취소 payment 지불, 지급 shipping 배송 eligible ~을 가질 수 있는 reluctant 꺼리는 be likely to ~할 것 같다

120

------- in Paris, Paris Airlines operates flights all over France as well as some international destinations.
(A) Remained
(B) Based
(C) Stored
(D) Moved

Paris에 본사를 둔, Paris Airlines는 몇몇 국제적인 지역들뿐만 아니라, 프랑스 전역으로 비행기를 운항한다.

해설 이 문제는 <based in + 지명(~에 본사를 둔)>을 알고 있다면 쉽게 해결되는 문제이다. 참고로 based on은 '~에 근거한'이라는 의미이다.

어휘 operate 작동하다 as well as ~에 대하여

121

If you need to make any ------- to your order, you can remove an item in the cart by clicking the 'X.'
(A) conversions
(B) commissions
(C) announcements
(D) adjustments

만약 당신이 당신의 주문에 어떠한 수정을 필요로 한다면, 당신은 X를 클릭함으로써 장바구니에 담긴 아이템을 제거할 수 있다.

해설 빈칸은 앞의 make와 뒤의 전치사 to 사이에 의미가 어울리는 명사가 들어갈 자리이다. make adjustments to는 '~에 수정을 가하다'라는 표현을 알아두면 해결이 간단한 유형이다. 선택지 중에서 announcements는 make announcements(공지하다)로 자주 쓰이며, to your order(당신의 주문에)와는 의미연결이 어색하다.

어휘 remove 제거하다 conversion 전환 commission 위원회, 수수료 adjustment 수정

122
Heat and humidity can ------- lots of items, such as electronics, musical instruments, and antique furniture.
(A) damages
(B) damage
(C) damaging
(D) damaged

열과 습도는 전자제품, 악기, 골동품 가구와 같은 많은 물건에 손상을 입힐 수 있다.

해설 조동사 뒤의 빈칸은 동사원형자리이다. 선택지 중 동사원형은 (B) damage(손상시키다)이다.
어휘 antique 고풍스러운 humidity 습도 instrument 악기

123
Directors have to address a few barriers if they want their employees to work together -------.
(A) productively
(B) productivity
(C) productive
(D) productiveness

감독관들은 직원들이 함께 생산적으로 일하기를 원한다면 몇 가지 방해 요소들을 처리해야 한다.

해설 빈칸은 문장의 끝에 어울리는 품사가 들어갈 자리이다.
어휘 diversity 다양성 barrier 장벽, 방해 요소 productively 생산적으로 employee 직원

124
In case of emergencies such as fire, all hotel guests are requested to stay in their rooms ------- directed to evacuate by hotel employees.
(A) while
(B) unless
(C) whereas
(D) unlike

화재와 같은 비상상황 시에 모든 호텔 손님들은 만약 호텔 직원들에게 대피하도록 지시되지 않는 한 방에 머물러야 합니다.

해설 빈칸은 뒤의 분사구문을 받는 접속사자리이다. 분사구문을 취할 수 있는 접속사인 while(~인 반면)과 unless(~하지 않는다면) 중에서 (B) unless가 해석이 매끄럽다. unless directed to evacuate 대피하도록 지시되지 않는 한
어휘 evacuate 대피하다 in case of ~의 경우에 request 요청하다 stay 머무르다 whereas 반면 unlike ~와 다른

125

We regret to inform you that K4 Shuttle Service is not ------- for lost or stolen items.
(A) responsibility
(B) response
(C) responsive
(D) responsible

우리는 당신에게 K4 셔틀 서비스가 잃어버리거나 훔친 물건에 대해서는 책임이 없다는 것을 알리게 되어 유감입니다.

해설 빈칸은 be동사 뒤에 어울리는 형용사자리이다. 선택지 중 형용사는 responsible(책임 있는)과 responsive(응답하는)이다. 뒤의 전치사 for와 어울리는 형용사는 (D) responsible이다. be responsible for ~에 책임이 있다

어휘 regret to 유감스럽게도 steal 훔치다 response 대답, 응답 be responsible for ~에 책임이 있는

126

The specific terms and conditions of agreement for the merger of the two giant auto makers are ------- under consideration.
(A) more current
(B) current
(C) most current
(D) currently

두 개의 큰 자동차 제조업체의 합병을 위한 합의서의 구체적인 조항이 현재 고려 중이다.

해설 be동사 뒤에는 통상 형용사가 온다고 생각할 수 있지만 이 문장에서는 형용사가 들어가면 의미가 어색해진다. be동사 뒤에 바로 <전치사 + 명사>가 와야 의미가 자연스럽다. 즉, terms and conditions are under consideration(조건들이 고려 중이다)로 문장이 완성되며 빈칸에는 부사가 들어갈 수 있다. 즉, '조건들이 현재(currently) 고려 중이다'라는 문맥이 완성된다.

어휘 under consideration 고려중인 merger 합병 currently 현재

127

Miyaki, who along with the three other assistant superintendents ------- attends every board meeting, did not attend the last meeting.
(A) typically
(B) equally
(C) recently
(D) well

일반적으로 세 명의 다른 보조 감독관들과 함께 모든 이사회 미팅에 참석하는 Miyaki 씨가 지난 회의에 불참했다.

해설 빈칸은 동사 attend와 의미가 잘 어울리는 부사가 들어갈 자리이다. attend의 시제가 현재이며 반복적이거나 규칙적인 상황을 나타내야 하므로 (A) typically(일반적으로, 보통)가 적절하다.

어휘 superintendent 감독관 along with ~와 함께 superintendent 감독관 attend 참석하다 absent 결석한, 결근한

128

The device is one of the most important systems of a modern wind turbine, and it requires considerable -------.
(A) maintained
(B) maintains
(C) maintenance
(D) maintain

그 장치는 현대 풍력 발전용 터빈의 가장 중요한 시스템 중 하나이고 상당한 유지 보수를 요구한다.

해설 빈칸은 requires의 목적어자리이며 명사인 (C) maintenance(유지 보수)가 정답이다.

어휘 device 장치 modern 현대의 require 요구하다 considerable 상당한 maintenance 유지 보수

129

To ------- the registration process on your first visit, you may fill in your information below prior to coming in to our office.
(A) relieve
(B) acquire
(C) expedite
(D) equip

첫 번째 방문에 등록 절차를 신속히 처리하기 위하여 당신은 사무실로 방문하기 전에 아래에 있는 정보를 작성할 수 있습니다.

해설 빈칸은 the registration process(등록 과정)를 목적어로 취하는 타동사자리이다. 선택지 중 의미가 적절한 동사는 expedite(신속히 하다, 가속화하다)이다.

어휘 registration 등록 process 과정 visit 방문하다 fill in ~을 채우다 prior to ~에 앞서

130

------- better serve our valued customers in Europe, we are pleased to announce the opening of our branch office in Germany.
(A) In order to
(B) With regard to
(C) Notwithstanding
(D) Due to

유럽에 있는 소중한 고객들을 더 잘 모시기 위하여, 우리는 독일지사의 개장을 발표하게 되어 기쁩니다.

해설 빈칸 뒤의 동사원형 serve와 연결되는 형태는 to부정사이다. 선택지 중 동사원형을 받을 수 있는 형태는 (A) In order to밖에 없다. 나머지들은 전치사로 뒤에 명사가 와야 한다.

어휘 valued 가치 있는 be pleased to 기쁘다 branch 지점 in order to ~위하여 with regard to ~에 관해서는 notwithstanding ~에도 불구하고 due to ~ 때문에

Questions 131-134 refer to the following article.

Maryland (June 2) – During the Summer Festival, the city government is planning to ------- the entry of vehicles into the National Capital Park where the festivities will be held.
131.

From June 7 to 11, no vehicles will be allowed to enter the park except for buses. This rule will be in effect during the whole duration of the festival in order to prevent traffic congestion ------- the National Capital Park.
132.

-------. Another option to reach the venue is to use the public transportation system, ------- to accommodate a great number of local and foreign tourists expected to come to witness the festival highlights.
133. **134.**

Maryland (6월 2일) – 여름 축제 동안, 시 정부는 축제가 열리는 National Capital Park로의 차량 진입을 규제할 계획이다.

6월 7일부터 11일까지, 버스를 제외한 어떠한 차량도 공원으로 진입이 허용되지 않을 것이다. 이 규칙은 National Capital Park 주변에 교통 체증을 막기 위해 축제의 전체 기간 동안 효력을 유지할 것이다.

따라서 개별 차량을 이용하는 운전자들과 승객들은 공원 외곽에 주차하고, National Capital Park로 걸어와야 한다. 행사 장소에 도달할 또 다른 선택 사항은 축제의 하이라이트를 보러 올 것으로 예상되는 많은 지역과 해외 관광객을 수용하도록 갖추어진 대중교통 시스템을 이용하는 것이다.

어휘 entry 진입 enter 들어가다 except for ~을 제외하고 rule 규칙 in effect 효력을 발휘하는 prevent 예방하다 congestion 혼잡 venue 장소 public transportation 대중교통 accommodate 수용하다 tourist 관광객 witness 목격하다

131
(A) restrict
(B) make
(C) take
(D) enhance

해설 빈칸 뒤에 the entry of vehicles(차량 진입)를 목적어로 취하는 적절한 동사를 선택하는 문제이다. 축제로 인해 차량 입장이 제한되므로 (A) restrict가 정답이다.

132
(A) between
(B) on
(C) around
(D) after

해설 빈칸은 the National Capital Park과 어울리는 전치사 어휘가 들어갈 자리이다. National Capital Park에서 축제가 열리면 공원으로 들어가려는 차량으로 인해 '공원 주변'이 차량 정체되는 것이 상식적이다. 따라서 (C) around(주변에)가 정답이다.

133

(A) As a result, you should find alternative routes to commute to your work during that period.
(B) To this end, authorities decided to extend the operating hours of the public transportation.
(C) Therefore, drivers and passengers who use private vehicles should park their cars outside the park and walk to the National Capital Park.
(D) There are many ways to participate in the festival as a volunteer.

해설 본 문제처럼 문맥이 바뀐 경우는 앞 내용과 다른 내용을 언급하려는 의도이기 때문에 뒤 문장과의 관계에 초점을 맞추자. 빈칸 다음에 another option(또 다른 선택)을 보면 빈칸이 한 가지 option을 언급했음을 알 수 있다. 따라서 (C)가 가장 적절하다.

(A) 그 결과, 당신은 그 기간 동안 직장에 통근할 우회 경로를 찾아야 한다.
(B) 이렇게 하기 위해서, 관계기관은 대중교통 운영시간을 연장하기로 결정했다.
(C) 따라서, 개별 차량을 이용하는 운전자들과 승객들은 공원 외곽에 주차하고, National Capital Park로 걸어와야 한다.
(D) 자원봉사자로서 축제에 참가할 많은 방법이 있다.

134

(A) equipment
(B) is equipped
(C) equipped
(D) equips

해설 빈칸의 본동사는 is이다. 그러므로 접속사가 없는 상태에서 빈칸에 동사가 될 수 없으므로 (B), (D)는 탈락된다. 빈칸은 선행사인 the public transportation system(대중교통 시스템)을 수식하는 분사자리이므로 (C) equipped가 정답이다. 참고로 <be equipped with + 명사>, <be equipped to + 동사>형태를 기억하자.

Questions 135-138 refer to the following letter.

Dear Sir: This is in reference to the news article in Every News on January 13 related to the sale of a stolen motor vehicle at the QM Motors Incorporation. QM Motors Incorporation is a registered and well-established company that ------- by all laws of the country and is engaged **135.** in used car sales. Through the years, QM Motors Incorporation has constantly conducted business in accordance with the provisions of the law and has maintained the highest degree of legal and ethical standards in the conduct of its business. -------, QM Motors Incorporation has never engaged in a **136.** transaction contrary to the law, such as that ------- in your **137.** newspaper. A large number of QM Motors Incorporation customers can testify to our high level of professionalism. -------. We would like to restore the excellent reputation of QM **138.** Motors Incorporation. Thank you very much for your attention to this matter. Sincerely yours, Ms. Charlotte Stanley Counsel Officer QM Motors Incorporation	귀하께 이 편지는 QM Motors Incorporation에서 도난 차량 판매에 관한 Every News의 1월 13일자 기사에 관한 것입니다. QM Motors Incorporation은 국가의 모든 법률을 준수하고 중고차 판매업에 종사하는 등록되고 인정받는 회사입니다. 수년에 걸쳐, QM Motors Incorporation은 법률 조항에 따라 사업을 지속해왔고, 사업의 수행에 있어 가장 높은 수준의 법적 윤리적 기준을 유지해왔습니다. 이런 이유로, QM Motors Incorporation은 신문에 보도된 것처럼 법률에 반하는 거래에 절대 연관되지 않았습니다. 다수의 QM Motors Incorporation 고객들이 우리의 높은 전문성을 증언할 수 있습니다. 따라서, 우리는 귀하의 신문에서 기사를 철회하고 사과문을 발행하기를 요청합니다. QM Motors Incorporation의 뛰어난 명성을 되찾았으면 합니다. 이 문제에 관심을 가져줘서 대단히 감사합니다. 진심을 담아 Charlotte Stanley 변호인 QM Motors Incorporation

어휘 in reference to ~에 관한 stolen 도난당한 well-established 안정된, 정착된 engage in ~에 종사하다 constantly 끊임없이 in accordance with ~에 따라 provision 조항 degree 정도 ethical 도덕상의 contrary to ~과 대조적으로 testify 증명하다

135
(A) abides
(B) complies
(C) observes
(D) conforms

해설 빈칸은 전치사 by와 어울리는 동사가 들어갈 자리이다. '~을 준수하다'라는 표현 중에 전치사 by와 어울리는 동사는 (A) abides 이다. 참고로 동의어 comply with, conform to, adhere to, follow, obey, observe를 외워두자.

136
(A) Since then
(B) Even so
(C) For this reason
(D) In contrast to this

해설 빈칸 앞 내용과 빈칸 뒤 내용을 연결시키는 접속부사자리이다. 앞 내용은 '우리는 불법을 저지르지 않았다'는 주장에 대한 근거를 제시하고 있다. 뒤 내용은 '당신들의 실수에 대해 조치를 취한다'이므로 (C) For this reason이 가장 적절하다.

137
(A) was printed
(B) printer
(C) printed
(D) to be printed

해설 빈칸은 선행사 that을 수식하는 분사자리이다. 여기서 that은 지시대명사로 앞서 기사에 언급되었던 '도난된 차량'을 언급하므로 '당신의 신문에 인쇄된 그것'이 적절하기 때문에 수동형태인 (C) printed가 정답이다.

138
(A) Most of our investors are among our regular customers.
(B) So, let me recommend a professional technician for the position.
(C) We are offering them loyal customer benefits as a token of our appreciation.
(D) Therefore, we request that you publish a retraction and apology in your newspaper column.

해설 문장삽입문제는 글을 쓰고 있는 화자의 입장에서 바라보아야 한다. 앞 내용이 '잘못된 기사글로 인해 해당 기업이 이미지에 타격을 입었다'이고 뒤 내용이 '훌륭한 평판을 회복하고 싶다'이므로 그에 대한 조치사항인 (D)가 적절하다.

(A) 대부분의 투자자들은 단골들 중에 있습니다.
(B) 그래서, 제가 그 자리에 대해 전문기술자를 추천하도록 해주세요.
(C) 우리는 감사의 표시로서 그들에게 단골 고객 혜택을 제공합니다.
(D) 따라서, 우리는 귀하의 신문에서 기사를 철회하고 사과문을 발행하기를 요청합니다.

Questions 139-142 refer to the following advertisement.

Trendy Hotstyle, the newest magazine to be published in Geralton, welcomes freelance writers to contribute articles ------- local events. To be a contributor, a college degree is not required, but excellent writing skills are necessary.
139.

The magazine will also pay for articles submitted by experienced writers and ------- with high quality submissions.
140.

-------. However, permission of the author will be asked first
141.
before an important part of the article ------- by the editors.
142.

For more information, feel free to send an e-mail to editor@ trendyhotstyle.com.

Geralton에서 발행되는 새로운 잡지인 Trendy Hotstyle은 지역행사에 관한 기사를 투고할 자유기고가를 환영합니다. 기고가가 되기 위해, 대학 학위가 요구되는 것은 아니지만 뛰어난 작문 솜씨는 필수적입니다.

잡지는 경험 많은 작가에 의해 제출된 기사들과 높은 품질의 제출물을 가진 사람들에게 또한 비용을 지불할 것입니다.

항상 그러하듯, 잡지는 문법이 정확하고 의미가 명확한 것을 확실히 하기 위해 제출물들을 편집할 것입니다. 그러나 기사의 중요 부분이 편집자에 의해 변경되기 전에 먼저 작가의 허가가 요청될 것입니다.

추가정보가 필요하면 www.trendyhotstyle. com.으로 이메일을 보내주시기 바랍니다.

어휘 newest 최신의 welcome 환영하다 contribute 기고하다 pertaining to ~에 관해서 contributor 기고자 permission 허가

139 (A) pertaining to
(B) belonging to
(C) submitted to
(D) subscribing to

해설 빈칸은 명사 local events(지역 행사들)를 목적어로 취하는 전치사자리이다. 빈칸 앞 기사글에 대한 주제가 지역 행사들이므로 주제나 목적을 나타내는 전치사 (A) pertaining to가 정답이다. 동의어인 regarding, concerning도 함께 외워두자.

140 (A) these
(B) those
(C) both
(D) whose

해설 알맞은 대명사 어휘를 선택하는 문제이다. 빈칸은 with high-quality submissions(높은 품질의 제출물을 가진)의 수식을 받아서 writers(작가들)과 동등한 의미를 나타내는 (B) those가 정답이다. those who(~하는 사람들), those with(~을 가진 사람들)를 외워두자.

141

(A) As always, the magazine will edit submissions to ensure that the grammar is correct and the meaning is clear.
(B) The magazine has a right to keep all profits from distribution.
(C) Articles submitted should contain at least 300 letters.
(D) Payments will be credited to their accounts by the end of the month.

해설 빈칸은 뒤 문장과의 문맥을 살펴보아야 한다. However(그러나) 다음 문장이 '변경되기 전 작가의 허락을 요청할 것이다'이므로 빈칸은 '내용을 변경하겠다'는 내용이 적절하다. 따라서 (A)가 정답이다.

(A) 항상 그러하듯, 잡지는 문법이 정확하고 의미가 명확한 것을 확실히 하기 위해 제출물들을 편집할 것입니다.
(B) 잡지가 배포에서부터 모든 수익을 가질 권리를 가집니다.
(C) 제출된 기사들은 적어도 300자 이상이어야 합니다.
(D) 지불금은 월말까지 계좌로 입금될 것입니다.

142

(A) was changed
(B) is changed
(C) will be changed
(D) will be changing

해설 빈칸은 알맞은 동사시제를 선택하는 문제이다. 문맥을 살펴보면 빈칸의 내용이 아직 일어나지 않았음을 알 수 있다. 빈칸은 미래 시제가 적절하지만 시간·조건 부사절의 경우 현재가 미래를 대신하므로 (B) is changed가 정답이다.

Questions 143-146 refer to the following e-mail.

TO: Erick Miller <miller@mail.net> FROM: Mark Denver<mdenver@tsd.org> DATE: Monday, March 10 SUBJECT: Training Classes Dear Mr. Alexander, We would like to thank you for ------- for two of our training **143.** courses. Your enrollment for the oil sampling class for March 27 has been confirmed. -------, due to the unfortunate fact that **144.** only a few people enrolled in the May 1 class you wish to enroll in, we have to remove it from the schedule. Our policy requires us ------- classes that have not reached at least 40 percent **145.** capacity. -------. Ms. Oswin will be teaching the same class, **146.** and there are still openings for that class. If you wish to register, please inform us by sending me an e-mail as soon as you can.	수신: Erick Miller 〈miller@mail.net〉 발신: Mark Denver〈mdenver@tsd.org〉 날짜: 3월 10일 월요일 제목: 훈련 수업 Alexander 씨께 두 개의 훈련과정을 신청해주셔서 감사합니다. 3월 37일 오일 샘플링 수업의 등록은 확정되었습니다. 그러나, 등록을 원한 5월 1일 수업은 적은 인원이 등록했다는 안타까운 사실 때문에, 우리는 일정에서 그 수업을 빼야 합니다. 우리의 정책은 적어도 40%의 인원을 채우지 못한 수업은 취소하도록 되어 있습니다. 하지만 수업 일정에서 나타난 것처럼 다른 날짜도 있습니다. Oswin 씨가 동일한 수업을 할 것이고, 그 수업에 여전히 빈자리가 있습니다. 만일 등록을 원한다면, 가능한 한 빨리 이메일로 알려 주시길 바랍니다.

어휘 apply to 지원하다 enrollment 등록 confirm 확인하다 remove 제거하다 policy 정책 reach 도달하다 capacity 정원, 용량 opening 공석

143
(A) **applying**
(B) subscribing
(C) contributing
(D) approaching

해설 빈칸은 전치사 for와 어울리는 동명사 어휘가 들어갈 자리이다. apply for(~에 지원하다)가 적절하므로 (A)가 정답이다. 참고로 subscribe to(~에 정기구독하다) contribute to(~에 기여하다)를 외워두자.

144
(A) Therefore
(B) Instead
(C) In that case
(D) **However**

해설 빈칸은 앞뒤 문장을 의미상으로 연결하는 접속부사자리이다. 앞 내용은 '당신의 등록이 확정 되었다'이고 뒤 내용은 '이 수업은 등록 인원이 부족해서 없어졌다'이므로 역접관계를 나타내는 (D) However가 정답이다.

145

(A) cancel
(B) canceled
(C) to cancel
(D) that cancel

해설 빈칸은 require(요구하다)의 목적보어자리이다. require는 to부정사를 목적보어로 취하므로 (C) to cancel이 정답이다.

146

(A) For that reason, we changed the instructor.
(B) The class you enrolled in is scheduled to be opened next month because of the instructor's health problems.
(C) But as the class schedule indicates, there is another date.
(D) You should have registered for the class which was suitable for your level.

해설 앞뒤 문장을 살펴보고 알맞은 문장은 선택하자. 앞 문장은 '인원수 부족으로 수업이 취소된다.'이고 뒤 문장은 '같은 날 다른 수업도 있다'고 언급하며 취소되는 수업에 대한 대안을 제시하고 있다. 따라서 빈칸은 대안을 제시하는 내용을 말한 (C)가 가장 적절하다.

(A) 그런 이유로, 우리는 강사를 변경했습니다.
(B) 당신이 등록한 수업은 강사의 건강 문제로 다음 달에 개설될 예정입니다.
(C) 하지만 수업 일정에서 나타난 것처럼 다른 날짜도 있습니다.
(D) 당신은 수준에 맞는 수업에 등록을 했었어야 했습니다.

ACTUAL TEST 01 ACTUAL TEST 02 ACTUAL TEST 03 ACTUAL TEST 04 ACTUAL TEST 05

PART 5

101

Daily News Quantified ------- business news and market data from over 2,300 of the most market-impacting daily news items.
(A) analyzes
(B) analyze
(C) to analyze
(D) analyzer

Daily News Quantified는 시장에 가장 영향을 주는 2,300개 이상의 매일 뉴스로부터 비즈니스 뉴스와 시장 데이터를 분석한다.

해설 주어 뒤의 빈칸에는 동사가 와야 하고, 주어가 3인칭 단수이므로 동사에 -s가 붙은 (A) analyzes가 정답이다.

어휘 business news 경제 뉴스 market-impacting 시장에 영향을 미치는 analyze 분석하다

102

Generally speaking, scientists have developed four ------- methods of determining the age of the earth.
(A) difference
(B) differences
(C) differently
(D) different

일반적으로 말해서 과학자는 지구의 나이를 결정하는 네 가지 다른 방법을 개발했다.

해설 명사 앞의 빈칸은 형용사자리이므로 정답은 (D) different(다른)이다.

어휘 determine 알아내다, 밝히다 generally speaking 일반적으로 말해서 method 방법 difference 차이

103

We are always ------- to deliver our products in the London Tube area at a time that is convenient for you.
(A) complete
(B) rich
(C) ready
(D) skilful

당신이 편리한 시간에 London Tube 지역에 저희 상품을 배달할 준비가 항상 되어 있습니다.

해설 be동사 are와 to부정사 사이의 빈칸에는 형용사가 온다. 문맥상 (C) ready가 적절하며, ready는 be ready to(~할 준비가 되다)로 쓰인다.

어휘 convenient 편리한 complete 완벽한 skillful 솜씨 있는

104

You can take this medication ------- as directed by your physician.
(A) finely
(B) mistakenly
(C) only
(D) closely

당신은 단지 의사에 의해 지시받은 대로 이 약을 복용할 수 있다.

해설 빈칸은 의미가 적절한 부사자리이다. as 이하는 '당신의 의사에 의해 지시받은 대로'이므로 (C) only(단지)가 어울린다.

어휘 medication 약 physician 의사, 의료진 as directed 지시된 대로 finely 훌륭하게 mistakenly 실수로 closely 면밀히, 밀접하게

105

From 10 A.M. to 2 P.M., scenic boat rides ------- the Seine River will be offered for free at the city's waterfront.
(A) below
(B) among
(C) apart
(D) along

오전 10시부터 오후 2시까지 Seine강을 따라서 '경치 좋은 보트 타기'가 도시 해안가에서 무료로 제공될 것이다.

해설 빈칸 뒤의 센강(the Seine River)과 어울리는 전치사는 (D) along(~을 따라서)이다.

어휘 scenic 경치 좋은 for free 무료로 waterfront 해안가

106

A filter removes harmful foreign substances from the water -------, so further purification processing is not required.
(A) chemicals
(B) chemist
(C) chemical
(D) chemically

필터는 물에서 해로운 이물질을 화학적으로 제거하고, 그래서 추가적인 정화처리는 요구되지 않는다.

해설 완전한 문장에 추가로 들어갈 수 있는 품사는 부사이다. 이 문장은 주어(filter) 동사(removes) 목적어(substances)가 있는 완전한 문장이므로 빈칸은 부사자리이다. chemically 화학적으로

어휘 harmful 해로운, 유해한 purification 정화 foreign substance 이물질 further 추가적인 purification 정화 processing 처리 chemical 화학물질

107

All arriving passengers are required to have valid travel
------- including passport and visa.
(A) documented
(B) document
(C) documents
(D) documenting

해설 빈칸은 동사 have에 대한 목적어로 어울리는 단어가 들어갈 자리이다. 복합명사인 travel document(여행 문서)가 적합하다. document는 셀 수 있는 명사이므로, 관사가 없는 경우 복수형태로 사용된다. 따라서 복수형태인 (C) documents가 정답이다.

어휘 passenger 승객 valid 유효한 travel document 여행 문서 including 포함하여

도착하는 모든 승객들은 여권과 비자를 포함하여 유효한 여행 문서를 소지하도록 요구된다.

108

Direct Deposit is now mandatory for all employees, so if you
have not yet submitted a direct deposit request form, you
must do so -------.
(A) immediately
(B) formerly
(C) clearly
(D) almost

해설 완전한 문장이므로 전체 문맥에 맞는 부사를 골라보자. 앞부분의 so 이하를 보면, if ~ not yet submitted(아직 제출하지 않았다면)이고 must do so(그렇게 해야 한다)로 연결되므로 즉시(immediately) 제출해야 한다는 의미가 적절하다.

어휘 mandatory 의무적인 formerly 이전에 clearly 분명히, 명백히

Direct Deposit은 모든 직원들에게 현재 필수적이다. 따라서 만약 당신이 Direct Deposit 요청양식을 제출하지 않았다면 즉시 제출해야 한다.

109

To ------- safety on the job, each employee is expected to
use all personal protective equipment provided.
(A) ensure
(B) protect
(C) insure
(D) assure

해설 빈칸 뒤의 safety를 목적어로 취하는 동사어휘를 골라보자. '보장하다'는 의미로 ensure, insure, assure가 모두 비슷해 보이지만, ensure는 <ensure + 목적어> 또는 <ensure that + 주어 + 동사>의 구조를 사용되며, insure는 '보험에 가입하다'라는 의미이다. assure는 <assure + 사람 + that + 주어 + 동사>의 구조로 '사람에게 무엇을 보장하다'라는 의미이다. 따라서 safety를 목적어로 취하는 (A) ensure가 정답이다.

어휘 safety 안전 ensure 보장하다 insure 보험에 가입하다 assure 확신시키다

그 직업에서 안전을 보장하기 위하여, 각 직원들은 제공된 모든 개인 보호장비를 사용할 것으로 예상된다.

172

110

Lakeview Pictures offers internships to applicants -------
want to acquire work experience in a photo studio.
(A) themselves
(B) whom
(C) whoever
(D) who

Lakeview Pictures는 사진 스튜디오에서 근무 경험을 원하는 지원자들에게 인턴십을 제공한다.

해설 빈칸은 선행사 applicants를 취하는 관계대명사자리이다. 선행사가 사람이고, 빈칸 뒤에 동사가 나오므로 주격관계대명사인 (D) who가 정답이다.

어휘 acquire 얻다, 습득하다 studio 작업실 whoever 누구든지

111

The questionnaire indicated that businesses in the food
industry are ------- optimistic about future prospects.
(A) fairly
(B) fair
(C) fairest
(D) fairness

설문지는 음식산업 업체들이 미래 전망에 대해서 상당히 낙관적임을 나타냈다.

해설 형용사 optimistic(낙관적인) 앞의 빈칸은 부사자리이므로 (A) fairly(꽤, 공평하게)가 정답이다.

어휘 questionnaire 설문지 prospect 가망, 전망 optimistic 낙관적인 fairly 꽤, 공평하게

112

------- the heavy rain, more than a hundred people formed in
a long line in front of the store on the opening day of our new
Brisbane store.
(A) Despite
(B) Nevertheless
(C) Due to
(D) Because

폭우에도 불구하고, 100명 이상의 사람들이 새로운 Brisbane Store의 개장일에 가게 앞에 길게 줄을 섰다.

해설 빈칸은 명사 the heavy rain과 연결되는 전치사자리이다. 전치사인 despite(~에도 불구하고)와 due to(~ 때문에) 중에 정답을 선택해보자. 문맥상 '폭우에도 불구하고 백 명 이상의 사람들이 줄을 섰다'가 의미연결이 자연스럽다.

어휘 heavy rain 폭우, more than ~이상 form 구성하다, 형성하다 nevertheless 그럼에도 불구하고 due to 때문에

173

113

Customer reports of damaged goods must be made ------- two working days from date of delivery, or a claim cannot be processed.
(A) against
(B) since
(C) within
(D) into

손상된 물건의 고객 보고서는 배달 날짜로부터 영업일 2일 내로 작성되어야 하고, 그렇지 않으면 청구는 처리될 수 없다.

해설 빈칸은 뒤의 two working days를 받는 전치사자리이다. 선택지 중 기간명사 앞에 쓰이는 전치사는 (C) within(~ 이내에)이다.
어휘 damaged goods 손상된 제품 working days 영업일 claim 주장, 청구

114

Network connections which clearly ------- and speed up working procedures are a must in the industrial world today.
(A) simplify
(B) simple
(C) simplicity
(D) simply

작업 공정을 분명히 단순화하고 빠르게 할 네트워크 연결은 오늘날 산업계에서 필수 사항이다.

해설 빈칸 뒤에 등위접속사 and가 있고, 그 뒤에 동사 speed가 보이므로, 빈칸은 동사(simplify '단순화 하다)자리라는 것을 알 수 있다.
어휘 connection 연결 clearly 분명히, 명백히 simply 단순히 speed up 가속화하다 procedure 절차, 공정 must 필수 사항, 절대로 필요한 것

115

W&W is a company ------- strong-willed, driven individuals are rewarded and recognized.
(A) then
(B) where
(C) which
(D) that

W&W는 의지가 강하고, 의욕 있는 사람들이 보상을 받고 인정을 받는 회사이다.

해설 빈칸 앞의 a company와 뒤 문장을 적절하게 연결해주는 단어가 들어갈 자리이다. 부사 then은 문장 연결기능이 없다. 관계대명사로 보이는 which와 that의 경우 뒤 문장이 불완전해야 하는데 빈칸 뒤의 문장이 수동태로 빠진 문장 성분이 없다. 따라서 두 문장을 연결하면서 빈칸 앞의 company라는 장소를 받는 관계부사인 (B) where가 정답이다. 관계대명사인 who, which, that과 관계부사인 when, where, how, why의 차이는 관계대명사가 이끄는 문장은 불완전하고, 관계부사가 이끄는 절은 완전하다는 데 있다.
어휘 strong willed 의지가 강한, 확고한 driven 의욕이 넘치는 reward 보상하다

116

There has been a ------- improvement in agricultural productivity, which has increased incomes for a number of farmers.
(A) multiple
(B) crowded
(C) respective
(D) marked

농업 생산성에서 현저한 개선이 있었는데, 그것은 많은 농부들을 위해 수입을 증가시켰다.

해설 빈칸은 뒤의 명사 improvement(개선)과 의미연결이 적절한 형용사가 들어갈 자리이다. 선택지 중 이에 어울리는 형용사는 (D) marked(현저한, 뚜렷한)이다.

어휘 agricultural productivity 농업 생산성 income 소득 multiple 다양한 crowded 붐비는 respective 각각의 marked 현저한

117

To repair your transmission problems, you must have a great deal of mechanical -------.
(A) timing
(B) decision
(C) importance
(D) expertise

전송 문제를 수리하기 위해 당신은 많은 기계적 전문지식을 가져야 한다.

해설 빈칸은 형용사 mechanical(기계적인)과 의미가 잘 연결되는 명사자리이다. 선택지 중에서 이에 적합한 명사는 (D) expertise(전문지식)이다. mechanical expertise 기계적인 전문지식

어휘 transmission 전송 a great deal of 많은 ~ expertise 전문지식

118

Alexix Muttoni, who works at the ------- acclaimed Madrine's Coffee, is the recipient of this year's Outstanding Barista Award.
(A) critically
(B) criticism
(C) critical
(D) criticized

비평가들에게 극찬을 받은 Madrine's Coffee에서 근무하는 Alexix Muttoni 씨는 올해의 뛰어난 바리스타상의 수상자이다.

해설 빈칸은 acclaimed라는 형용사와 어울리는 부사자리이다. 선택지 중 부사는 (A) critically이다. 빈칸의 위치를 통해 문제를 해결해도 되지만, critically acclaimed(아주 찬사를 받는)으로 묶어서 외워 두면 부사를 찾는 문제로 접근하지 않아도 바로 정답을 고를 수 있다.

어휘 acclaimed 찬사를 받은, 호평 받은 acclaimed 찬사를 받는 recipient 수령인, 수상자 critical 중요한, 비판적인

119

We have to wait ------- evaluate Mr. Wilson's ability until we have heard back from all his co-workers.
(A) toward
(B) to
(C) on
(D) for

우리는 모든 그의 직장 동료들로부터 소식을 들을 때까지, Wilson 씨의 능력을 평가하기 위하여 기다려야 한다.

해설 본동사가 존재하기 때문에 evaluate를 to부정사 형태로 바꿔줘야 한다.

어휘 evaluate 평가하다 ability 능력

120

When applying for reimbursement of travel expenses ------- less than $ 18, don't itemize it in your report.
(A) totalled
(B) being totalled
(C) will total
(D) totalling

총 18달러보다 더 적은 출장비 상환을 요청할 때 보고서에 항목별로 적지 마세요.

해설 빈칸부터 콤마까지(------- less than $ 18)가 travel expenses(출장비)를 수식해준다. expenses 뒤에 which are가 생략된 구조이므로 동사의 -ed 또는 -ing 형태가 빈칸에 들어가야 한다. total은 타동사로 '합계가 얼마이다'라는 의미이다. 빈칸 뒤에 목적어($ 18)가 있으므로, -ing 형태인 (D) totalling이 정답이다.

어휘 reimbursement 배상, 상환 itemize 항목별로 적다, 명세서를 작성하다 travel expense 출장 경비 total 합계가 ~가 되다

121

The feasibility of constructing a connecting bridge between the two islands has been ------- researched and the results have been posted at www.contractors.org.
(A) permanently
(B) consecutively
(C) extensively
(D) roughly

두 개의 섬을 잇는 다리의 건설 가능성은 광범위하게 조사되었고 결과는 www.contractors.org에 게시되었다.

해설 동사 research(조사하다)와 의미가 어울리는 부사는 (C) extensively(광범위하게)이다.

어휘 feasibility 실행 가능성 post 게시하다 permanently 영구적으로 consecutively 연속해서 extensively 광범위하게 roughly 대략

122

El Najhad is a three-time recipient of an award at Oxford for
------- in teaching economic history.
(A) excellent
(B) excellence
(C) excelled
(D) excel

El Najhad 씨는 경제사 교수법에 탁월해서
Oxford에서 상을 세 차례 수상한 사람이다.

해설 전치사 for 뒤는 명사자리이므로 정답은 (B) excellence이다.

어휘 recipient 받는 사람, 수령자 excellence 우수함

123

Yamakasi Motors guarantees its repairs for four years, so feel
free to contact the service desk if you have ------- problems.
(A) any
(B) many
(C) no
(D) all

Yamakasi Motors는 4년 동안 수리를 보장
합니다. 그러므로 문제가 생기면 서비스 데
스크로 연락 주세요.

해설 명사 problems를 적절하게 수식해주는 형용사어휘를 고르는 문제이다. 빈칸 앞에 있는 if절은 (A) any와 의미연결이 자연스럽
다. any는 if ~ any, not ~ any, ~any?의 형태로 자주 쓰인다.

어휘 guarantee 보장하다 feel free to 마음대로 ~하다 contact 연락하다

124

The president of the company ------- the opening ceremony
which will be held in the conference hall of the Lakeview
Hotel.
(A) attends
(B) attended
(C) will attend
(D) will be attended

회사 대표는 Lakeview Hotel 회의 홀에서
개최될 개장식에 참석할 것이다.

해설 문맥상 적절한 동사의 형태를 묻고 있다. 빈칸 뒤에 목적어(the opening ceremonies)가 있기 때문에 수동형인 will be attend-
ed는 우선 탈락이다. the opening ceremonies(개장식)는 관계대명사절인 which will be held(개최될)의 수식을 받으며 문맥상 개최
될 개장식이 미래를 나타내므로, 참석도 당연히 미래에 하게 될 것이다. 그래서 정답은 (C) will attend이다.

어휘 president 대표 opening ceremony 개장식, 개업식 attend 참석하다

ACTUAL TEST 06 ACTUAL TEST 07 ACTUAL TEST 08 ACTUAL TEST 09 ACTUAL TEST 10

177

125

The housing shortage this year in Beaverton County is more serious than ------- experienced last year.
(A) this
(B) those
(C) these
(D) that

올해 Beaverton County의 주택 부족은 작년에 경험했던 것보다 더 심각하다.

해설 빈칸은 한 문장에서 반복되는 어휘를 다시 받는 지시대명사자리이다. this와 these는 앞 문장의 내용을 다시 받을 때 쓰는 단어들로 우선 오답이 된다. 본 문장에서는 housing shortage(주택 부족)를 받기 때문에 단수 지시대명사인 (D) that이 정답이다.

어휘 housing 주택 shortage 부족 serious 심각한

126

Environmental activists have advocated the use of more diverse energy sources ------- solar, wind and hydrogen power.
(A) equally
(B) similarly
(C) likewise
(D) such as

환경운동가는 태양, 바람, 수소에너지와 같은 더 다양한 에너지 자원의 사용을 지지한다.

해설 빈칸은 diverse energy sources(다양한 에너지원)와 solar, wind and hydrogen power(태양열, 풍력, 수소)를 연결해주는 역할을 한다. 선택지 중 명사 연결이 매끄러운 단어는 (D) such as(예를 들면)이다. 나머지는 부사이기 때문에 명사를 받을 수 없다.

어휘 advocate 지지하다 activist 운동가 diverse 다양한 source 원천 hydrogen power 수소 동력

127

The candidate for the Hawk Media manager position will ------- excellent communication skills and a positive attitude.
(A) assign
(B) state
(C) review
(D) possess

Hawk Media의 매니저직 지원자는 뛰어난 의사소통 능력과 긍정적인 태도를 갖추어야 할 것이다.

해설 주어 candidate(후보자, 지원자)와 목적어 excellent communication skills and a positive attitude(뛰어난 의사소통 능력과 긍정적인 태도)의 관계를 볼 때, 기술과 태도들은 후보자가 갖추어야 할 소양들이라는 의미이므로 (D) possess(가지다, 소유하다)가 정답이다.

어휘 candidate 후보자, 지원자 communication skill 의사소통 기술 positive 긍정적인 attitude 태도

128

According to the U.K. Department of Labour, employees must receive additional pay when ------- work in excess of 38 hours a week.
(A) they
(B) them
(C) their
(D) theirs

영국 노동부에 따르면, 직원들은 주당 38시간을 초과해서 근무할 때 추가수당을 받아야 한다.

해설 빈칸은 접속사 when 뒤에 그리고 동사 work 앞에 어울리는 주어가 들어갈 자리이다. 주어자리이기 때문에 주격 대명사인 (A) they가 정답이다.

어휘 according to ~에 따르면 pay 급여 in excess of ~을 초과하여

129

After much -------, the committee would like to recommend the following project to be funded.
(A) deliberated
(B) deliberate
(C) deliberately
(D) deliberation

많은 심사숙고 후에, 위원회는 자금이 공급되는 다음 프로젝트를 추천하기를 바랍니다.

해설 much 뒤에는 셀 수 없는 명사(불가산명사)가 와야 한다. 선택지 중 불가산명사는 (D) deliberation(심사숙고)이다.

어휘 committee 위원회 following 다음의 fund 자금을 공급하다 deliberate 심사숙고하다 deliberately 고의로 deliberation 심사숙고

130

At the A.U. Postal Service, mail is sorted by automated equipment, therefore, it is important for your mail to be addressed -------.
(A) corrected
(B) correctly
(C) correct
(D) correcting

A.U. Postal Service에서 우편물은 자동화된 장비에 의해서 분류되므로 우편물의 주소가 정확하게 기재되는 것이 중요하다.

해설 수동태(be + p.p) 뒤의 빈칸은 부사자리라는 것을 알고 있다면 (B) correctly(정확하게)를 쉽게 고를 수 있다.

어휘 sort 분류하다, 정리하다 automated 자동화된 therefore 따라서 correctly 정확하게

PART 6

Questions 131-134 refer to the following e-mail.

From: Mary Fitzherbert

To: Maria Clare

Date: December 8

Subject: Change of plans

Hi, Maria

I was informed earlier today that I have been chosen to attend a mortgage advisor training seminar which ------- on Fridays in **131.** March and April from 9:00 A.M. to 12:00 P.M. -------, I will not **132.** be able to cover for you on Fridays after all. However, I can still fill in for you on some of the Tuesday hours while you are out of the office as we have already agreed upon.

I will be on vacation leave this week, so Peter and I have discussed this matter already today. -------. Please send Peter **133.** an e-mail if this ------- is okay with you. **134.**

발신: Mary Fitzherbert
수신: Maria Clare
날짜: 12월 8일
제목: 계획 변경

안녕하세요, Maria

저는 오늘 아침 3월과 4월 금요일마다 오전 9시부터 12시 사이에 있을 대출자문 훈련세미나에 참석하도록 선택되었다고 통지받았습니다. 그러한 이유로 금요일에 당신을 대신할 수 없을 것입니다. 그러나 우리가 이미 동의한 대로, 당신이 출장 가는 화요일 시간에는 대신할 수 있습니다.

저는 이번 주에 휴가를 갈 것입니다. 그래서 Peter와 저는 이 문제를 이미 오늘 논의했습니다. 그가 원래 자원했던 화요일뿐 아니라 금요일에 당신을 대신해 줄 수 있다고 언급했습니다. 만약 이 조정이 당신에게 괜찮다면, Peter에게 이메일로 알려주길 바랍니다.

어휘 mortgage 대출 agree upon ~에 동의하다. enroll in ~에 등록하다 cover 다루다, 돈을 대다, 누군가의 일을 대신해주다 fill in ~을 작성하다, 누군가의 일을 대신해주다 arrangement 준비, 조정

131
(A) was held
(B) are held
(C) will be held
(D) held

해설 동사의 수, 태, 시제를 묻는 문제이다. 주격 관계대명사절의 동사는 선행사에 수일치시키고 선행사(a mortgage advisor training seminar)가 단수이므로 복수동사 (B)는 정답이 될 수 없다. 빈칸 뒤에 목적어가 없기 때문에 동사는 수동태를 취해야 하므로 능동태인 (D)도 탈락한다. 마지막 시제 일치에서 편지를 쓴 시점은 12월이지만 세미나가 개최되는 것은 3, 4월, 즉 미래이기 때문에 미래시제 (C)가 정답이다.

132

(A) **As such**
(B) Because
(C) Instead
(D) Furthermore

해설 접속부사를 묻는 문제는 앞뒤 문맥을 파악하여 가장 어울리는 것을 선택한다. 빈칸 앞으로는 세미나에 참석하게 되었다는 내용이고 뒤로는 수신자의 일을 대신해줄 수 없을 것이라는 내용이 이어지므로 결과의 접속부사 (A) As such(그러한 이유로)가 정답이다.

133

(A) But he was also scheduled to fly to the Arizona headquarters on those Fridays.
(B) We decided to recruit a new assistant to help promote our mortgage products.
(C) **He mentioned that he can fill in for you on those Friday hours as well as the Tuesdays he originally volunteered for.**
(D) He said that it is possible to work overtime on Tuesday.

해설 빈칸 뒤로 this arrangement라는 명사구가 존재한다. 지시형용사 this는 앞에서 언급된 명사 앞에서 사용 가능하므로 빈칸에는 명사 arrangement로 받을 만한 내용이 있어야 한다. arrangement는 '준비, 정리, 합의' 등의 뜻이 있으므로 (C)가 가장 적절하다.

(A) 하지만 우리는 또한 금요일마다 애리조나 본사로 갈 예정이었습니다.
(B) 우리는 우리의 주택담보대출 상품을 홍보하는 것을 도울 새로운 보조를 채용하기로 결정했습니다.
(C) 그가 원래 자원했던 화요일뿐 아니라 금요일에 당신을 대신해 줄 수 있다고 언급했습니다.
(D) 그는 화요일에 초과근무를 하는 것이 가능하다고 말했습니다

134

(A) flight
(B) **arrangement**
(C) compensation
(D) replacement

해설 133번 문제와 연결되는 문제이다. 지시형용사 this의 쓰임에 초점을 맞추고 앞 내용(여행을 가게 되어 당신의 일을 대신 해줄 수가 없다)을 조정하는 표현인 (B)가 정답이다.

ACTUAL TEST 06 ACTUAL TEST 07 ACTUAL TEST 08 ACTUAL TEST 09 ACTUAL TEST 10

181

Questions 135-138 refer to the following article.

Airline Merger Leaves Passengers Perplexed
 	
San Francisco (November 10) - A merger of two airlines caused confusion after the computer system for the joined companies failed. Chaos broke out when only the names of passengers of General Airlines appeared on the screen.
 	
As a result, boarding passes had to be issued manually to those who booked with Vita Air, and ------- were rescheduled. -------.
            135.   **136.**
 	
This shows that despite prior experience, no precautionary measures were put in place ------- the same kind of mishap
                                        137.
from happening again.
 	
"Computer analysts are ------- the cause of the problem and will
                      138.
submit a complete report soon, along with a recommendation," said the airline spokesperson.
	항공사의 합병이 당황한 승객들을 방치했다
	
	(샌프란시스코 11월 10일) 합병된 회사들의 컴퓨터 시스템이 고장 난 후에, 두 항공사의 합병이 혼란을 초래했다. 혼란은 General Airlines의 승객 이름만 화면이 나타났을 때 발생했다.
	
	그 결과 Vita Air로 예약한 승객들에 대해 탑승권은 수동으로 발행되어야 했다. 비행기들은 일정이 조정되었다. 이러한 문제는 합병된 몇몇 항공사에 의해 발생한다.
	
	이것은 이전의 경험에도 불구하고, 동일한 사고가 다시 발생하는 것을 막기 위한 사전 예방조치가 취해지지 않았다는 것을 보여준다.
	
	"컴퓨터 분석가들이 문제의 원인을 조사 중이고, 권유사항과 함께 곧 완성된 보고서를 제출할 것이다"라고 항공사 대변인이 말했다.

어휘 merger 합병 confusion 혼란, 혼동 fail 고장 나다 encounter 맞닥뜨리다, 마주치다 precautionary 예방의 measure 조치 mishap 실수 investigate 조사하다 complete 완전한, 끝난 along with ~와 함께 recommendation 제안, 권고사항 spokesperson 대변인

135
(A) workers
(B) tickets
(C) flights
(D) bills

해설 항공사 소프트웨어의 오작동으로 인해 일정이 조정될(rescheduled) 수 있는 것은 (C) flights(항공편)이다.

136
(A) However, as soon as we implemented a new program, scheduling conflicts no longer occurred.
(B) Passengers who have complaints regarding this problem may claim proper compensation.
(C) You need to provide us detailed information to claim your lost bags in the airport.
(D) This problem has been encountered by several airline companies that have merged.

해설 빈칸 앞으로 프로그램 오작동으로 인해 생겨난 현재의 상황에 대한 설명이 있었고 다음 단락으로 해결되었다는 내용은 이어지지 않았으므로 여전히 현재 상황에 대한 추가 설명이 들어가는 것이 적절하다. 그러므로 정답은 다른 합병된 회사들도 비슷한 상황을 겪었음을 첨가해주는 (D)가 된다.

(A) 그러나, 우리가 새로운 프로그램을 시행하자마자, 일정 충돌은 더 이상 발생하지 않았다.
(B) 이 문제에 관해 불만을 가진 승객들은 적절한 보상을 청구할 수 있다.
(C) 당신은 공항에서 분실된 가방에 대해 청구를 하기 위해 자세한 정보를 우리에게 제공할 필요가 있다.
(D) 이 문제는 합병된 몇몇 항공사에 의해 발생한다.

137
(A) to prevent
(B) to be prevented
(C) prevents
(D) preventing

해설 빈칸 앞으로 수동태 동사(were put)와 전치사구(in place)가 보인다. 즉, 빈칸 앞이 완전하므로 빈칸에는 부사적 용법의 to부정사 (A) to prevent 또는 (B) to be prevented가 답으로 들어가야 한다. 두 선택지의 차이는 동사의 태이므로 빈칸 뒤 목적어의 유무로 답을 고르면 정답은 능동태 to부정사인 (A)가 된다.

138
(A) removing
(B) investigating
(C) contacting
(D) protecting

해설 목적어인 the cause(원인)와 연결되는 가장 적절한 동사는 (B) investigating(조사하다)이다. 게다가 그 후에 보고서와 제안 사항들을 제출하겠다고 했으므로 (A) 제거하다는 어울리지 않는다.

Questions 139-142 refer to the following e-mail.

To: Josephine Charms From: International Organization of Seafarers Date: January 4 Subject: Approval of Your Application Dear Josephine, Welcome and thank you for joining the International Organization of Seafarers. This organization ------- the rights and promotes **139.** the welfare of people working on sea vessels. Our ------- mission is to extend help to seafarers who encounter **140.** problems while in foreign ports. We provide them some means to contact their families, transportation so that they can visit shopping areas or medical facilities, and counselling when needed. ------- the services mentioned, we have a web site that features **141.** up-to-date information on international laws and policies. Also, -------. **142.** We welcome the opportunity to assist you and safeguard your welfare. Thanks again for joining our organization.	수신: Josephine Charms 발신: International Organization of Seafarers 날짜: 1월 4일 제목: 지원 승인 Josephine 님께, International Organization of Seafarers에 참여해주신 여러분을 환영하며 감사를 드립니다. 이 단체는 선박에서 근무하는 사람들의 복지를 장려하고 권리를 지원합니다. 우리의 주요 임무는 해외 항구에 있는 동안 문제에 직면한 선원들에게 도움을 주는 것입니다. 우리는 그들의 가족들에게 연락할 수단, 쇼핑지역이나 의료시설에 갈 수 있도록 번역, 그리고 필요할 때 상담을 제공합니다. 언급된 서비스 외에도, 국제법과 정책에 대한 최신 정보를 특징으로 하는 홈페이지가 있습니다. 또한, 우리는 이 단체의 회원권의 혜택을 설명하는 문서를 첨부했습니다. 우리는 당신을 돕고 복리후생을 보호할 기회를 기꺼이 받아들입니다. 다시 한 번 우리 단체에 가입해주셔서 감사드립니다.

어휘 right 권리 promote 홍보하다 welfare 복지 primary 주요한 vessel 선박 encounter 맞닥뜨리다 seafarer 선원 port 항구 means (항상 복수형으로) 수단, 방법 transportation 교통수단 so that ~하기 위해서 facility 시설 aside from ~외에도 up-todate 최신식의 international 국제적인 safeguard 안전하게 지키다 organization 단체

139

(A) **supports**
(B) supporting
(C) supported
(D) having supported

해설 동사자리이기 때문에 동사가 아닌 (B)와 (D)는 탈락이다. 조직이 어떤 일을 하는지에 대한 설명은 현재의 사실로 보기 때문에 현재시제를 사용한 (A)가 정답이다. 게다가 등위접속사 and 뒤로 현재시제 동사인 promotes가 따라 나온다는 점을 확인했으면 쉽게 답을 찾을 수 있는 문제이다.

140
(A) previous
(B) primary
(C) early
(D) eager

해설 명사 mission(임무)을 수식하는 적절한 형용사를 찾는다. 조직에 대한 소개를 하는 내용이므로 '주요 임무'라는 의미로 연결되는 게 가장 잘 어울린다.

141
(A) Aside from
(B) In spite of
(C) Due to
(D) According to

해설 앞선 언급한 서비스 '외에도' 다른 서비스가 더 있음을 뒤에서 설명해주고 있다. 그러므로 전치사 (A)가 적절하다. aside from(전치사)은 본문처럼 명사 앞에 오기도 하지만 동명사 앞에 위치해 aside from -ing(~하는 것 외에도)의 형태로도 잘 쓰인다는 점을 기억하자.

142
(A) You can find the form that needs to be completed before you join.
(B) If you want to see that information, you should enroll as a member of the association.
(C) We have attached a document that explains the benefits of membership in this association.
(D) These are requirements for the access of confidential documents.

해설 빈칸 앞에 첨가의 접속부사 also가 존재하므로 빈칸은 앞 문장에 추가되는 내용이 와야 한다. 정보를 얻을 수 있는 홈페이지가 있다고 하므로 또 다른 정보를 얻을 수 있는 출처인 문서를 첨부했다고 하는 (C)가 정답이다.

(A) 가입하기 전에 작성해야 할 양식을 찾을 수 있다.
(B) 만약 그 정보를 보기를 원한다면, 당신은 단체 회원으로 등록해야 한다.
(C) 우리는 이 단체의 회원권 혜택을 설명하는 문서를 첨부했다.
(D) 이것들은 기밀문서의 접근에 대한 요구사항들이다.

Questions 143-146 refer to the following letter.

Defaunt- Nestene Banking Corporation

December 22
Rebecca Moore
3rd Avenue
Geraldton, West Australia 6530

Dear Ms. Marzonia,

You might have read in yesterday's newspaper that Defaunt Savings Bank and Nestene Finance Corporation are joining forces to serve you more efficiently. As of December 10, these two institutions -------.
143.

Our new name is Defaunt-Nestene Banking Corporation. -------.
-------, you can anticipate an increase in the range of products
145.
144.
you can use.

Please take time to read the brochure that comes with this letter so that you can familiarize yourself with some of our new -------.
146.

For more information with regard to all of our products, visit our web site (www.dnbc.com). We always look forward to serving you.

Defaunt- Nestene Banking Corporation

12월 22일
Rebecca Moore
3rd Avenue
Geraldton, West Australia 6530

Marzonia 씨께

어제 신문에서 Defaunt Savings Bank와 Nestene Finance Corporation이 더 효율적으로 당신을 모시기 위해 합병한다는 기사를 읽으셨을 것입니다.

우리의 새로운 명칭은 Defaunt-Nestene Banking Corporation입니다. 우리는 당신의 계좌에 어떠한 변경사항도 없을 것을 보장합니다. 뿐만 아니라, 당신은 이용할 수 있는 상품의 범위가 증가한다는 것을 기대할 수 있습니다.

당신이 몇몇 우리의 새로운 금융 상품들에 익숙해지기 위해 이 편지에 동봉된 소책자를 시간 내서 읽어보시길 바랍니다.

우리의 모든 상품에 관해 더 많은 정보를 얻으려면 홈페이지를 방문하시면 됩니다. 우리는 항상 당신을 모시기를 기대합니다.

어휘 force 세력, 힘 efficiently 효율적으로 institution 기관 merge 합병하다 anticipate 예상하다 range 범위 brochure 소책자 come with ~와 함께 오다 familiarize A with B A를 B에 익숙하게 만들다 look forward to -ing ~하기를 학수고대하다

143
(A) will merge
(B) can merge
(C) have merged
(D) is to merge

해설 편지를 쓴 날짜는 12월 22일이고 합병이 일어난 시점은 12월 10일이므로 지금으로부터 과거의 일임을 확인할 수 있다. 현재완료가 완료용법으로 사용될 때는 마치 과거시제처럼 '~했다'로 해석이 가능하므로 정답은 (C)이다.

144
(A) We assure you that no changes will be made to your accounts.
(B) Our new headquarters will be located on the site where the former city hall was.
(C) Nestene has lost its business to competitors over the last three years.
(D) We are in consultation with the union to increase work hours.

해설 두 금융업체가 합병했다는 내용의 기사글이다. 두 업체의 합병으로 인해 생겨날 일 중에서 빈칸 뒤로 이용할 수 있는 상품군이 증가할 것이라는 긍정적인 내용이 뒤따르고 있으므로 정답은 고객들 계좌에는 어떤 변경도 없을 것이라는 (A)가 가장 어울린다.

(A) 우리는 당신의 계좌에 어떠한 변경 사항도 없다는 것을 보장한다.
(B) 우리의 새로운 본사는 이전에 시청이었던 곳에 위치할 것이다.
(C) Nestene은 지난 3년간 경쟁 회사들에 거래처를 많이 뺏겼다.
(D) 우리는 근무시간을 늘리도록 노동조합과 협의 중이다.

145
(A) However
(B) For instance
(C) As such
(D) Furthermore

해설 144번 문제와 연결되고 있다. 두 개의 회사가 합병하면서 생겨날 일들 중에서 긍정적인 것들이 빈칸 앞뒤로 연결되고 있으므로 첨가의 접속부사 (D)가 가장 적합하다.

146
(A) offerings
(B) employees
(C) locations
(D) titles

해설 고객이 빈칸에 익숙해지도록 동봉된 소책자를 읽어 달라는 내용이 나왔다. 두 회사가 합병하면서 새롭게 제공할 '서비스, 제품, 여러 사항' 등을 확인해달라는 것이 가장 어울리므로 정답은 (A)이다. offering은 회사가 고객에게 제공하는 '서비스, 무료 선물, 제의, 제공' 등등 여러가지 뜻을 가졌으며 가산명사라는 점에 유의한다.

ACTUAL TEST 06 ACTUAL TEST 07 ACTUAL TEST 08 ACTUAL TEST 09 ACTUAL TEST 10

101

------ to the Moharvi Building should first register at the main security desk.
(A) Visiting
(B) Visitors
(C) Visit
(D) To visit

Moharvi Building에 방문하는 사람은 맨 먼저 메인 보안데스크에서 등록을 해야 합니다.

해설 동사는 register(등록하다)이고 등록할 수 있는 주체인 사람이 주어로 와야 한다. 사람명사인 (B) Visitors(방문객들)가 정답이다.

어휘 register 등록하다 security desk 보안데스크

102

Our clinic is located inside David Johns Mall which has ample parking spaces and is easily ------ by public transit.
(A) accessibility
(B) accessibly
(C) access
(D) accessible

우리 병원은 충분한 주차공간이 있고 대중교통과 쉽게 접근할 수 있는 David Johns Mall 안에 위치해 있다.

해설 빈칸은 부사 easily(쉽게)와 어울리는 품사가 들어갈 자리이다. 부사 뒤의 빈칸은 형용사자리이므로 정답은 (D) accessible(접근 가능한)이다.

어휘 ample 충분한 clinic 병원 easily 쉽게 public transit 대중교통 accessible 접근 가능한

103

Mishellan Library will be ------ from November 2 until December 22 while renovation works are carried out.
(A) paused
(B) closed
(C) nominated
(D) expired

Mishellan Library는 개조작업이 시행되는 동안 11월 2일부터 12월 22일까지 문이 닫힐 것입니다.

해설 while절은 '개조작업이 시행되는 동안'이므로, 도서관은 문을 닫게 된다는 의미연결이 적절하다. 따라서 (B) closed가 정답이다.

어휘 carry out ~을 수행하다, 시행하다 pause 멈추다 nominate 후보를 지명하다 expire 만료되다

104

The recently revised safety regulations ------- all the engineers wear safety helmets while working in the factory.
(A) assume
(B) mandate
(C) investigate
(D) organize

최근에 수정된 안전규정은 모든 엔지니어들이 공장에서 근무하는 동안 안전모를 착용할 것을 지시한다.

해설 빈칸은 동사자리이다. 주어인 regulations(규정)와 의미 연결이 적절한 동사는 (B) mandate(명령하다, 지시하다)이다.
어휘 regulation 규정, 규제 revised 수정된 put on ~을 착용하다 assume 추측하다 mandate 명령하다, 위임하다 investigate 조사하다 organize 조직하다

105

The addition of three assembly lines to its existing manufacturing plant is ------- of the growth occurring at Jake Corporation.
(A) substance
(B) evidence
(C) support
(D) appreciation

기존 제조공장에 3개의 조립라인 추가는 Jake Corporation에서 일어나고 있는 성장의 증거이다.

해설 of the growth(성장의 ~)와 의미연결이 매끄러운 단어는 (B) evidence(증거)이며 evidence of the growth는 '성장의 증거'라는 의미이다.
어휘 addition 추가 assembly line 조립라인 existing 현재 있는, 기존의 occur 발생하다 growth 성장 substance 물질 evidence 증거 appreciation 감사

106

The latest software significantly ------- the number of hours needed for employees to finish the task.
(A) reduction
(B) to reduce
(C) reduced
(D) reducing

최신 소프트웨어는 직원들이 업무를 끝내기 위해 요구되는 시간을 상당히 줄였다.

해설 빈칸은 주어 뒤에 동사가 와야 하는 위치이다. 선택지 중 동사로 적합한 형태는 (C) reduced이다.
어휘 latest 최신의 significantly 상당히 task 업무 reduction 감소

107

Applicants for the position of production manager must hand in a letter of ------- from previous supervisors.
(A) recommend
(B) recommending
(C) recommended
(D) recommendation

생산매니저 직책을 위한 지원자는 반드시 이전 상관에게 받은 추천서 한 부를 제출해야 합니다.

해설 전치사(of) 뒤는 명사자리이므로 정답은 (D) recommendation(추천)이다.

어휘 hand in ~을 제출하다 a letter of recommendation 추천서 previous 이전의

108

While the road is under construction, commuters are advised to use ------- when driving at night.
(A) cautions
(B) caution
(C) cautious
(D) cautiously

도로를 건설하는 동안 통근자들은 저녁에 운전할 때 조심하도록 권고됩니다.

해설 빈칸은 동사 use의 목적어자리이다. 선택지 중 목적어가 될 수 있는 단어는 명사인 (B) caution이다. use caution(주의를 기울이다)을 알고 있다면 쉽게 풀 수 있는 문제이다.

어휘 under construction 공사 중 commuter 통근자 be advised to 권고되다 use caution 주의를 기울이다 cautiously 조심스럽게

109

Errors found early in the development process can be fixed ------- easily than those identified toward the end.
(A) most
(B) more
(C) right
(D) very

개발과정에서 조기에 발견된 실수는 끝날 무렵에 발견된 실수보다 더 쉽게 수정될 수 있다.

해설 빈칸은 tha과 어울리는 비교급이 들어가야 한다. 선택지 중 비교를 나타내는 단어는 (B) more이다.

어휘 error 실수 early 조기에 process 과정 fix 고치다

110

Lampeter Inc. has ------- that applicants who have minimum 5 years of experience and knowledge of statistics will be considered for the managerial position.
(A) distinguished
(B) specified
(C) connected
(D) hired

Lampeter 사는 최소 5년의 경험이 있는 통계학 지식을 가진 지원자들이 관리 직책에 고려된다는 것을 명시했다.

해설 빈칸은 문장의 구조에 적절한 동사어휘가 들어갈 자리이다. 선택지 중에서 빈칸 바로 뒤의 that절을 받을 수 있는 동사는 specify (명시하다)이다.

어휘 statistic 통계학 consider 고려하다 distinguish 구별하다, 돋보이게 하다 specify 명시하다

111

The Tilamook Land Trust is dedicated to working ------- with landowners to conserve land for wildlife, scenic views, and local communities.
(A) cooperated
(B) cooperatively
(C) cooperate
(D) cooperative

Tilamook Land Trust는 야생, 전경, 지역 커뮤니티를 위한 토지를 보존하기 위하여 토지 소유주와 협조적으로 일하는 것에 전념한다.

해설 자동사(work)와 전치사(with) 사이의 빈칸은 부사자리이다.(cooperatively 협동적으로)

어휘 be dedicate to ~에 전념하다 conserve 보존하다 wildlife 야생 cooperatively 협동해서, 협조적으로

112

Semiconductors were America's third-leading manufactured export in 2019 ------- only airplanes and automobiles.
(A) among
(B) toward
(C) without
(D) behind

반도체는 단지 항공기와 자동차에 이어 2019년에 미국의 세 번째 선도적인 제조 수출품이었다.

해설 빈칸은 의미가 적절한 전치사가 들어갈 자리이다. 앞부분의 '반도체는 미국의 세 번째의 선도적인 제조 수출품'과 뒤부분의 '단지 항공기와 자동차'를 연결하면 '단지 항공기와 자동차 바로 뒤에 있는'이라는 문맥이므로 '~뒤'를 나타내는 (D) behind가 정답이다.

어휘 semiconductor 반도체 leading 선도하는 export 수출품 behind 뒤에 among ~ 사이에(셋 이상)

113

Telecom network operators are expected ------- more than $ 50 billion from LTE 4G services in 2019, according to recent telecom market research.
(A) generating
(B) will generate
(C) generated
(D) to generate

최근 텔레콤 시장조사에 따르면, 통신망 운영사들은 2019년에 LTE 4G서비스로부터 대략 500억 달러를 창출할 것으로 예상된다.

해설 expect는 <expect + 목적어(to부정사)>의 구조를 취하며 수동태일 경우 be expected to(~할 것으로 예상되다)의 형태가 된다. 따라서 to부정사인 (D) to generate가 정답이다.

어휘 telecom network 통신망 operator 운영 회사 market research 시장 조사 generate 생기게 하다, 산출하다

114

Your reservation may be cancelled with a full refund, ------- notification of the cancellation is received in writing.
(A) provided that
(B) together with
(C) regardless of
(D) according to

취소 통지가 서면으로 받아지는 점을 고려한다면, 예약은 전액 환불로 취소될 수도 있다.

해설 빈칸은 뒤의 문장을 받을 접속사자리이다. 선택지 중 접속사는 provided that(~한다면)이고 나머지 선택지(전치사구)들은 뒤에 명사만 받을 수 있다.

어휘 full refund 전액 환불 notification 통지 in writing 서면으로 provided that ~라면 together with ~와 함께 regardless of ~에 관계없이

115

When you register, you will have the opportunity to enter your ------- flight details on the registration form.
(A) preferentially
(B) preferred
(C) prefer
(D) preference

등록을 할 때, 등록양식에 선호하는 비행편 세부사항을 입력할 기회가 있다.

해설 빈칸은 명사(flight details)와 어울리는 형용사가 와야 한다. 선택지 중 형용사는 (B) preferred(선호되는)이다.

어휘 register 등록하다 enter 입력하다 preferred 선호하는

116

Romanson has a ------- of expertise across a number of sectors and the board is delighted with his appointment as new Chief Executive Officer.
(A) height
(B) fame
(C) wealth
(D) field

Romanson 씨는 다방면에 걸쳐 풍부한 전문지식을 가지고 있으며 이사회는 새로운 CEO로서 그의 약속에 기뻐한다.

해설 빈칸은 뒤의 of expertise와 의미가 연결되는 단어가 들어갈 자리이다. a wealth of expertise는 '풍부한 전문 지식'이라는 의미로 문맥상 적절하다.

어휘 wealth 풍부함 expertise 전문지식 be delighted with ~을 기뻐하다 appointment 임명 height 높이 fame 명성 field 분야

117

Each luggage tag is made of durable plastic with a flexible strap that can be ------- attached to any bag.
(A) security
(B) securely
(C) securing
(D) secure

각각의 수하물 태그는 어떤 가방에도 안전하게 부착될 수 있는 유연한 끈이 달린 내구성이 강한 플라스틱으로 만들어졌다.

해설 be pp의 수동태 사이의 빈칸은 부사(securely 안전하게, 안정적으로)자리이다.

어휘 luggage 수화물 tag 표 be made of ~로 만들어지다 durable 내구성이 있는 flexible 유연한 strap 줄 attach 붙이다 securely 안전하게, 단단히

118

The applicant must provide academic transcripts, three letters of recommendation, and three writing samples ------- the completed application.
(A) along with
(B) moreover
(C) however
(D) in addition

지원자는 작성된 지원서와 함께 성적표, 추천서 3부와 작문 샘플을 제공해야 한다.

해설 빈칸은 뒤의 명사를 연결해 주는 전치사자리이다. (A) along with(~와 함께)가 명사를 받을 수 있다. in addition은 뒤에 명사를 받기 위해서는 to를 붙여 in addition to의 형태가 되어야 가능하다.

어휘 academic transcripts 성적표 along with ~와 함께 moreover 게다가 in addition 뿐만 아니라

119

Everyone involved was greatly ------- of the new equipment that was needed to help the new trees thrive.
(A) appreciated
(B) appreciation
(C) appreciate
(D) appreciative

관련된 모든 사람들은 새로운 나무들이 잘 자라는데 필요한 새로운 장비에 매우 감사해했다.

해설 빈칸은 be동사 was 뒤에 어울리는 형태의 단어가 들어갈 자리이다. be동사 뒤에는 수동형으로 pp형태나, 주격보어로 형용사가 올 수 있다. 선택지 중에서 appreciated와 appreciative가 정답 후보인데, 형용사 appreciative는 전치사 of와 어울려 be appreciative of로 쓰인다. 평소 be appreciative of(~을 감사히 여기다)를 알고 있다면 수동형과 혼동되지 않는다.

어휘 involved 관련된 greatly 매우 thrive 잘 자라다, 번창하다 appreciate 감사히 여기다

120

You can save ------- three percent on heating costs for every one degree you lower the thermostat.
(A) approximately
(B) consecutively
(C) substantially
(D) meticulously

온도조절장치를 1도씩 낮추면 난방요금을 대략 3퍼센트 정도 절약할 수 있다.

해설 빈칸은 뒤의 three percent와 의미연결이 적절한 부사자리이다. 숫자와 의미연결이 적절한 부사는 (A) approximately(대략)이다.

어휘 save 절약하다 heating cost 난방비 degree 도 lower 낮추다 thermostat 온도조절장치 approximately 대략 consecutively 연속해서, 뒤이어 substantially 상당히 meticulously 꼼꼼히, 세심히

121

All employees are responsible for a safe and efficient working environment with ------- on a cooperative attitude with fellow workers.
(A) emphasized
(B) emphasize
(C) emphasizes
(D) emphasis

모든 직원들은 동료 직원들과 협조적인 태도를 강조하는 안전하고 효과적인 근무환경을 만들 책임이 있다.

해설 전치사 뒤는 명사자리이다. with와 잘 연결되는 명사는 (D) emphasis(강조)이다.

어휘 be responsible for ~에 책임지다 efficient 효율적인 working environment 근무환경 attitude 태도 cooperative 협력하는 fellow worker 동료 직원 emphasis 강조

122

If your computer does not switch on, consult page 8 of the user's manual ------- calling a customer support center.
(A) along
(B) though
(C) during
(D) before

만약 컴퓨터가 켜지지 않는다면, AS센터에 전화하기 전에 사용자 설명서의 8페이지를 참조하세요.

해설 문맥상 '서비스센터에 전화 걸기 전에(before) 설명서의 8페이지를 참고하세요'가 자연스럽다.

어휘 consult 참조하다 user's manual 사용자 설명서 along ~을 따라서 though 비록 ~일지라도

123

Research shows that parents who are artists often encourage ------- children to play a musical instrument.
(A) themselves
(B) their own
(C) them
(D) theirs

연구는 예술가인 부모가 종종 자녀들이 악기를 연주하는 것을 장려한다는 것을 보여준다.

해설 명사 앞에 어울리는 대명사의 격은 소유격이므로 (B) their own이 정답이다. 중간에 own은 소유격을 강조하는 의미로 쓰인다.

어휘 encourage 격려하다, 장려하다 musical instrument 악기

124

Leonardo Cario was nominated as Outstanding Employee of the Year after his marketing strategy led to an ------- 35 percent increase in company revenue.
(A) extraneous
(B) unprecedented
(C) anxious
(D) imminent

Leonardo Cario 씨는 그의 마케팅 전략이 회사 수익에 유례없는 35%의 증가로 이어져서 올해의 뛰어난 직원으로 지명되었다.

해설 빈칸은 뒤의 명사 increase(증가)를 수식해주는 형용사자리이다. 문맥상 '유례없는 증가(unprecedented increase)'가 적절하다.

어휘 nominate 후보 지명하다 lead to ~로 이어지다 revenue 수익 extraneous 외부의 unprecedented 유례없는 anxious 걱정하는 imminent 절박한

125

Food products must be handled and cooked in a ------- that keeps them from getting contaminated or spoiled.
(A) manner
(B) performance
(C) type
(D) behavior

음식은 오염되거나 상하는 것을 막는 방법으로 취급되고 요리되어야 한다.

해설 빈칸은 that절의 수식을 받는 선행사자리이며 that절의 의미와 연결이 되어야 한다. '음식 제품들이 오염되거나 상해지는 것을 막는'으로 해석되므로 '방법'이라는 의미의 (A) manner가 정답이다.

어휘 handle 다루다, 처리하다 keep A from B A가 B하는 것을 막다 contaminate 오염시키다 spoil 상하다, 망치다 manner 방법 performance 수행, 성과 behavior 행동

126

Please e-mail your summary from this morning's board meeting to all managers ------- the end of the day.
(A) on
(B) of
(C) in
(D) at

오늘 아침 미팅에서 나온 요약본을 모든 매니저들에게 오늘까지 이메일로 전송해주십시오.

해설 빈칸은 the end of the day와 의미가 어울리는 단어가 들어갈 자리이다. 선택지 중 at이 들어가서 at the end of the day(오늘까지)의 의미로 적합하다.

어휘 board meeting 이사회 summary 요약, 개요

127

To assemble the purchased wooden desk, you must ------- the instructions in the enclosed manual.
(A) feature
(B) follow
(C) look
(D) direct

구매된 나무 책상을 조립하기 위하여, 당신은 동봉된 설명서 안의 지시사항을 따라야 합니다.

해설 빈칸은 the instructions(지시사항)을 목적어로 취하는 적합한 의미의 동사가 들어갈 자리이다. 선택지 중에서 (B) follow(~을 따르다)가 가장 적합하다. (A) feature ~을 특징으로 하다 (C) look ~을 보다 (D) direct ~을 지시하다

어휘 assemble 조립하다 purchased 구매된 enclosed 동봉된 instruction 설명, 지시사항 manual 설명서

128

If ------ enrolls in the management workshop, the session may be rescheduled.
(A) no one
(B) one another
(C) some
(D) few

만약 아무도 경영 워크숍에 등록하지 않는다면, 그 모임은 재조정될지도 모른다.

> **해설** 빈칸은 접속사 If 뒤에 어울리는 주어가 들어갈 자리이다. 대명사인 one another(서로서로)는 의미상 적절하지 않다. 뒤에 enroll이 3인칭 단수형태인 enrolls이므로 복수동사를 취하는 some과 few도 오답이다. 그래서 남은 선택지 (A) no one이 빈칸에 적절한 형태의 정답이다.

> **어휘** enroll in ~에 등록하다 one another 서로서로

129

Grocery stores in the area have started selling a wider variety of organic fruit and vegetables in ------ to customer demand.
(A) respond
(B) response
(C) responded
(D) responsive

이 지역의 식료품 가게는 고객 요구에 대응하여 매우 다양한 유기농 채소와 과일을 팔기 시작했다.

> **해설** 빈칸은 전치사 뒤에 적절한 형태의 단어가 들어갈 자리이다. 전치사 뒤의 빈칸은 명사자리이므로 정답은 (B) response(응답)이다.

> **어휘** grocery store 식료품 가게 a wider variety of 폭 넓게 다양한 ~ organic 유기농 in response to ~에 응답하여 demand 수요

130

Our call center is open 24 hours a day and our service crew can help you ------ you encounter car troubles.
(A) whomever
(B) whoever
(C) whatever
(D) whenever

콜센터는 하루 24시간 동안 이용 가능하고 서비스 직원은 자동차에 문제가 생길 때마다 당신을 도울 수 있다.

> **해설** 빈칸의 뒤의 문장 연결에 의미가 적합한 단어가 들어갈 자리이다. 문장 앞 부분은 '콜 센터는 연중 내내 문을 열고 당신을 도울 수 있다'이고 뒷부분은 '자동차에 문제가 생긴다'로 연결된다. 즉, '자동차에 문제가 생길 때는 언제든지(whenever) 당신을 도울 수 있다'는 의미가 적절하다.

> **어휘** encounter 직면하다 whoever 누구든지 whatever 무엇이든 whenever 언제든지

ACTUAL TEST 06 ACTUAL TEST 07 ACTUAL TEST 08 ACTUAL TEST 09 ACTUAL TEST 10

PART 6

Questions 131-134 refer to the following information.

Part 3, Section D: Handsfree calling	파트 3, 섹션 D: 핸즈프리 콜링
The Altman Tablet PC has the capacity to store ------- 64GB of information. **131.**	Altman 태블릿은 최대 64기가의 정보를 저장할 용량을 가진다.
You can use your voice to give commands to your tablet PC by pushing the button that looks like a microphone. Different voice commands will appear, like finding maps, searching the Internet, or sending e-mail. -------. Commands must be given by one **132.** person because if there are several people recording, the tablet PC will not recognize ------- voice. **133.**	마이크처럼 보이는 버튼을 누름으로써 태블릿에 명령하기 위해 당신의 음성을 사용할 수 있다. 지도를 찾는 것, 인터넷을 검색하는 것 또는 이메일을 보내는 것과 같은 다양한 음성 명령이 들릴 것이다. 인터넷을 사용하기 위해서, 당신이 찾는 단어나 구를 말하고 나면 홈페이지가 열릴 것이다. 몇몇 사람이 녹음한다면, 태블릿은 한 사람 이상의 음성을 인식할 수 없기 때문에 명령은 한 사람이 해야 한다.
Speak slowly and clearly when giving commands because if the words are not -------, the tablet PC will not do as ordered. **134.**	명령을 할 때 천천히 그리고 명확히 말하라. 왜냐하면 단어들이 명확하지 않다면, 태블릿은 지시된 대로 작동하지 않을 수 있기 때문이다.

어휘 capacity 수용량 up to ~까지 command 명령 appear 나타나다 recognize 인정하다, 인지하다 more than ~ 이상의

131
(A) up to
(B) as to
(C) except
(D) without

해설 숫자 앞에서 최대(maximum)을 나타내는 표현은 (A) up to(~까지)이다. 본문에서는 태블릿이 최대 64기가까지의 용량을 저장할 수 있다는 내용이므로 정답은 (A)가 된다.

132

(A) To use the Internet, say the word or phrase that you are looking for and a web page will open.
(B) You need to be familiar with a new commander.
(C) What you have to do is just type the title of books you want to search for.
(D) However, the tablet PC doesn't have these features at all.

해설 전반적으로 태블릿 PC의 사용법을 설명하고 있다. 구체적으로는 음성을 통한 명령을 언급하고 있다.

(A) 인터넷을 사용하기 위해서, 당신이 찾는 단어나 구를 말하고 나면 홈페이지가 열릴 것이다.
(B) 당신은 새로운 지휘관에 익숙해질 필요가 있다.
(C) 당신이 해야 하는 것은 단지 검색을 원하는 책의 제품을 입력하는 것이다.
(D) 그러나 태블릿은 이런 기능들을 전혀 가지고 있지 않다.

133

(A) its
(B) your
(C) more than one
(D) apart

해설 빈칸 앞을 살펴보면 명령을 내리는 음성이 오직 한 명에 의해서만 녹음되어야 한다는 내용이 있다. 그 이유는 태블릿 PC가 한 명 이상의 목소리는 인식하지 못하기 때문이므로 정답은 (C) more than one(하나 이상의)이다.

134

(A) distinct
(B) technical
(C) identical
(D) prospective

해설 앞서 음성 명령을 내릴 때는 천천히, 명확하게 말해달라는 내용이 있었다. 이유는 단어가 '뚜렷하지' 않으면 명령을 내린 대로 작동하지 않을 것이기 때문이다.

Questions 135-138 refer to the following e-mail.

To: Rucino Publishing Employees
From: Abigail Greene
Subject: Annual Employment Survey Request
Date: August 13

We hope that all the expectations you have for every ------- of
135.
your employment at Rucino Publishing have been met, but we
also know that our company still has room for improvement.
In line with this, we request you submit your annual feedback
about our benefits, rules and regulations, management and
administrative systems, products, and marketing approaches.

The HR team requests that you complete the questionnaire
for ------- satisfaction ------- August 17. -------. To access the
136.   **137.**   **138.**
questionnaire provided by DDB Consulting on its web site, click
here. Please be reminded that, as always, all your responses
remain confidential, as the forms bear no identifying information
and are directly sent to third-party consultants. They will analyze
all the responses from the forms submitted and render their
suggestions to our HR department.

Abigail Greene
HR Team Manager

수신: Rucino Publishing 직원
발신: Abigail Greene
제목: 연례 고용 설문조사 요청
날짜: 8월 13일

Rucino Publishing 사는 각각의 고용측면
에서 모든 기대가 만족되기를 바라지만 회
사 또한 개선의 여지가 있다는 걸 알고 있
습니다. 이에 따라, 우리는 회사의 복지 혜
택, 규칙과 규정, 경영과 관리시스템, 제품,
그리고 마케팅 접근에 대한 연간 의견을 제
출하도록 요청합니다.

인사팀에서는 당신이 직업만족에 대한 설
문지를 8월 17일까지 작성하기를 요청합니
다. 이것은 Rucino Publishing 직원들의 경
험이 만족스럽다는 것을 보장하기 위한 것
입니다. DDB Consulting의 홈페이지에 제
공된 설문지에 접근하기 위해서, 여기를 클
릭하세요. 항상 그렇듯이, 양식서가 어떤 식
별 정보도 가지고 있지 않기 때문에 당신
의 모든 응답은 기밀 상태로 유지되고, 제3
의 상담가에게 직접 보내진다는 점을 유념
하시기 바랍니다. 그들이 제출된 양식서로
부터 모든 응답을 분석하고 인사과로 제안
을 할 것입니다.

Abigail Greene
인사팀 관리자

어휘 aspect 측면 improvement 개선 in line with ~와 일치하여 benefit 이익, 혜택 regulation 규정 management 관리 administrative 관리상의 marketing approach 시장접근법 request 요구하다 complete 작성하다 questionnaire 설문조사 job satisfaction 직업 만족도 access 접근하다 Please be reminded that ~라는 점을 유념하세요 confidential 기밀의 bear 지니다 identifying 신분을 식별하는 third-party 제3자 analyze 분석하다 render 만들다, 제공하다

135

(A) aspect
(B) phase
(C) pace
(D) team

해설 회사에서 고용의 모든 '측면'에 대한 기대가 충족되었길 바란다는 내용이므로 정답은 (A)가 적절하다.

136

(A) job
(B) customer
(C) application
(D) statistics

해설 빈칸 뒤의 satisfaction과 복합명사를 만드는 명사를 찾는다. 일단 (A)가 들어가면 '직무 만족도'가 되고, (B)가 들어가면 '고객 만족도'가 된다. 내용상 직원이 회사에 대한 만족도가 어느 정도인지를 알아보기 위해 설문조사를 시행하는 상황이므로 정답은 (A)이다.

137

(A) to
(B) until
(C) within
(D) by

해설 설문지를 작성할 마감기한을 나타내는 전치사 by가 정답이다. 흔히 학생들이 (B) until(~까지)와 (D) by(~까지)를 헷갈려 하는데 '~까지 동작을 지속(계속)하다'는 until을 사용하고, '~까지 동작을 완료하다'는 전치사 by를 사용한다.

138

(A) This is to ensure the experience of employees at Rucino Publishing is a satisfying one.
(B) The results from the survey will be utilized for improving our customer service.
(C) Moreover, it is mandatory for you to attend the safety course provided by DDB consulting.
(D) Along with it, at least two references from your previous supervisor are required for the application.

해설 앞서 직원들의 업무 만족도에 관한 설문조사를 시행한다고 언급했으므로 설문조사의 목적을 설명하는 (A)가 가장 적합하다. 직원들을 대상으로 직원을 위한 설문조사이기 때문에 고객에게 이득이 된다는 내용은 어울리지 않는다.

(A) 이것은 Rucino Publishing 직원들의 경험이 만족스럽다는 것을 보장하기 위한 것입니다.
(B) 설문결과는 우리의 고객서비스를 개선하는 데 이용될 것입니다.
(C) 게다가, 당신이 DDB consulting이 제공하는 안전과정에 참석하는 것은 의무적입니다.
(D) 그것과 함께, 이전 상사로부터 적어도 두 장의 추천서가 지원하기 위해 요구됩니다.

Questions 139-142 refer to the following article.

Toronto (September 4) - The City Parking Authority ------- new
139.
powers by the City Council to tow away any cars they deem to
be impeding the flow of traffic.

Traffic has recently become so bad in the city core that for
about 6 hours a day between Monday and Friday cars come to
a complete standstill. As Mayor Trumbee put it, "With no room
for traffic, we are going to aggressively ------- the parking laws
140.
already on the books." -------.
141.

It is hoped that the new subway line set to open next year will
make the city ------- more commuter-friendly as well.
142.

토론토 (9월 4일) – 도시 주차당국은 교통 흐름을 방해한다고 여겨지는 어떠한 차량이든지 견인할 수 있는 새로운 권한이 시의회에 의해 부여되었다.

시내 중심가에 교통이 너무 악화되어, 월요일부터 금요일 하루에 6시간 정도, 차들은 완전히 멈춰 서 있다. 시장 Trumbee가 말한 것처럼 "교통량에 대한 여유가 없어, 우리는 이미 책자에 있는 주차법규를 적극적으로 시행할 것이다." 그것은 당신이 150달러의 벌금과 견인의 위험을 무릅쓰지 않고는 주차를 할 수 없을 것이라는 것을 의미한다.

내년에 운행할 예정인 새로운 지하철 노선이 또한 도시를 더욱 통근자 친화적으로 만들어 주기를 바란다.

어휘 deem (~로) 여기다 tow 견인하다 impending 임박한 core 중심 standstill 정지, 멈춤 aggressively 공격적으로 commuter-friendly 통근자 친화적인

139
(A) have given
(B) has been given
(C) will give
(D) giving

해설 빈칸은 동사자리이므로 동사가 아닌 (D)는 맨 먼저 탈락된다. 주어(The City Parking Authority)가 단수이기 때문에 복수동사인 (A)도 정답에서 제외된다. 동사 give는 수여동사이므로 목적어의 유무를 통해 동사의 태를 판단하기보다는 해석을 통해 문제를 풀도록 하자. 시 주차 당국은 권한을 새로이 부여'받은 것'이고 게다가 빈칸 뒤로 by the City Council이라는 수동태의 행위자 표현도 따라 나오고 있으므로 정답은 (B)가 된다.

140
(A) retain
(B) perform
(C) comply
(D) enforce

해설 동사 enforce는 법률이나 규정 따위를 '시행하다'라는 뜻이 있으므로 정답이 될 수 있다. 오답인 (B)와 비슷해 보이지만 (B) perform은 일이나 과제 업무 등을 '수행하다'는 의미이므로 정답이 될 수 없다.

141

(A) Therefore, we are soliciting any proposals to reduce commuting hours.
(B) That means that you won't be able to park your car without risking a 150 dollar ticket and a tow.
(C) However, you can be exempt from fines.
(D) You need to arrange alternative routes.

해설 앞서 심각한 교통난 때문에 적극적으로 주차 규제를 시행할 것이라 했으므로 정답은 불법 주차를 했을 때 겪을 수 있는 벌금과 견인에 관해 설명하는 (B)가 된다.

(A) 따라서, 우리는 통근 시간을 줄일 제안서를 요청하고 있다.
(B) 그것은 당신이 150달러의 벌금과 견인의 위험을 무릅쓰지 않고는 주차를 할 수 없을 것이라는 것을 의미한다.
(C) 그러나, 당신은 벌금이 면제될 수 있을 것이다.
(D) 당신은 우회 도로를 준비할 필요가 있다.

142

(A) so
(B) such
(C) few
(D) much

해설 빈칸 뒤의 비교급인 more을 강조하는 부사를 묻는 문제이다. 선택지 중 비교급 강조부사는 (D) much밖에 없다. 그밖에 다른 비교급 강조부사로는 even, still, far, a lot(훨씬)이 있으며 markedly(눈에 띄게), significantly(상당히) 등도 비교급 강조부사이다.

Questions 143-146 refer to the following e-mail.

FROM: Information Center <info@bestinvestcorp.com>

TO: employees@bestinvestcorp.com

SUBJECT: Corporate Upkeep

Access to e-mails and electronic calendars of the company will be ------- between 5:00 P.M. and 7:00 P.M this Thursday.
143.
The Information Technology Department will be conducting their scheduled system maintenance on all related electronic applications.

In the coming week, the client management databank -------
144.
as well. Upon using your computer, you will be prompted to download the updated version of the software. -------.
145.

If you have problems with upgrading or are not able to -------
146.
the update, you can call the Information Center for help.

발신: 인포메이션 센터 〈info@bestinvest-corp.com〉
수신: employees@bestinvestcorp.com
제목: 회사 유지

회사의 이메일과 전자달력에 대한 접근은 이번 목요일 오후 5시부터 7시 사이에 불가능합니다. IT부서가 모든 관련 전자프로그램에 대한 예정된 시스템 유지보수 작업을 할 것입니다.

다가오는 주에, 고객관리데이터 또한 재정리될 것입니다. 컴퓨터를 사용할 때 소프트웨어의 업데이트된 버전을 다운로드하도록 권유될 것이다. 새로운 소프트웨어와 관련된 모든 설명은 이 이메일에 첨부되었습니다.

만일 업그레이드에 문제가 있거나 업데이트를 할 수 없다면, 도움을 받기 위해 정보센터에 연락할 수 있습니다.

어휘 access 접근(성) electronic 전자의 maintenance 유지보수 inquiry 문의, 질문 reorganize 재편성하다 prompt 촉발하다, 유발하다 upon -ing ~하자마자

143
(A) convenient
(B) unavailable
(C) deserving
(D) allowable

해설 시스템 유지보수 작업을 시행하게 되면 그 시간 동안 회사의 해당 서비스는 '이용 불가능한' 상태가 될 것이다.

144
(A) to be reorganized
(B) will be reorganized
(C) reorganized
(D) was to reorganize

해설 빈칸은 동사자리이고 시제표현인 in the coming week(다음 주에)에서 단서를 얻을 수 있다. 앞으로 일어날 유지보수 작업이 어떤 일을 포함할 것인지를 설명하고 있으므로 미래시제로 표현한 (B)가 정답이다.

145
(A) Whether to upgrade or not has yet to be decided.
(B) It should be renewed annually to extend your subscription to our anti-virus services.
(C) There will be restructuring after the acquisition.
(D) All instructions associated with the new software are attached in this e-mail.

해설 빈칸 앞으로 업데이트된 시스템을 다운받아 직접 업데이트를 실행하라는 내용이 있었다. 그러므로 자세한 방법의 설명서가 첨부되어 있음을 알리는 (D)가 정답이다.

(A) 업그레이드할지 말지는 아직 결정되지 않았습니다.
(B) 우리의 바이러스 방지서비스에 구독 연장은 매년 갱신되어야 합니다.
(C) 인수 합병 뒤에 구조조정이 있을 것입니다.
(D) 새로운 소프트웨어와 관련된 모든 설명은 이 이메일에 첨부되었습니다.

146
(A) perform
(B) assume
(C) cover
(D) turn out

해설 목적어로 update를 취하는 동사어휘를 찾는다. 만약 업데이트를 '수행할 수' 없거나 문제가 있다면 연락하라는 내용이므로 정답은 (A)가 된다.

101

If Jeannette Glover from Torret Corporation arrives at the airport, please inform ------- immediately.
(A) my
(B) mine
(C) me
(D) I

만약 Torret Corporation에서 근무하는 Jeannette Glover 씨가 공항에 도착하면 나에게 즉시 알려주십시오.

해설 빈칸은 동사 inform의 목적어자리이므로 목적격인 (C) me가 정답이다.
어휘 arrive 도착하다 inform 알리다 immediately 즉시

102

Please contact Mr. Scott if you need ------- with your enrollment.
(A) assisted
(B) assist
(C) assistance
(D) assistant

만약 등록하는 데 도움이 필요하다면, Scott 씨에게 연락해주세요.

해설 빈칸은 동사 need의 목적어자리이다. 목적어로 명사가 와야 하므로 assistance(도움)와 assistant(보조자)가 가능하다. 단, 사람을 나타내는 경우 관사가 붙거나, 복수형태가 되어야 하므로 (C) assistance(도움)가 정답이다.
어휘 enrolment 등록 assistance 도움 assistant 보조자

103

Recent advances in telecommunications have made it convenient for cell phone users to send clear images to other users -------.
(A) easy
(B) easier
(C) ease
(D) easily

전기통신에서의 최근의 진보는 휴대폰 사용자들이 선명한 이미지를 다른 사용자들에게 쉽게 전송하는 것을 편리하게 했다.

해설 빈칸은 문장의 끝에 어울리는 품사가 들어갈 자리이다. 완전한 문장에 추가적으로 올 수 있는 품사는 부사(easily 쉽게)이다.
어휘 recent advances in ~에서의 최근의 발전 telecommunication 통신 easily 쉽게

104

Fire Chief Jason Nick will retire on September 28, and Ted Miller will serve as interim chief ------- a replacement is named.
(A) outside
(B) within
(C) until
(D) from

소방서장인 Jason Nick 씨는 9월 28일에 은퇴할 것이고, Ted Miller 씨가 후임자가 지명될 때까지 임시 소방서장으로서 역할을 할 것입니다.

해설 빈칸은 두 문장을 적절하게 연결시켜주는 접속사자리이다. 선택지 중 접속사는 (C) until뿐이고 나머지는 전치사들이다.

어휘 retire 은퇴하다 serve as ~로서 역할을 하다 interim 임시의 replacement 후임자 name 지명하다

105

Confusion remains over whether the tour group had ------- to be in the area of the Sahara Desert.
(A) request
(B) permission
(C) decision
(D) cost

투어그룹이 사하라 사막 지역에 들어갈 허가를 받았는지 아닌지에 대한 혼동이 있다.

해설 빈칸은 의미가 적절한 명사가 들어갈 자리이다. whether 문장에서 주어인 tour group(단체 관광객)이 '사막지역에 들어가는 것'에 대한 내용이므로 '허가'를 의미하는 (B) permission이 정답이 된다. permission은 셀 수 없는 명사(불가산명사)로 관사 없이 사용 가능하다. 반면 request, decision, cost는 보통 셀 수 있는 명사 취급을 한다.

어휘 confusion 혼란 remain 계속 ~이다 request 요청 permission 허락

106

Nomper Tech's main objectives are to increase its share of the market in computer sales, and to ------- its range of products.
(A) diversify
(B) diversely
(C) diverse
(D) diversity

Nomper Tech의 주요한 목적은 컴퓨터 판매에서 시장 점유율을 증가시키는 것이고 상품의 범위를 다양화하는 것이다.

해설 등위접속사 and 다음에 to -------가 있고 and 앞부분에 to increase가 등장하므로 빈칸은 to부정사자리라는 것을 알 수 있다. 정답은 동사원형인 diversify(다양화하다, 다각화하다)이다.

어휘 objective 목적 share 점유율 range 범위 diversify 다각화하다, 다양화하다

107

Because of a ------- conflict, the CEO of Yodobashi Steel Inc. regrettably declined the offer to speak at the local business conference.
(A) scheduled
(B) scheduler
(C) schedule
(D) schedules

일정 충돌 때문에, Yodobashi Steel의 최고경영자는 유감스럽게도 지역 경제회의에서의 연설 제안을 거절했다.

해설 빈칸 뒤의 conflict(충돌)와 의미가 어울리는 단어가 들어갈 자리이다. 일정이 겹치거나 꼬일 때 쓰는 표현은 schedule conflict(일정 충돌)이다.

어휘 schedule conflict 일정 충돌 regrettably 유감스럽게도 decline 거절하다

108

Later this month, the Olympic Committee is expected to narrow down the list of U.K. cities being ------- as an Olympic host.
(A) categorized
(B) known
(C) remained
(D) considered

이번 달 말에, 올림픽 위원회는 올림픽 개최지로 고려되고 있는 영국 도시들의 목록을 좁힐 것으로 예상됩니다.

해설 narrow down the list of U.K. cities(영국 도시들의 목록을 좁힌다)와 as an Olympic host(올림픽 주최지로서) 사이에 의미연결이 적절한 어휘는 consider(고려하다, 여기다)이다. known as는 '~로서 유명하다, 잘 알려져 있다'는 의미로 문맥상 어울리지 않는다.

어휘 categorize 분류하다 remain 상태를 유지하다 consider 여기다, 고려하다 narrow down (선택 가능한 수효를) 좁히다, 줄이다

109

Any big merchandise bought at Jamy Hardware requires ------- handling so as not to damage product components.
(A) careful
(B) grateful
(C) previous
(D) typical

Jamy Hardware에서 구매한 큰 상품은 부품에 손상을 입히지 않기 위해 취급 주의를 요합니다.

해설 명사 handling과 의미가 자연스럽게 연결되는 형용사어휘를 고르는 문제이다. 선택지 중 handling(처리)과 의미 연결이 매끄러운 단어는 careful(주의 깊은)이다.

어휘 merchandise 상품 handling 처리 so as not to ~하지 않기 위해서 damage 손상시키다 component 부품 careful 주의 깊은

110

Liverpool is one of the safest British cities to live in according to a report ------- in the April issue of BK's magazine.
(A) publish
(B) to publish
(C) publishing
(D) published

BK 잡지의 4월호에 실린 기사에 따르면, Liverpool은 살기에 가장 안전한 영국 도시 중 한 곳입니다.

해설 명사 a report(기사, 보고서)를 수식해주는 형용사를 고르는 문제이다. 기사는 실리는 것이므로 과거분사 형태인 (D) published가 적절하다.

어휘 according to ~에 따르면 publish 발행하다

111

We use production machines imported ------- France and automated quality control systems to ensure all our products are of high quality.
(A) from
(B) about
(C) abroad
(D) against

우리는 모든 상품이 고급 품질임을 보장하기 위하여 프랑스로부터 수입된 생산기계와 자동화된 품질 제어시스템을 사용합니다.

해설 빈칸은 imported(수입된)와 의미연결이 적절한 전치사자리이다. 수입은 '~로부터 되는 것'이므로 전치사 (A) from이 가장 적합하다.

어휘 import 수입하다 automated 자동화된 of high quality 질 좋은

112

Efforts to ------- work procedures at our Paris plant may lead to lowering production costs.
(A) simplify
(B) contact
(C) proceed
(D) overweigh

파리 공장에서 근무절차를 간소화하려는 노력은 생산비를 낮출지도 모른다.

해설 빈칸은 work procedures(업무절차)를 목적어로 취하는 동사자리이다. 절차를 '간소화하다'라는 의미의 (A) simplify가 정답이다.

어휘 effort 노력 procedure 절차 lead to ~로 이어지다, 초래하다 lower 낮추다 simplify 간소화 하다 overweigh ~보다 무겁다

113

Raw material prices rose ------- again last month, but most economists expect a sharp decrease in the coming months.
(A) seldom
(B) previously
(C) slightly
(D) highly

원재료 가격은 작년에 다시 약간 올랐지만 대부분의 경제학자들은 앞으로 급격한 감소를 예상한다.

해설 빈칸은 앞의 동사 rose(rise의 과거형, 오르다)와 의미 연결이 적절한 부사자리이다. 선택지 중에서 오르고 내림의 정도를 나타내는 단어는 (C) slightly(약간)이다. highly(크게, 대단히)는 강조의 의미로 쓰인다.

어휘 raw material 원자재 rise 오르다 coming 다가오는 slightly 약간 highly 매우

114

------- the firm's official Code of Conduct, employees must obtain their supervisor's permission in advance when taking a day off work.
(A) In accordance with
(B) As well as
(C) Agreeing
(D) On behalf of

회사의 공식적인 행동수칙에 따르면, 직원들은 하루 휴가를 내기 전에 상사의 허가를 미리 얻어야 합니다.

해설 빈칸은 Code of Conduct(행동 수칙)과 의미가 잘 연결되는 전치사자리이다. 선택지 중에서 규칙이나 규정과 연결이 매끄러운 표현은 (A) In accordance with(~을 따라서, ~을 준수하여)이다. (C)의 경우 agree(동의하다)가 자동사이므로 agreeing(분사구문) 뒤에 on 등의 전치사가 필요하다.

어휘 in advance 미리 obtain 얻다 take a day off wok 하루 쉬다 in accordance with ~에 따라 as well as ~뿐만 아니라 on behalf of ~을 대신하여

115

Harro Ranter has successfully completed the educational program and is now ------- for a promotion to general director.
(A) possible
(B) considerable
(C) decisive
(D) eligible

Harro Ranter는 성공적으로 교육 프로그램을 끝냈고 현재는 총괄이사로 승진할 자격이 있다.

해설 be동사 is와 전치사 for 사이는 형용사자리이다. 선택지 중 eligible이 가장 적절하다. eligible은 be eligible for(~에 자격이 있다)로 자주 출제된다.

어휘 successfully 성공적으로 promotion 승진 considerable 상당한 decisive 결정적인, 단호한 eligible 자격 있는

116

After starting work at Eastern Express Railway, Michale Richards ------- to serve as its vice-president for twelve years.
(A) met with
(B) pick up
(C) arrived at
(D) went on

Eastern Express Railway에서 근무를 시작한 후에, Michale Richards는 12년 동안 부사장으로서 역할을 계속했다.

해설 빈칸은 문장의 의미에 적절한 동사가 들어갈 자리이다. meet with는 '만나다' pick up은 '수거하다, 사다, 태우다' arrive at은 '도착하다' go on은 '계속하다'의 의미로 쓰인다. 문맥상 go on의 과거형태인 (D) went on이 정답이다.

어휘 serve as ~의 역할을 하다 pick up 수거하다, 마중가다 go on 계속하다

117

The Mathematics Dialogue promotes mathematical research in Germany and acts as a ------- for discussing issues related to mathematical education.
(A) forum
(B) vision
(C) round
(D) variety

Mathematics Dialogue는 독일에서 수학적 연구를 장려했고 수학교육과 관련된 문제를 논의하는 토론회의 역할을 합니다.

해설 for discussing issues(문제들을 토론하는 것에 대한)와 의미 연결이 자연스러운 명사가 들어갈 자리이이다. 문제를 토론하는 것과 어울리는 표현은 (A) forum(포럼, 공개 토론, 회의)이다.

어휘 promote 장려하다 mathematical 수학적 act as ~로서 역할을 하다 related to ~와 관련하여 forum 포럼, 토론회 vision 시력, 전망, 통찰 round 회, 정해진 일상

118

Mr. Watson Smith, the Managing Director gave a welcome speech, and took the opportunity to introduce the newly ------- Marketing Manager, Ms. Showna Lim,
(A) appoints
(B) appointing
(C) appoint
(D) appointed

경영이사인 Watson Smith 씨는 환영 연설을 했고, 새롭게 임명된 마케팅 매니저인 Showna Lim 씨를 소개할 기회를 가졌다.

해설 빈칸은 명사 앞에 어울리는 품사가 올 자리이다. 명사 앞의 빈칸은 형용사자리이므로 선택지 중에서 '임명된'의 의미인 (D) appointed가 정답이다.

어휘 welcome speech 환영 연설 appoint 임명하다 take the opportunity to ~할 기회를 가지다

ACTUAL TEST 06   ACTUAL TEST 07   ACTUAL TEST 08   ACTUAL TEST 09   ACTUAL TEST 10

119

The Metro Pole center has more than 150 volunteers, ------- are students participating in various activities to improve awareness of environment.
(A) the reason
(B) following as
(C) most of whom
(D) because of them

Metro Pole 센터는 150명 이상의 자원봉사자가 있고, 그들 중 대부분은 환경의 인식을 증진시키기 위하여 다양한 활동에 참석하는 학생들입니다.

해설 빈칸은 앞뒤 문장을 연결해주는 단어가 들어갈 자리이다. 선택지 중 두 문장을 이어주는 역할을 하는 형태는 관계대명사가 들어간 (C) most of whom이다.

어휘 various 다양한 activity 활동 awareness 인식 participate in ~에 참가하다

120

In order to receive the appropriate visa, all ------- documents and forms must be forwarded to the embassy two weeks prior to the intended departure date.
(A) skilled
(B) compared
(C) required
(D) interested

적절한 비자를 받기 위하여, 모든 요구된 문서와 양식은 예정된 출발일 2주 전에 대사관으로 보내져야 합니다.

해설 빈칸은 뒤의 명사 documents와 의미가 적절한 형용사가 들어갈 자리이다. skilled(숙련된)와 interested(관심 있는)는 사람이 어떠한 상태를 보일 때 쓰는 표현이다. 나머지 선택지 중 documents(문서)와 의미 연결이 적절한 단어는 (C) required(요구된)이다. required documents 요구된 문서

어휘 in order to ~하기 위해서 appropriate 적절한 forward 보내다 embassy 대사관 prior to 앞서 intended 예정된, 의도된 skilled 숙련된 compared 비교된 required 요구되는 interested 관심 있는

121

If Nokio continues its steady decline in sales, it will ------- be the leading electronics provider in the market.
(A) anymore
(B) not enough
(C) other
(D) no longer

만약 Nokio 판매가 꾸준히 감소한다면, 더 이상 이 시장에서 선도하는 전자제조업체가 아닐 것입니다.

해설 빈칸은 문장 전체의 의미와 어울리는 부사자리이다. 앞 문장은 '꾸준히 판매가 감소한다'이고 뒤 문장은 '선두적인 전자제품 공급회사'라고 말하고 있다. 문맥상 '더 이상 선도하는 전자업체가 아니다'는 의미가 적절하므로 no longer(더 이상 ~않다)가 자연스럽다.

어휘 steady 꾸준한 decline 감소 leading 선도하는

122

Make sure to fill out the application form completely before ------- it to our office.
(A) to submit
(B) submitted
(C) submitting
(D) submission

우리 사무실로 지원서를 제출하기 전에, 지원서가 완벽하게 작성되었다는 것을 확실히 해주십시오.

해설 전치사 before 뒤에 어울리는 품사를 고르는 문제이다. 빈칸 뒤에 it이라는 목적어가 등장하기 때문에 빈칸은 뒤에 목적어를 취하는 동명사 형태인 (C) submitting이 정답이 된다. 또한, 다른 관점에서 before를 접속사로 보고 빈칸 바로 뒤에 주어와 be동사가 빠진 분사구문으로 파악해도 뒤에 it이라는 목적어가 있기 때문에 빈칸은 submitting이 들어갈 수 있다. 즉, before를 전치사로 보든, 접속사로 보든 정답은 (C) submitting이 되는 것이다.

어휘 make sure ~을 확실히 하다 fill out ~을 작성하다 completely 완전히

123

Beverages can be obtained from vending machines located ------- the office building.
(A) without
(B) throughout
(C) with
(D) into

음료는 사무실 빌딩 곳곳에 위치된 자판기로부터 얻을 수 있다.

해설 빈칸은 located와 the office building 사이를 적절하게 연결해주는 전치사자리이다. 선택지 중 '곳곳에, 전역에'라는 의미의 throughout이 적절하다. located throughout the office building 사무실 건물 전역에 위치된

어휘 beverage 음료 obtain 얻다, 획득하다 vending machine 자판기 locate 위치하다

124

Jeremy Hicks and other top executives will meet on Saturday to discuss new business plans and marketing -------.
(A) initiatives
(B) deadlines
(C) explanations
(D) conversations

Jeremy Hicks 씨와 다른 최고경영자들은 새로운 사업 계획과 마케팅 계획을 논의하기 위하여 토요일에 만날 것이다.

해설 빈칸은 앞의 marketing과 의미가 어울리는 명사자리이다. marketing initiative 마케팅 계획

어휘 discuss 논의하다 business plan 사업 계획 initiative 계획 deadline 마감일 explanation 설명 conversation 대화

125

At the reception for new employees, the food will be served ------- the firm's president finishes his speech.
(A) most
(B) away
(C) almost
(D) once

신입직원을 위한 연회에서, 일단 회사 대표가 연설을 마치면 음식이 제공될 것입니다.

해설 빈칸은 뒤의 문장(주어+동사)을 연결하는 접속사자리이다. 선택지 중 접속사는 once(일단 ~하면)밖에 없다.

어휘 reception 연회 serve 제공하다

126

------ traffic problems are frequent on this road, the San Francisco Transportation Department has decided not to put in a traffic signal.
(A) Although
(B) So that
(C) Both
(D) In case

이 도로에서 교통문제가 빈번할지라도, San Francisco 교통부는 신호등을 설치하지 않기로 결정했다.

해설 빈칸은 두 문장을 이끄는 접속사가 들어갈 자리이다. 접속사인 although(비록 ~일지라도), so that(~하기 위해서), in case(~인 경우에 대비해서) 중에서 의미상 적절한 접속사는 (A) Although이다.

어휘 frequent 빈번한 traffic signal 신호등

127

Any application for a building ------- must be submitted to the Municipal Inspector in writing.
(A) to permit
(B) permits
(C) permit
(D) permitting

건축 허가증을 위한 어떠한 지원서라도 서면으로 지역 감독관에게 제출되어야 합니다.

해설 빈칸은 앞의 명사 building과 의미연결이 적절한 명사자리이다. 앞에 관사(a)가 있으므로 단수형태가 들어가야 한다. 이 둘을 충족시키는 선택지는 permit이다. permit은 동사, 명사 둘 다 될 수 있는 단어이다.

어휘 in writing 서면으로 permit 허가증

214

128

------- the tremendous success of Dr. Lowang's aesthetics clinic, she is planning to open another salon on the east side of town.
(A) Resulted
(B) As a result of
(C) Resulting
(D) To result

Dr. Lowang 미용클리닉의 엄청난 성공의 결과, 그녀는 시의 동쪽에 또 다른 살롱을 개장할 계획이다.

해설 빈칸은 뒤의 '엄청난 성공'과 어울리는 형태의 단어가 들어갈 자리이다. result와 관련된 다양한 형태의 선택지들이 있는데 result 는 자동사로 뒤에 전치사 in 또는 from과 어울린다. 따라서 resulted, resulting, to result는 모두 탈락이다. 남은 선택지 as a result of(~의 결과로서)가 정답이다.

어휘 tremendous 엄청난 success 성공 aesthetics clinic 피부 미용실 salon 미용실 as a result of ~의 결과로서

129

Many prominent professors accepted Ms. Leon's ------- for a report on effective educational methods.
(A) approval
(B) renewal
(C) contact
(D) proposal

많은 저명한 교수들은 효과적인 교육 방법에 대한 Leon 씨의 제안서를 받아들였다.

해설 빈칸은 동사 accept(수락하다, 받아들이다)에 대한 목적어로 어울리는 명사가 들어갈 자리이다. 선택지 중 (D) proposal(제안서)이 잘 어울린다.

어휘 prominent 유명한, 저명한 effective 효과적인 method 방법 approval 승인 renewal 갱신

130

------- wanting to enroll in the Nice EXPO have to confirm their arrangements with Ms. Eloise.
(A) This
(B) Them
(C) That
(D) Those

Nice EXPO에 등록하길 원하는 사람들은 Eloise 씨와 준비사항을 확인해야 합니다.

해설 빈칸은 뒤의 분사형태인 wanting과 연결이 가능한 단어가 들어갈 자리이다. 그리고 수식 부분인 wanting부터 EXPO를 제외하면 동사가 have이므로 복수형태의 단어가 빈칸에 와야 한다. 이 조건들을 충족시키는 선택지는 (D) Those이다. Those (who are wanting to enroll in the Nice EXPO) have to의 구조로 보면 이해가 쉬울 것이다.

어휘 enroll in 등록하다 confirm 확인하다 arrangement 준비

ACTUAL TEST 06 ACTUAL TEST 07 ACTUAL TEST 08 ACTUAL TEST 09 ACTUAL TEST 10

Questions 131-134 refer to the following letter.

Dear Mr. Nicole,

We received a letter from you on June 2 ------- an estimate
131.
of the costs involved in ------- the building at 3656 Covington
132.
Avenue into a residential condominium. -------. Enclosed is our
133.
calculation of the conversion cost. RENO Home Builders offers
competitive rates, which include labor and material costs. We
------- to give our clients complete satisfaction.
134.

The building conversion can begin as early as June 30. Before
starting the project, we require a 20% deposit and a signed
contract.

Thank you for choosing RENO Home Builders. We look forward
to hearing from you soon.

Sincerely,

Simon Luke

Nicole 씨께,

우리는 3656 Covington Avenue에 있는 건물을 주거용 아파트로 개조하는 것과 관련한 비용 견적을 요청하는 편지를 6월 2일에 받았습니다. 우리는 6월 8일에 현장 평가를 했습니다. 개조 비용의 계산이 동봉되었습니다. RENO Home Builders는 인건비와 재료비를 포함한 경쟁력 있는 가격을 제공합니다. 우리는 고객들에게 완전한 만족을 주도록 노력합니다.

건물 개조 작업은 빨라야 6월 30일에 시작 가능합니다. 프로젝트를 시작하기 전에, 우리는 20%의 보증금과 서명된 계약서를 요구합니다.

RENO Home Builders를 선택해 주신 것에 감사드립니다. 우리는 곧 연락받기를 기대합니다.

진심을 담아

Simon Luke

어휘 estimate 추정(치), 견적 be involved in ~에 관련되다 conversion 개조, 전환 residential 거주의 condominium 콘도 calculation 계산 competitive 경쟁력 있는 labor 노동

131
(A) requests
(B) requested
(C) requisite
(D) requesting

해설 빈칸은 동사자리가 아니므로 동사인 (A)는 우선 제외한다. 구조상 a letter(편지)를 후치 수식하는 형용사자리이고 from you on June은 수식어구이다. 형용사의 역할을 하면서 목적어를 이끌 수 있는 현재분사인 (D)가 정답이다.

132
(A) relocating
(B) converting
(C) furnishing
(D) constructing

해설 목적어인 building을 이끌 수 있는 동사어휘를 고른다. 앞서 견적서를 언급했기 때문에 건물을 '개조하다'의 의미로 연결되어야 한다. 동사 convert는 convert A into B(A를 B로 개조하다)의 형태로 사용될 수 있다.

133
(A) Unfortunately, we consider it impossible to demolish the existing condominium.
(B) We conducted an onsite assessment on June 8.
(C) We have been in business for the last 30 years.
(D) You need to vacate the building before repair works begin.

해설 빈칸 앞으로 건물 개조를 위한 견적서를 요청했다는 내용이 나오고 뒤로는 해당 견적서를 첨부했다고 했으므로 빈칸에는 현장 조사를 끝냈다는 내용의 (B)가 정답이 된다.

(A) 안타깝게도, 우리는 기존 아파트를 철거하는 것이 불가능하다고 생각합니다.
(B) 우리는 6월 8일에 현장 평가를 했습니다.
(C) 우리는 지난 30년간 운영을 해 왔습니다.
(D) 당신은 수리작업을 시작하기 전에 건물을 비울 필요가 있습니다.

134
(A) charge
(B) respond
(C) agree
(D) strive

해설 빈칸은 to부정사를 목적어로 취하는 동사자리이다. 선택지 중 가능한 동사는 (C) agree, (D) strive가 있는데 문맥상 고객에게 만족을 주기 위해 '노력하다, 고군분투하다'가 어울리므로 정답은 (D)가 된다.

Questions 135-138 refer to the following notice.

Corporate Museum Cards

The city museum is extending admission privileges to the corporate community. Employees of any organization in our city are entitled to receive a corporate card. -------. Government **135.** employees and nonprofit organizations are exempt from these fees.

Corporate cards are intended for employees and up to 2 family members, who are ------- to free admission to the museum **136.** throughout the year.

------- a corporate card, simply visit the city museum. Applicants **137.** must show photo identification to confirm their ------- status. **138.** The annual fee for the corporate museum card must be paid at the time of application.

If you have any questions about the corporate card program, please contact us at corporatecards@citymuseum.com.

박물관 기업 카드

시립박물관은 기업 단체들에게 입장 혜택을 주고 있습니다. 도시 내의 단체 직원들은 기업 카드를 받을 자격이 있습니다. 단체의 직원에게 발급되는 각 카드에 대한 연회비는 10달러입니다. 공무원들과 비영리단체 직원들은 이 비용이 면제입니다.

기업 카드는 직원들과 가족 2명까지를 대상으로 하는데, 연중 내내 박물관 무료로 입장할 수 있는 자격이 주어집니다.

기업 카드를 받기 위해서, 박물관을 방문하면 됩니다. 지원자들은 그들의 고용 상태를 확인하기 위한 사진 신분증을 제시해야 합니다. 기업 카드에 대한 연회비는 지원 시에 지불되어야 합니다.

만일 당신이 기업 카드 프로그램에 질문이 있다면, 우리에게 corporatecards@citymuseum.com로 연락하기를 바랍니다.

어휘 extend 연장하다, 주다 privilege 특권 organization 조직, 단체 be entitled to do ~할 자격이 있다 nonprofit 비영리의 be exempt from ~로부터 면제되다 be intended for ~를 대상으로 하다 corporate 기업 applicant 지원자 identification 신분(증) at the time of ~의 때에

135
(A) This card must be presented at the gate.
(B) Card holders can use the fitness center at no cost.
(C) There is no entrance fee to the gallery in celebration of it 10th anniversary.
(D) The annual fee for each card issued to an employee of an organization is $10.00.

해설 빈칸 뒤의 these fee에 집중한다. 지시형용사 these를 사용했기 때문에 빈칸에는 fee와 관련된 내용이 있어야 하므로 연회비에 대해 언급하고 있는 (D)가 정답이다.

(A) 이 카드는 입구에서 제시되어야 합니다.
(B) 카드 소지자들은 무료로 체육관을 이용 가능합니다.
(C) 개관 10주년을 기념해서 미술관 입장료는 없습니다.
(D) 단체의 직원에게 발급되는 각 카드의 연회비는 10달러입니다.

136
(A) encouraged
(B) eligible
(C) allowed
(D) entitled

해설 be ~ to N과 어울리는 과거분사를 찾는다. 선택지 중에서 그러한 구조로 사용 가능한 것은 (D)이다. be entitled to N(~를 받을 자격이 있다) 또는 be entitled to do(~할 자격이 있다)의 형태로 사용한다.

137
(A) Receive
(B) Received
(C) To receive
(D) Receipt of

해설 빈칸 뒤의 a corporate card를 목적어로 취하며 부사구 역할을 할 수 있는 to부정사가 정답이다. to부정사의 부사적 용법은 '~ 하기 위해서'로 해석된다.

138
(A) employment
(B) residence
(C) investment
(D) reference

해설 빈칸 뒤의 status와 복합명사를 이루는 명사가 정답이다. 기업 카드를 발행하기 위해 요청할 만한 것으로는 '고용 상태(증명)'이다.

Questions 139-142 refer to the following e-mail.

To: Karina Bhat
From: Ken Suzuki
Subject: Job application
Date: March 19

Dear Mr. Bhat,

I saw Tracker's job posting in the Bratton Post. I am writing to apply for a suitable position at your new factory in Bratton. Please allow me to introduce myself and to present my -------.
139.

My experience and various skills would serve as an excellent contribution to your company's growth. I am fluent in the Indonesian language, which is my native language. I am also proficient in English, ------- university in Sydney, Australia.
140.
There, I studied and graduated with a degree in Accounting. Over the last three years, I ------- at several companies as an
141.
accountant. -------.
142.

Thank you for taking the time to read this letter. I hope to hear from you soon regarding my enclosed application.

Sincerely,

Ken Suzuki

수신: Karina Bhat
발신: Ken Suzuki
제목: 일자리 지원
날짜: 3월 19일

Bhat 씨께,

저는 Bratton Post에서 Tracker사의 구인 광고를 봤습니다. 새로운 Bratton 공장의 적절한 자리에 지원하기 위해 이 글을 쓰고 있습니다. 제 자신을 소개하고, 자격을 보여 주도록 해주셨으면 합니다.

제 경험과 다양한 기술들은 귀사의 성장에 뛰어난 기여를 할 것입니다. 저는 모국어인 인도네시아어에 능숙하고 또한 호주, 시드니에서 대학을 다녀서 영어에도 능통합니다. 거기서, 회계학을 전공하고 졸업을 했습니다. 지난 3년간, 회계사로서 몇몇 회사들에 고용되었습니다. 이력서에 적었다시피, 저는 Tracker에서 관리직으로 고려되길 원합니다.

이 편지를 시간 내어 읽어 주셔서 감사합니다. 저는 동봉된 지원서에 대해 곧 연락을 받기를 희망합니다.

진심을 담아

Ken Suzuki

어휘 apply for ~에 지원하다, 신청하다 suitable 적합한, 적절한 various 다양한 contribution 기여 be fluent in ~에 유창하다 be proficient in ~에 능숙하다 degree 학위 accountant 회계사

139
(A) demonstrations
(B) credentials
(C) positions
(D) samples

해설 이 글은 지원서이며 빈칸의 문장 내에 본인에 대한 소개를 하겠다 했으니 그와 함께 '자격'을 보여주겠다는 의미이다.

140
(A) attendant
(B) attended
(C) having attended
(D) attentive

해설 빈칸에는 완전한 문장을 후치 수식해줄 수 있는 부사구가 들어가야 한다. 목적어를 취하며 부사구의 역할을 하는 분사구문인 (C)가 정답이다. having p.p는 완료형 분사구문으로 주절의 동사시제보다 한 시점 전의 일을 나타낸다.

141
(A) am employed
(B) have employed
(C) have been employed
(D) employed

해설 같은 문장 속에 시제의 단서인 over the last three years(지난 3년 동안)가 존재한다. 그러므로 현재완료시제인 (C)가 정답이다. 참고로 be employeed at은 '~에 고용되다'보다는 '~에서 일하다'정도로 해석된다.

142
(A) As I noted in my résumé, I would like to be considered for a managerial position at Tracker.
(B) I'm so delighted to start my career with such a reputable company like yours.
(C) So I would like to keep working on that project.
(D) Jim Harrison, my direct supervisor, nominated me for this promotion.

해설 빈칸 앞으로 발신자의 여러 자격요건과 학력 등이 나열되고 있다. 그러므로 본인이 어느 직책을 원하는지를 알리는 내용인 (A)가 가장 적절하다. 지원만 했지 아직 고용된 것은 아니므로 고용 후에 일어날 수 있는 내용을 언급하는 나머지 선택지는 모두 정답이 될 수 없다.

(A) 이력서에 적었다시피, 저는 Tracker에서 관리직으로 고려되고 싶습니다.
(B) 저는 당신 회사와 같은 명성 있는 회사에서 일을 시작하게 되어 너무나 영광입니다.
(C) 그래서 저는 그 프로젝트에 대해 계속 작업을 하고 싶습니다.
(D) 직속상사 Jim Harrison은 저를 승진에 지명했습니다.

ACTUAL TEST 06 ACTUAL TEST 07 ACTUAL TEST 08 ACTUAL TEST 09 ACTUAL TEST 10

To: Matthew Moy

From: Williams Reed

Date: Friday, November 3

Subject: News

Dear Matthew,

Thank you very much for organizing my trip to Madrid last week. I had a wonderful time, and it was a pleasure to meet our new clients.

During my stay, you ------- interest in relocating to Berlin to
                         143.
be closer to your mother. -------. We are looking for sales
                          144.
associates who have at least five years' experience and an educational background similar to yours. The work itself is very similar to what you have been doing in Madrid.

The openings will be ------- posted at the end of next month. If
                     145.
you are interested in one of the positions, please let me know ------- I can tell Miranda Leary, who is in charge of recruitment,
146.
to schedule an interview with you.

Kind regards,

Williams Reed

수신: Matthew Moy

발신: Williams Reed

날짜: 11월 3일 금요일

제목: 뉴스

Matthew 씨께,

지난주 마드리드로의 여행을 준비해줘서 무척 감사합니다. 저는 멋진 시간을 보냈고, 새로운 고객을 만나서 만족스러웠습니다.

제가 머무는 동안, 당신은 모친과 가까이 있기 위해 베를린으로 옮기는 것에 관심을 표했다. 우리의 베를린 사무소는 총 4개의 공석이 있다고 알려드립니다. 우리는 적어도 5년의 경험과 당신과 비슷한 학력을 가진 판매담당자를 찾고 있습니다. 업무는 마드리드에서 해온 것과 아주 비슷합니다.

공석은 다음 달 말에 공개적으로 게시될 것입니다. 만일 당신이 그 자리에 관심이 있다면, 채용담당인 Miranda Leary 씨와 면접 일정을 잡을 수 있게 저에게 알려주세요.

마음을 담아

Williams Reed

어휘 organize 준비하다, 조직하다 pleasure 기쁨, 만족 relocate 이전하다 sales associate 판매 직원 educational background 학력 openings 공석, 빈자리 be in charge of ~를 담당하다

143
(A) focused
(B) appeared
(C) applied
(D) expressed

> 해설 목적어 interest(관심)와 어울리는 동사를 찾는다. 관심은 '표현하는' 것이 적절하므로 정답은 (D)이다. 참고로 나머지 선택지들은 모두 자동사이므로 목적어를 취할 수 없다.

144
(A) There are better jobs available in other companies in Berlin.
(B) In my childhood, my family also lived in Berlin.
(C) I am happy to inform you that our Berlin office has a total of four openings.
(D) To provide your background and qualifications, please submit resumes along with the job application form.

> 해설 앞서 수신자가 베를린 지역으로 이전하길 원한다는 내용이 나왔고 빈칸 뒤로 어떤 직원을 구하는지 상세한 설명이 뒤따르고 있으므로 정답은 공석이 있음을 알리는 내용인 (C)가 가장 적절하다.

(A) 베를린에 다른 회사들에 가능한 더 나은 일자리들이 있습니다.
(B) 어린 시절에, 제 가족들은 또한 베를린에 거주했습니다.
(C) 우리의 베를린 사무소에는 총 4개의 공석이 있다는 것을 알려드립니다.
(D) 당신의 경력과 자격을 제공하기 위해, 지원서와 함께 이력서를 제출하세요.

145
(A) public
(B) publicly
(C) publicize
(D) publicity

> 해설 빈칸은 be동사와 p.p 사이의 부사자리이다. 선택지 중 유일한 부사는 (B)이다.

146
(A) as soon as
(B) since
(C) now that
(D) so that

> 해설 선택지가 모두 접속사이므로 해석을 통해 정답을 골라보자. 문맥상 채용 담당자에게 말해주기 '위해서' 공석에 관심이 있으면 알려달라는 내용이 어울리므로 정답은 (D)가 된다. 참고로 so that 접속사는 문두에 사용하지 않으며 조동사 can(may, will)이 뒤따른다는 특징이 있다.

101

Mr. Gilitsh had to change his schedule for the business trip to Miami because he arrived ------- for his flight.
(A) lately
(B) later
(C) late
(D) latest

Gilitsh 씨는 비행기 때문에 늦게 도착했으므로 Miami의 출장 일정을 변경해야만 했다.

해설 빈칸은 자동사 arrive 뒤에 어울리는 부사자리이다. 문장에 비교급이나 최상급의 표현이 없으므로 later, latest는 우선 탈락이다. 나머지 선택지 중 부사인 lately는 '최근에, 얼마 전에', late는 형용사로 '늦은, 지각한', 부사로 '늦게'로 쓰이므로 정답은 (C) late(늦게)이다.

어휘 business trip 출장 lately 최근에 later 나중에

102

When ------- have finished encoding all the data, store the file in our shared drive.
(A) yours
(B) you
(C) your
(D) yourself

모든 데이터를 암호화하는 것을 끝냈을 때, 공유 드라이브에 파일을 저장하십시오.

해설 빈칸은 문장에서 주어가 들어갈 자리이다. 선택지 중 주어가 되는 주격 대명사인 (B) you가 정답이다.

어휘 encode 암호화하다 store 저장하다 shared drive 공유 드라이브

103

The paper shredder in the conference room on the third floor needs to be ------- because it runs too slowly.
(A) replacing
(B) replaced
(C) replace
(D) replaces

3층 회의실에 있는 파쇄기는 너무 느리게 작동하기 때문에 교체될 필요가 있습니다.

해설 빈칸은 앞의 be동사 뒤에 어울리는 형태의 단어가 들어갈 자리이다. be동사 뒤에 동사는 -ing나 -ed의 형태가 되어야 하는데, replace(교체하다)는 타동사이므로 뒤에 명사가 없는 경우는 수동태의 형태가 되어야 한다. 그래서 정답은 (B) replaced이다.

어휘 shredder 파쇄기 run 작동하다 slowly 느리게 replace 교체하다

104

------- of the employee benefits of the Holguin Publishing Company is a $ 150-gift card towards book purchases.
(A) One
(B) Every
(C) Some
(D) All

Holguin Publishing Company의 직원 복리후생 중 하나는 도서 구매에 따른 150달러의 기프트카드이다.

해설 우선 선택지 중 every는 of the를 받을 수 없다. one of the, some of the, all of the의 형태가 가능하다. 빈칸이 주어자리이고 동사가 is이므로 주어는 단수형태가 되어야 한다는 점을 고려하면 정답이 one이 됨을 알 수 있다.(one of the + 복수명사 + 단수동사)
어휘 employee benefits 직원 복지 혜택 gift card 상품권 카드

105

Vamos Corporation ------- staff members five additional days for vacation if they have worked for the company for more than eight years.
(A) grant
(B) granting
(C) grants
(D) are granted

Vamos Corporation은 만약 직원들이 회사에서 8년 이상 근무했다면, 그들에게 5일 휴가를 추가로 제공합니다.

해설 빈칸은 문장에서 동사가 들어갈 자리이다. 주어가 단수이므로 동사에 s를 붙인 grants가 정답이다.
어휘 additional 추가적인 more than ~이상 grant 주다, 수여하다

106

All scissors manufactured by Dixon, Inc. come apart ------- to allow sharpening and thorough cleaning.
(A) effortlessly
(B) attentively
(C) accurately
(D) exactly

Dixon 사에서 제조된 모든 가위들은 날갈이와 철저한 세척을 위하여 쉽게 분리됩니다.

해설 동사 come apart(분리하다)와 의미연결이 적절한 부사는 effortlessly(손쉽게, 어려움 없이)이다. come apart effortlessly 손쉽게 분리하다
어휘 scissor 가위 manufacture 제조하다 come apart ~을 분리하다 sharpening 연마, 날갈이 thorough 철저한 effortlessly 손쉽게 attentively 세심하게 accurately 정확하게

107

Before laying a carpet, employees of Bonheur Clothing accurately measure the exact ------- of the rooms.
(A) figures
(B) styles
(C) dimensions
(D) rates

카펫을 갈기 전에, Bonheur Clothing의 직원들은 방의 정확한 치수를 정밀하게 측정합니다.

해설 빈칸은 형용사 exact(정확한)와 뒤의 of the rooms(방들의) 사이에 의미가 적절한 명사가 들어갈 자리이다. 내용 연결이 가장 매끄러운 선택지는 dimensions(치수)이다. the exact dimensions of the rooms 방들의 정확한 치수

어휘 lay 놓다, 깔다 accurately 정확하게 measure 측정하다 figure 수치 dimension 치수 rate 속도, 비율, 요금

108

Mr. Jaime has asked that employees ------- the benefits and the risks seriously before investing in the start-up company.
(A) considers
(B) consider
(C) is considering
(D) considering

Jaime 씨는 직원들이 신생기업에 투자하기 전에 이익과 위험을 더 심각하게 고려해야 한다고 요청했다.

해설 빈칸은 적절한 형태의 동사가 들어갈 자리이다. that절 앞에 동사가 ask가 보인다. ask는 요구·주장·제안동사로서 that절을 받을 때 주어 뒤에 should를 생략한 동사원형을 쓴다. 즉, <ask that 주어 + (should) 동사원형>의 형태가 되어야 한다. 따라서 정답은 동사원형인 (B) consider이다.

어휘 seriously 진지하게, 심각하다 start-up 신생 기업

109

Customer service representatives of Maxo Cable Company should promptly ------- to all inquiries regarding the recently updated cable channels.
(A) respond
(B) conduct
(C) collect
(D) invite

Maxo Cable Company의 고객서비스 담당자는 최근에 업데이트된 케이블 채널에 관한 모든 질문에 즉각적으로 응답해야 합니다.

해설 빈칸은 문장에 적절한 동사가 들어갈 자리이다. 빈칸 뒤에 전치사 to가 보이므로 선택지 중 자동사인 (A) respond가 정답으로 적절하다. respond to ~에 응답하다

어휘 promptly 즉각적인, 지체 없이 inquiry 문의 사항 respond 응답하다 conduct 시행하다 collect 모으다 invite 권유하다

226

110

We offer a ------- range of career opportunities for highly motivated professionals dedicated to improving product quality and customer service.
(A) competitive
(B) diverse
(C) various
(D) several

우리는 상품 품질과 고객서비스를 개선시키는 데 전념하는, 매우 의욕적인 전문가들을 위한 다양한 고용 기회를 제공합니다.

해설 빈칸은 range라는 명사를 수식하는 적절한 의미의 형용사가 들어갈 자리이다. a range of와 어울리는 형용사는 (B) diverse이고 a diverse range of는 '아주 다양한 ~'라는 의미이다. various(다양한)와 several(몇몇의) 뒤에는 복수명사가 온다.

어휘 career opportunity 일자리 기회 highly motivated 매우 역동적인, 동기가 부여된 competitive 경쟁적인 diverse 다양한

111

------- leading medical organizations recommend breaking up sedentary time in the office, most workers still have no choice but to sit at their desks all day.
(A) Although
(B) Nevertheless
(C) But
(D) Only if

비록 선도하는 의학기관이 사무실에서 앉아서 일하는 시간을 줄이자고 권했지만 대부분의 직원들은 여전히 하루 종일 책상에 앉아 있을 수밖에 없다.

해설 빈칸은 의미가 적절한 접속사가 들어갈 자리이다. 우선 두 문장의 맨 앞에 쓸 수 없는 Nevertheless와 But은 탈락이다. 나머지 Although(비록 ~일지라도)와 Only if(단지 ~인 경우에만) 중에 문맥상 자연스러운 접속사는 (A) Although이다.

어휘 leading 선도하는 break up 나누다 sedentary 주로 앉아서 하는 have no choice but to ~할 수밖에 없다 all day 하루 종일

112

As construction work becomes more ------- on the use of complex equipment, the construction workers are expected to have enhanced competency in understanding technology.
(A) depends
(B) dependable
(C) dependent
(D) depend

공사작업이 복잡한 장비사용에 더 의존하기 때문에 공사 노동자들은 장비를 이해하는 데 향상된 능력을 갖출 것으로 기대됩니다.

해설 become은 형용사를 보어로 취하기 때문에 dependable(믿을 만한)과 dependent(의존하는)가 가능하다. 빈칸 뒤에 전치사 on이 보이므로, dependent on(~에 의존하는)의 형태가 적절하다.

어휘 complex 복잡한 enhanced 향상된 competency 능력 dependable 믿을 수 있는 dependent 의존하는

113

NAU airports have excellent facilities for keeping ------- goods within the optimum temperature range between four and five degrees Celsius.
(A) constructive
(B) confusing
(C) perishable
(D) plentiful

NAU 공항은 상하기 쉬운 물건을 최적 온도 범위 이내인 섭씨 4~5도 사이로 유지하기 위한 훌륭한 시설을 보유하고 있다.

해설 빈칸은 명사 goods와 의미연결이 적절한 형용사가 들어갈 자리이다. 빈칸에 perishable(상하기 쉬운)을 넣으면 excellent facilities for keeping perishable goods는 '상하기 쉬운 물건들을 보관하는 데 훌륭한 시설'이라는 의미가 된다.

어휘 keep 보관하다 goods 물건 optimum 최적의 celsius 섭씨 constructive 건설적인 confusing 혼란을 주는 perishable 상하기 쉬운 plentiful 풍부한

114

While many shoppers remain ------- cautious, gift spending is expected to rise 23 percent from last year.
(A) financed
(B) financing
(C) financial
(D) financially

많은 쇼핑객들이 금전적으로 신중하긴 하지만 선물 소비는 작년부터 23% 오를 것으로 예상됩니다.

해설 형용사(cautious) 앞 빈칸은 부사(financially)자리이다.

어휘 cautious 신중한, 조심스러운 financially 재정적으로

115

For users of previous versions, a discounted upgrade offer is ------- until the end of the year.
(A) beneficial
(B) complicated
(C) frequent
(D) available

이전 버전의 사용자들을 위해 할인된 업그레이드의 제공은 올해 말까지 이용 가능합니다.

해설 빈칸은 문장에서 의미가 어울리는 형용사가 들어갈 자리이다. 주어인 '할인된 업그레이드의 제안'과 뒤의 '연말까지' 사이에서 의미연결이 매끄러운 표현은 (D) available(가능한)이다.

어휘 previous 이전의 discounted 할인된 beneficial 유익한 complicated 복잡한 frequent 빈번한

116

The restaurant Fresh Food is very popular for a variety of delicious ------- inexpensive food.

(A) yet
(B) once
(C) despite
(D) because

Fresh Food 식당은 맛있지만 비싸지 않은 다양한 종류의 음식으로 아주 유명합니다.

해설 빈칸은 앞의 형용사 delicious와 뒤의 inexpensive 사이에 어울리는 등위접속사가 들어갈 자리이다. 그래서 선택지 중 접속사인 yet(하지만)이 적절하다. yet은 부사로 '아직'이란 의미이고, 접속사로는 '하지만'이라는 의미이다.

어휘 popular 인기 있는 a variety of 다양한 ~ delicious 맛있는 inexpensive 저렴한

117

Please ------- reference books to the second floor so they will be available for the next user.

(A) return
(B) renew
(C) research
(D) replace

참고 도서를 2층으로 반납하시면 다음 사용자들이 이용 가능할 것입니다.

해설 빈칸은 명령문에 어울리는 의미의 동사가 들어갈 자리이다. 빈칸 뒤에 목적어 reference books(참조 도서)가 있고 뒤에 전치사 to가 나오므로, 이런 형태를 가질 수 있는 단어는 return A to B의 구조가 되는 (A) return밖에 없다.

어휘 reference book 참조 도서 renew 갱신하다 replace 교체하다

118

Upon receiving your shipment, inspect the content to determine if it may ------- have been damaged while in transit.

(A) possibilities
(B) possibility
(C) possible
(D) possibly

선적물을 받자마자, 그것이 수송 중에 파손되었는지 아닌지를 결정하기 위하여 내용물을 확인해주십시오.

해설 빈칸은 조동사 may와 have 사이에 어울리는 품사의 단어가 들어갈 자리이다. 문장 성분상 없어도 되는 자리이므로 빈칸은 부사가 적당하다. 그래서 선택지 중 (D) possibly(아마, 혹시)가 정답이다.

어휘 upon ~하자마자 content 내용물 determine 알아내다 while in transit 운송 동안

ACTUAL TEST 06 ACTUAL TEST 07 ACTUAL TEST 08 ACTUAL TEST 09 ACTUAL TEST 10

119

It is necessary for all tour visitors to wear the life jacket provided and listen ------- to the safety procedure.
(A) attention
(B) attentively
(C) attends
(D) attend

모든 여행객들이 제공된 구명조끼를 착용하는 것과 안전절차를 주의 깊게 듣는 것이 필요하다.

> 해설 자동사(listen)와 전치사(to) 사이에는 부사가 와야 하므로 정답은 (B) attentively(주의 깊게, 세심하게)이다.
> 어휘 lafe jacket 구명조끼 compulsory 강제적인, 의무적인 safety procedure 안전절차 attentively 세심하게, 주의 깊게

120

The two eastbound lanes on the Napoleon's Gate Bridge that were closed ------- emergency repairs have reopened after nearly six hours.
(A) as a result
(B) in order to
(C) so that
(D) owing to

긴급 수리 때문에 차단되었던 Napoleon's Gate Bridge에 있는 동쪽으로 향하는 두 차선을 거의 6시간 후에 다시 개통했다.

> 해설 빈칸은 뒤의 emergency repairs와 의미연결이 적절한 단어가 들어갈 자리이다. 빈칸 뒤가 문장처럼 보이지만 that부터 repairs까지는 앞의 lanes를 수식한다. 전치사이면서 의미상 자연스러운 (D) owing to(~ 때문에)가 정답이다. owing to emergency repairs 긴급한 수리 작업 때문에
> 어휘 eastbound 동쪽으로 향하는 lane 차선 nearly 거의 as a result 그 결과 owing to ~ 때문에

121

Your order will be processed and shipped within 3 business days ------- the date it is placed.
(A) when
(B) under
(C) than
(D) from

당신의 주문은 처리될 것이고 주문된 날로부터 영업일 3일 이내로 발송될 것입니다.

> 해설 빈칸은 뒤의 the date와 의미연결이 적절한 단어가 들어갈 자리이다. 선택지 중 날짜와 어울리는 전치사는 (D) from이다.
> 어휘 process 처리하다 ship 발송하다

122

The road ------- has caused much inconvenience to travellers who have to find alternative routes.
(A) closure
(B) closed
(C) closes
(D) close

도로 차단은 우회 도로를 찾아야 하는 여행자들에게 많은 불편함을 야기해왔다.

(해설) 빈칸은 주어자리이며, road와 어울리는 명사가 와야 하는 자리이다. 선택지 중 명사인 (A) closure(폐쇄)가 정답이다.
(어휘) closure 폐쇄 cause 야기하다 inconvenience 불편 alternative route 우회 도로

123

Synops Airlines will provide $180 to customers ------- flights were delayed more than three hours due to its system failures.
(A) when
(B) those
(C) whose
(D) their

Synops Airlines는 회사의 시스템 고장 때문에 3시간 이상 비행이 지연된 승객들에게 180달러를 제공합니다.

(해설) 빈칸에 접속사 when을 넣어 보면 의미연결이 되지 않으므로, 앞의 명사 customers(고객들)를 선행사로 취하는 관계대명사 whose가 적합하다. whose는 소유격 관계대명사이므로 선행사에 '~의'를 붙여 whose 뒤의 명사와 연결되는지 확인해봐야 한다. 문맥상 '고객들의 비행기'라고 연결할 수 있다.
(어휘) more than 이상 due to ~ 때문에 failure 고장, 오작동

124

Benjamin Frank's Coffee House offers a wide ------- of gift items, such as coffee cups, ornamental spoons and beautiful bowls.
(A) preference
(B) selection
(C) part
(D) compound

Benjamin Frank의 Coffee House는 커피컵, 장식용 숟가락과 아름다운 그릇과 같은 매우 다양한 선물용 아이템을 제공한다.

(해설) 빈칸은 a wide ~ of의 표현에 어울리는 명사가 들어갈 자리이다. 선택지에서 selection(선택, 선별)이 의미가 적절하다. a wide selection of 폭넓게 다양한 ~
(어휘) such as 예를 들어 ornamental 장식용 preference 선호 selection 선정 compound 혼합물

ACTUAL TEST 06 ACTUAL TEST 07 ACTUAL TEST 08 **ACTUAL TEST 09** ACTUAL TEST 10

231

125

The users are expected to be ------- of any hazards and precautions regarding the chemicals that they use.
(A) alert
(B) aware
(C) present
(D) serious

사용자들은 그들이 사용하는 화학물질에 관하여 위험과 예방조치를 인지할 것으로 예상됩니다.

해설 빈칸은 be동사와 전치사 of 사이에 어울리는 형용사가 들어갈 자리이다. 선택지 중 aware(알고 있는, 인식하는)는 be aware of(~을 알고 있다)로 쓰인다.

어휘 be aware of 알다, 인식하다 hazard 위험 precaution 예방조치, 예방책 alert 방심 않는 serious 심각한, 진지한

126

Please ------- our web site for complete details of our services and price lists of all of our products.
(A) refer
(B) look
(C) notify
(D) consult

우리 서비스의 전체 세부사항과 모든 제품의 가격표를 위해서 웹사이트를 참조하십시오.

해설 빈칸은 명령문과 의미가 어울리는 동사자리이다. refer와 look은 자동사로 뒤에 전치사가 와야 하고, notify는 사람목적어를 취하므로 오답이 된다. 그래서 남은 consult(참조하다, 상담하다)가 정답이다. (A) refer 언급하다 (B) look 보다 (C) notify ~을 통지하다

어휘 complete details 전체 세부사항 price list 가격표

127

By the time he retires, Mrs. Maeva ------- for more than sixteen years as director of the company.
(A) will have served
(B) has served
(C) had served
(D) been served

Maeva 씨가 은퇴할 때쯤이면, 그는 회사의 부장으로서 16년 이상 근무하게 될 것입니다.

해설 빈칸은 문장에서 적절한 동사형태가 들어갈 자리이다. 맨 앞의 By the time이 접속사로 쓰이는 경우, ① By the time + 현재시제, 미래완료시제 ② By the time + 과거시제, 과거완료시제로 쓰인다. 본 문제에서는 By the time절이 현재이므로, 빈칸이 있는 문장은 미래완료시제가 와야 한다. 그래서 정답은 (A) will have served이다.

어휘 by the time ~할 무렵 serve 근무하다 more than ~이상

128

To post your job opening on Valley Industry's website, ------- fill out an online application form and you will receive your receipt via e-mail.
(A) finally
(B) sparsely
(C) simply
(D) such

웹사이트 Valley Industry에 공석을 게시하기 위하여, 간단히 온라인 지원서를 작성하면 이메일을 통하여 영수증을 받을 것입니다.

해설 빈칸은 뒤의 fill out과 의미연결이 적절한 부사자리이다. simply는 '단순히, 간단히'의 의미로, 별 부담 없이, 성가심 없이 한다는 의미일 때 많이 쓰는 표현이다. simply fill out 간단히 작성하다

어휘 post 게시하다 job opening 공석 fill out 작성하다 via 통하여 finally 마침내 sparsely 드물게 simply 단순히, 간단히

129

As principal administrative officer, Mr. Thomas has unlimited ------- to the performance evaluation files.
(A) access
(B) accessing
(C) accesses
(D) accessed

관리부장으로서, Thomas 씨는 실적 평가 파일에 자유롭게 접근할 수 있다.

해설 빈칸은 형용사 unlimited(무제한의, 자유로운)와 어울리는 명사자리이다. access는 '접근'이라는 셀 수 없는 명사(불가산명사)이므로 복수로 쓰이지 않는다. 따라서 정답은 (A) access이다.

어휘 principal 주요한 unlimited 무제한의 performance evaluation 성과 평가 access 접근

130

------- impresses investors the most is that Muttoni Company has achieved international fame with its brand this year.
(A) What
(B) Neither
(C) When
(D) Nothing

투자자들을 가장 감명시켰던 것은 Muttoni Company가 올해 이 브랜드로 국제적인 명성을 얻었다는 것이다.

해설 빈칸은 문장의 주어를 이끌 수 있는 단어가 들어갈 자리이다. 명사절을 이끌 수 있는 선택지는 선택지 (A) What(~ 것)이다.

어휘 impress 감동시키다 fame 명성

PART 6

Questions 131-134 refer to the following notice.

Attention Staff: Underground Parking Lot Reopening It has taken several months longer than ------, but the **131.** Greenearth Paper company has finally started to reopen its underground parking lot. ------- means employees will no longer **132.** need to park their vehicles across the street at the abandoned mill. The parking lot will reopen in sections starting in the first week of June. ------. Any employees ------ have difficulty **133.** **134.** with mobility will be given priority for the first section of parking spots. If you suffer from problems with mobility, contact the building manager to reserve a spot in the first section.	주목: 지하주차장 재개장 계획된것보다몇달더걸렸지만,Greenearth Paper는 지하주차장을 마침내 재개장했습니다. 그것은 직원들이 더 이상 길 건너 폐공장에 주차할 필요가 없다는 것을 의미합니다. 주차장은 6월 첫 주부터 구역별로 다시 열 것입니다. 7월말까지, 전체 주차장이 재개장하고 모든 직원들이 다시 지하에 주차가 가능할 것입니다. 이동에 제약이 있는 직원들은 주차 장소의 첫 구역에 우선순위가 주어질 것입니다. 만일 이동하는 문제로 어려움을 겪는다면, 첫 구역에 자리를 지정할 수 있게 건물관리인에게 연락 바랍니다.

어휘 underground 지하 no longer 더 이상 ~가 아니라 abandoned 버려진 mill 공장, 제분소 have difficulty with ~에 어려움을 겪다 mobility 이동성 priority 우선사항, 우선권 suffer from ~로 고통받다

131 **(A) planned**
(B) planer
(C) planless
(D) planning

해설 빈칸 앞에 전치사이자 접속사의 역할을 하는 than이 보인다. 전치사가 보인다고 바로 명사를 고르지 않도록 조심하자. 전치사 than은 비교급에서 비교 대상 앞에 사용되지만 접속사 than은 분사구문으로 than p.p의 형태로도 잘 쓰인다. 특히 p.p 자리에는 '기대하다, 예측하다' 등의 의미의 과거분사들이 잘 들어가며 than expected(예상보다), than anticipated(기대보다), than predicted(예상보다)의 구조를 만든다.

132 (A) What
(B) Those
(C) These
(D) That

해설 빈칸이 속한 문장에 동사는 will no longer need 하나밖에 없으므로 빈칸은 단순 주어의 역할을 하는 명사나 대명사의 자리이다. 선택지 중 접속사인 (A)는 우선 제외된다. 문맥상 앞 문장 전체를 대신 받는 대명사가 들어가야 어울리므로 그러한 쓰임이 있는 지시대명사인 (D) that이 정답이 된다.

133

(A) The old underground parking lot was so old that the renovation was necessary.
(B) The construction took longer than expected due to a delay in material supply.
(C) All employees must use an alternative parking lot until the parking lot reopens.
(D) By the end of July, the entire parking lot will be reopened and everyone can again park underground.

해설 재개장 계획이 나열되고 있다. 빈칸 앞 문장에서 6월에는 구역별로 개장될 것임을 언급했으므로 빈칸에는 전체 주차장이 7월에 개장할 것임을 설명하는 (D)가 가장 적절하다. 특히 문장삽입문제는 시점 표현(6월, 7월) 등이 중요한 단서가 될 수 있다.

(A) 이전 지하 주차장은 너무 낡아서 수리가 필요했습니다.
(B) 건설은 재료 공급에 지연 때문에 예상보다 오래 걸렸습니다.
(C) 모든 직원들은 주차장이 다시 개장할 때까지 대체 주차장을 사용해야 합니다.
(D) 7월말까지, 전체 주차장이 재개장하고 모든 직원들이 다시 지하에 주차가 가능할 것입니다.

134

(A) whose
(B) they
(C) who
(D) which

해설 관계대명사를 묻는 문제이다. 우선 선행사로 사람(employees)이 왔고 빈칸 뒤로 동사(have difficulty)가 연결되고 있으므로 빈칸은 사람을 선행사로 취하는 주격 관계대명사의 자리가 된다.

From: Joshua Radnor <sales@buildersmaterial.com>

To: Taylor Moy <moy@diyconstruction.com>

Subject: Order #35987

Date: Thursday, April 19

Dear Mr. Moy,

We are processing your order, which we received on April 13. You indicated that you were interested in receiving the ceramic tiles ------- the end of the week. -------, the color you ordered
     135.   **136.**
will not be available from the manufacturer for another month. We apologize for the delay and ask for your understanding.

-------. They are slightly lighter in color, but we have plenty in
137.
stock. If you are interested, you can compare product colors on our website www.buildersmaterial.com or just visit our store.

For the moment, the cost of the ceramic tiles has been -------
                                        138.
from your order. You should receive the in-stock items by tomorrow. We thank you for choosing Builders Material.

발신: Joshua Radnor ⟨sales@builders-material.com⟩

수신: Taylor Moy ⟨moy@diyconstruction.com⟩

제목: 주문 #35987

날짜: 4월 19일 목요일

Moy 씨께,

우리는 4월 13일에 받은 당신의 주문을 처리 중입니다. 당신은 주말까지 타일을 받는 것에 관심을 보였습니다. 안타깝게도, 당신이 주문한 색상은 한 달 동안 제조업자로부터 이용 가능하지 않습니다. 우리는 지연에 사과드리고, 이해해주시길 요청드립니다.

우리는 당신이 주문한 같은 스타일을 베이지 색상으로 보유하고 있습니다. 그것들은 색상이 약간 밝습니다. 하지만 재고량이 많습니다. 만일 관심이 있다면, 홈페이지에서 제품 색상을 비교하거나 우리 가게를 방문할 수 있습니다.

현재, 타일 비용은 주문에서 빠져 있습니다. 재고가 있는 물건은 내일까지 받을 것입니다. Builders Material을 선택해주셔서 감사드립니다.

어휘 process 처리하다 indicate 나타내다 ceramic 도자기 by the end of ~의 끝에, 말에 unfortunately 불행히도 available 이용 가능한 manufacturer 제조사 understanding 이해 slightly 약간 compare 비교하다 in-stock 재고가 있는

135
    (A) from
    (B) by
    (C) of
    (D) until

해설 빈칸 뒤의 시점 표현인 the end of the week와 어울리는 전치사를 찾는다. '주말까지'라는 의미로 정답은 (B)가 된다. 참고로 at the end of the week는 '주말에'의 의미로도 잘 쓰인다.

136
(A) Alternatively
(B) Subsequently
(C) Unfortunately
(D) Approximately

해설 문맥상 어울리는 접속부사를 찾는 문제이다. 빈칸 앞에는 주문에 감사한다는 내용이 있었지만 빈칸 뒤로는 주문한 제품이 이용 가능하지 않다는 내용이 따라오므로 정답은 '불행히도, 안타깝게도'라는 의미의 (C)가 된다.

137
(A) Any defective tiles will be replaced with new ones.
(B) The cost of out-of-stock items will be refunded within 10 working days.
(C) Another retailer sells the same products in the area.
(D) We have the same style that you ordered in beige.

해설 빈칸 뒤에 they라는 대명사가 있는 것으로 보아 빈칸에는 일단 복수명사가 포함된 문장이 있어야 하고, 뒷내용에 색상은 약간 더 밝지만 재고가 많이 있다는 내용이 나온다. 빈칸에는 당신이 주문한 같은 스타일의 제품을 다른 색상으로 보유하고 있다는 (D)가 가장 적당하다.

(A) 어떤 결함 있는 타일들은 새것으로 교체될 것입니다.
(B) 재고 없는 물품들의 비용은 10영업일 이내에 환불될 것입니다.
(C) 다른 소매점이 그 지역에서 같은 제품을 판매합니다.
(D) 우리는 당신이 주문한 같은 스타일을 베이지색으로 보유하고 있습니다.

138
(A) promoted
(B) removed
(C) determined
(D) evolved

해설 지금은 재고가 없어서 판매할 수가 없는 타일 가격은 주문에서 제외(removed)될 것이다.

Questions 139-142 refer to the following letter.

Dear Mr. Capron,
 	
This is to submit my resignation as an assistant photographer from the Colbert Weekly News, ------- March 2, as I seek to broaden my career. I am ------- you with one month's notice as stipulated in my employment contract.
      139.   **140.**
 	
For some time, I have been considering ------- my own photography business. -------. The $40,000 grand prize I won has enabled me to start my own photography studio.
  141. **142.**
 	
I will truly miss working at the Colbert Weekly News with all of you. I wish you and the company continued success.
 	
Sincerely,
 	
Jeffrey Sparshott
	Capron 씨께,
	
	이 편지는 제가 경력을 넓히고 싶기 때문에, 3월 2일부터 Colbert Weekly News에서 보조 사진기자직의 사직서를 제출하기 위한 것입니다. 당신에게 고용계약서에 명시된 대로 한 달간의 사전 공지를 합니다.
	
	한동안, 저는 사진 사업을 시작하려고 고민해왔습니다. 석 달 전, 풍경사진으로 International Photographers Club으로부터 상을 받았습니다. 제가 받은 4만 달러의 상금으로 사진 스튜디오를 시작할 수 있었습니다.
	
	저는 정말 Colbert Weekly News에서 당신들 모두와 일한 것을 그리워할 것입니다. 당신과 회사의 계속적인 성공을 바랍니다.
	
	진심을 담아
	
	Jeffrey Sparshott

어휘 submit 제출하다 assistant 비서, 보조 photographer 사진작가 broaden 넓히다, 넓어지다, 퍼지다 stipulate 규정하다, 명시하다 enable 가능하게 하다

139
    (A) outside
    (B) effective
    (C) afterward
    (D) instead of

해설 빈칸 뒤로 날짜 표현이 따라오고 있다. 선택지들 중 날짜 앞에 사용할 수 있는 전치사는 (B) effective이다. effective는 일반 형용사로 '효과적인'이라는 의미가 있을 뿐만 아니라 시점의 전치사로 시점 표현 앞에서 '~부로'라는 의미로 사용되기도 한다. 이 용법으로 사용될 때 동의어로는 starting, beginning, as of 등이 있다.

140
(A) writing
(B) providing
(C) showing
(D) prohibiting

해설 선택지 중에서 사람목적어를 쓸 수 있는 동사어휘를 찾는다. 그리고 빈칸 뒤의 문장구조(사람 + with + 사물)가 단서가 된다. [provide 사람 with 사물], [provide 사물 to/for 사람]의 구조를 기억하자.

141
(A) to start
(B) start
(C) starting
(D) started

해설 빈칸은 my own photography business를 이끌며 동사 consider의 목적어가 될 수 있는 동명사자리이다. 이처럼 동명사목적어를 취하는 동사로는 discontinue(중단하다), finish(끝내다), avoid(피하다), recommend(권하다) 등이 있다.

142
(A) Finally, I decided to open my photography studio in May.
(B) Fortunately, the Wacom investment company has funded my own business.
(C) Three months ago, I won an award from the International Photographers Club for my landscape photography portfolio.
(D) As you know, our industry is increasingly competitive.

해설 빈칸 뒤로 상금 $40,000가 언급되고 있다. 그것을 밑천으로 스튜디오를 연다는 내용이 나온다. 따라서 빈칸에는 상금의 출처가 언급되는 것이 어울리므로 정답은 (C)다.

(A) 마침내, 저는 5월에 저의 작업실을 열기로 결정했습니다.
(B) 다행스럽게도, Wacom 투자사가 제 사업에 자금을 제공했습니다.
(C) 석 달 전, 풍경사진으로 International Photographers Club으로부터 상을 받았습니다.
(D) 당신도 알다시피, 우리 산업은 점점 경쟁적입니다.

Questions 143-146 refer to the following e-mail.

To: Jim Patel <jpatel@Mckinney.com> From: Julie Sarandon <jsarandon@Mckinney.com> Date: Monday, March 1 Subject: Welcome Dear Mr. Patel, Welcome to Mckinney Electronics! We are glad to have you with us, and we, especially the Sales and Marketing Team, all look forward to working with you. ------- this is your first day with the company, we would like to **143.** have you join us in the main conference room to meet ------- officials and key people of Mckinney Electronics. -------. **144.** **145.** This meeting has been set for 10:00 A.M. today. After the short meeting, we will take you on a tour of our office facilities. The company president will then ------- welcome you at a lunch to **146.** be attended by other top managers. We will see you later. Julie Sarandon	수신: Jim Patel 〈jpatel@Mckinney.com〉 발신: Julie Sarandon 〈jsarandon@ Mckinney.com〉 날짜: 3월 1일 월요일 제목: 환영 Patel 씨께, Mckinney Electronics에 오신 당신을 환영합니다. 우리는 당신과 함께하게 되어 기쁘고 특히 우리 판매·마케팅팀 모두는 당신과 함께 일하기를 기대합니다. 오늘이 회사의 첫날이기 때문에, 주회의실에서 다른 간부들과 Mckinney Electronics의 핵심 인물들을 함께 만나기를 바랍니다. 이것은 후일에 함께 근무할 사람들과 친해지게 할 것입니다. 이 미팅은 오늘 오전 10시로 예정되어 있습니다. 간단한 미팅 뒤에, 당신을 사무실 견학에 데려갈 것입니다. 그러고 나서 사장님이 다른 관리자들이 참석하는 점심 행사에서 당신을 공식적으로 환영할 것입니다. 나중에 뵙겠습니다. Julie Sarandon

어휘 especially 특히 look forward to -ing ~하기를 학수고대하다 official 고위 간부, 공무원 key people 주요 인사

143
(A) Even though
(B) Once
(C) As
(D) In order that

해설 문맥상 어울리는 접속사를 찾는 문제이다. 원인이 수신자가 회사의 첫 출근이고, 결과가 이 회사의 다른 간부들과 주요 인사들과 만남을 가지는 것이다. 그러므로 이유의 접속사 as가 가장 어울린다.

144
(A) the other
(B) another
(C) others
(D) the one

해설 빈칸은 officials(복수명사)를 수식하는 형용사자리이다. 우선 (B) another는 단수명사만 수식하므로 정답이 될 수 없다. (C) others는 복수명사로 쓰이고 명사를 수식할 수 없다. (D) the one은 그 자체로 명사이다. one이 가산단수명사를 수식하긴 하지만 그때는 한정사의 역할을 하므로 관사 the와 함께 쓰이지 않는다. 정답은 '나머지의'라는 의미로 복수명사나 불가산명사를 수식하는 (A) the other이다.

145
(A) The president called a special meeting to discuss Mckinney Electronics's strategy.
(B) This will help you get acquainted with the people who will be working with you in the coming days.
(C) The executives of Mckinney Electronics look forward to meeting you and celebrating your promotion.
(D) Considering your past experience, you are highly qualified for the position with Mckinney Electronics.

해설 앞서 첫 출근일에 회사의 간부들과 주요 인사들을 만나게 될 것이라 언급했다. 정답 문장의 주어인 this가 앞문장의 내용을 대신 받는 대명사로 사용되었고 그것이 앞으로 함께 일할 사람들과 친해지도록 도울 것이라는 내용인 (B)가 정답이다.

(A) 사장님이 Mckinney Electronics의 전략을 논의하기 위해 특별회의를 소집했습니다.
(B) 이것은 후일에 함께 근무할 사람들과 친해지게 할 것입니다.
(C) Mckinney Electronics의 중역들은 당신을 만나고 승진을 축하하기를 기대합니다.
(D) 당신의 지난 경험을 고려해 볼 때, 당신은 Mckinney Electronics의 자리에 매우 자질이 있습니다.

146
(A) formally
(B) periodically
(C) customarily
(D) solely

해설 첫 출근일에 사장이 식사 자리에서 환영할 것은 '공식적인' 일이므로 이와 가장 잘 어울리는 부사는 (A) formally이다. 오답인 (B) periodically와 (C) customarily는 주로 현재시제와 함께 쓰인다는 것에 유의하자.

PART 5

101

Mr. Smith told ------- that his company is currently supplying several kinds of construction materials for the new museum.
(A) I
(B) myself
(C) me
(D) mine

Smith 씨는 그의 회사가 현재 새로운 박물관에 몇 가지 종류의 건설자재를 공급한다고 나에게 말했다.

해설 빈칸은 동사 told의 목적어자리이다. 선택지 중에 목적격인 (C) me가 정답이 된다.

어휘 currently 현재 construction material 건설자재

102

Riverdale Hotel is planning to ------- its parking space to reduce traffic congestion during the weekends.
(A) enlarge
(B) distract
(C) accomplish
(D) communicate

Riverdale Hotel은 주말 동안에 교통체증을 줄이기 위하여 주차공간을 확장할 계획이다.

해설 빈칸은 뒤의 parking space(주차공간)를 목적어로 취하는 동사자리이다. 선택지 중에서 의미가 잘 연결되는 단어는 (A) enlarge(확장하다)이다.

어휘 reduce ~을 줄이다 traffic congestion 교통 혼잡 enlarge 확장하다 distract 산만하게 하다 accomplish 성취하다 communicate 의사소통을 하다

103

Najad's expertise of the local economy ------- by that of no other economist.
(A) to surpass
(B) is surpassed
(C) surpassable
(D) surpassing

지역경제에 대한 Najad의 전문지식은 다른 경제학자의 전문지식을 능가했다.

해설 빈칸은 문장의 동사가 들어가야 하는 자리이다. surpass는 '능가하다'는 의미의 타동사인데, 빈칸 뒤에 목적어가 없으므로 수동형태가 빈칸에 와야 한다. 그래서 정답은 is surpassed이다.

어휘 expertise 전문 지식 surpass 능가하다

104

Nowadays, rail transportation has been described as the most affordable and ------- means of transportation.
(A) correct
(B) reliable
(C) portable
(D) cooperative

요즘, 철도교통은 교통수단의 가장 합리적이고 믿을만한 수단으로서 설명되고 있다.

해설 빈칸은 뒤의 means와 의미가 어울리는 형용사자리이다. means(수단, 방법)와 어울리는 형용사는 reliable(믿을 만한)이다.

어휘 nowadays 요즘 rail transportation 철도 운송 describe 묘사하다 affordable (가격이) 알맞은 means 수단 correct 정확한 portable 휴대가 능한 cooperative 공동의

105

To unlock the door, turn the dial clockwise slowly and ------- until the dial comes to a stop.
(A) nearly
(B) gently
(C) openly
(D) timely

문을 열기 위해 다이얼이 멈출 때까지 시계방향으로 천천히 그리고 부드럽게 돌리십시오.

해설 빈칸은 and 앞의 부사 slowly와 의미가 연결되는 부사자리이다. 앞의 내용을 보면 '다이얼을 시계방향으로 천천히 그리고 ~'라고 문맥이므로 '부드럽게'라는 의미의 gently가 정답이다.

어휘 unlock 열다 clockwise 시계 방향으로 come to a stop 멈추다 gently 부드럽게 nearly 거의 openly 공개적으로

106

At your -------, your appointment with Dr. Watson has been moved up to 6:30 P.M. on Friday, November 6.
(A) claim
(B) conflict
(C) paper
(D) request

당신의 요청에 따라, Dr. Watson과의 약속은 11월 6일 금요일 저녁 6시 30분으로 옮겨졌습니다.

해설 전치사 at과 연결되는 명사어휘를 고르는 문제이다. 토익빈출 표현인 at your request(당신의 요청에 따라)를 잘 챙겨두자.

어휘 move up to ~로 옮기다 claim 주장 conflict 충돌, 마찰 request 요청

107

Ruzzie Consulting has a main office in Paris and will ------- be opening a branch office in Nice.

(A) shortly
(B) almost
(C) initially
(D) equally

Ruzzie Consulting은 Paris에 본사가 있으며 곧 Nice에 지사를 개설할 것이다.

해설 빈칸은 문장의 의미에 어울리는 부사가 들어갈 자리이다. 빈칸이 있는 문장의 시제가 미래이므로, 이에 어울리는 부사는 (A) shortly(곧)이다.

어휘 main office 본사 branch office 지점, 지사 shortly 곧 initially 초기에 equally 동등하게

108

British and French translations of Mr. Choi's speech ------- marketing strategy should be available online on January 14.

(A) regarded
(B) regard
(C) regards
(D) regarding

마케팅 전략에 대한 Choi 씨 연설의 영국과 프랑스어 번역은 1월 14일 온라인으로 이용 가능할 것이다.

해설 빈칸은 뒤의 marketing strategy를 받는 전치사자리이다. 선택지 중에 전치사는 (D) regarding(~에 관하여)이다.

어휘 translation 번역 strategy 전략 regarding 관한

109

Please understand ------- we will not be able to process refunds or exchanges until the first week of February because it is so busy.

(A) where
(B) whom
(C) what
(D) that

너무 바쁘기 때문에, 2월 첫 주까지 환불이나 교환을 해줄 수 없다는 것을 이해해 주십시오.

해설 understand는 that절을 목적어로 취하는 동사이다. 따라서 정답은 (D) that이 된다.

어휘 process 처리하다 exchange 교환

110

The Neo Institute of Visual Arts will feature a variety of presentations by leaders of the ------- design companies.
(A) most prominent
(B) more prominently
(C) prominence
(D) prominently

Neo Institute of Visual Arts는 가장 저명한 디자인회사 리더들의 다양한 발표를 특징으로 할 것입니다.

해설 빈칸은 design companies를 수식해주는 형용사자리이다. 부사인 more prominently, prominently, 명사인 prominence를 제외하면 (A) most prominent가 남는다.
어휘 feature 특징으로 하다 a variety of 다양한 presentation 발표 prominent 유명한, 저명한

111

BK's Personnel Training Academy always ------- constructive suggestions, which we assume are helpful to further improve the training programs.
(A) collaborates
(B) welcomes
(C) introduces
(D) correspond

BK's Personnel Training Academy는 우리가 가정하기에 훈련프로그램을 더 개선하기 위하여 도움이 되는 발전적인 제안을 항상 환영합니다.

해설 빈칸은 constructive suggestions(발전적인 제안)를 목적어로 취하는 동사자리이다. constructive suggestions와 의미 연결이 잘 되는 동사는 welcome(반기다)이다. 자동사인 collaborate(협력하다)와 correspond(서신 연락하다)는 오답이다.
어휘 constructive 건설적인 assume 추정하다 helpful 도움이 되는 further 더욱더 collaborate 협동하다 correspond 서신으로 연락하다

112

The president decided to hire a consulting firm to help ------- potential business partners.
(A) investigated
(B) investigate
(C) investigator
(D) investigation

사장은 잠재적인 사업 파트너를 조사하는 것을 돕기 위해 자문회사를 고용하기로 결정했다.

해설 동사 help 뒤에 어울리는 단어 형태를 고르는 문제이다. help는 <help + 목적어 + to부정사>, <help + 목적어 + 동사원형>, <help + 동사원형>의 구조를 갖는다. 이 문제에서는 <help + 동사원형>의 구조를 취해야 하므로 선택지 중 동사원형인 (B) investigate (조사하다)가 정답이다.
어휘 potential 잠재적인 investigate 조사하다

ACTUAL TEST 06 | ACTUAL TEST 07 | ACTUAL TEST 08 | ACTUAL TEST 09 | **ACTUAL TEST 10**

113

ESPY Sports TV will have full ------- of Judy Emilton's press conference tomorrow afternoon.
(A) occurrence
(B) response
(C) coverage
(D) announcement

ESPY Sports TV는 내일 오후에 Judy Emilton의 기자회견을 처음부터 끝까지 보도할 것이다.

해설 빈칸은 have의 목적어자리이다. 앞에 있는 형용사 full과의 의미 연결도 살펴봐야 한다. 그런데, 문장에서 주어가 ESPY Sports TV라는 방송사이고 이와 연결해서 의미가 적절한 목적어(명사)는 coverage(보도, 방송)이다. full coverage는 처음부터 끝까지 전부 방송을 해 준다는 의미가 된다.

어휘 press conference 기자회견 occurrence 발생 response 응답 coverage 보도범위 announcement 공지

114

------- a few minor flaws, the construction of the building was smooth and efficient.
(A) As to
(B) Together
(C) Except that
(D) Aside from

약간의 작은 흠집을 제외하고 빌딩의 건설은 순조롭고 효율적이었다.

해설 선택지 중 전치사인 as to(~에 관하여)와 aside from(~을 제외하고) 중에서 aside from이 문맥상 어울린다.

어휘 flaw 결함 construction 건설 smooth 순조로운 efficient 효율적인 as to ~에 관해 except that ~이라는 것 이외는 aside from ~을 제외하고

115

In a TV interview, Chief Executive Officer Richard Hudson claimed that his ------- accomplishment was his success in negotiating the merger with Bixson Publishers.
(A) gratified
(B) most gratifying
(C) gratifyingly
(D) more gratified

TV 인터뷰에서, CEO인 Richard Hudson은 가장 만족스러웠던 업적이 Bixson Publishers와의 성공적인 합병 협상이었다고 주장했다.

해설 빈칸은 명사 accomplishment(성취)와 의미가 어울리는 형용사자리이다. 빈칸 앞에 소유격이 보이므로, 최상급을 나타내는 관사 the 대신에 소유격이 왔음을 알 수 있다. 형용사이고, 최상급의 의미로 적합한 선택지는 most gratifying(가장 만족을 주는)이다.

어휘 Chief Executive Officer 최고 경영자 claim 주장하다 accomplishment 성취 merger 합병 gratifying 만족을 주는

116

According to the schedule, the new company ID will be distributed to all employees ------- the end of this month.
(A) on
(B) by
(C) of
(D) as

일정에 따라, 새로운 회사 ID는 모든 직원들에게 이번 달 말까지 나눠줄 것이다.

해설 빈칸은 the end of this month와 의미연결이 적절한 전치사가 들어갈 자리이다. 정답을 떠나 빈칸은 before the end of(~말 전에), at the end of(~말에), by the end of(~ 말까지) 등의 표현이 가능하다. 정답은 선택지에 있는 (B) by이다.

어휘 according to ~에 따르면 distribute 분배하다

117

Despite the recent ------- in sales, the CEO of Cramax Electronics believes that his company will be profitable within a few months.
(A) conference
(B) overhead
(C) appraisal
(D) decline

최근의 판매 감소에도 불구하고, Cramax Electronics의 CEO는 그의 회사가 몇 달 내로 수익을 낼 것이라 믿는다.

해설 빈칸은 의미가 적절한 명사가 들어갈 자리이다. 뒤에 in sales(판매에서)와 의미연결을 보면 '감소'를 나타내는 decline이 적절하다. decline in sales 판매에서의 감소

어휘 profitable 수익이 있는 overhead 운영비 appraisal 평가 decline 감소

118

------- to our survey, Riverside residents are overwhelmingly in favor of adding walk lanes along the beach.
(A) Including
(B) Concerning
(C) Considering
(D) According

우리의 설문조사에 따르면, Riverside 거주민들은 해변을 따라서 인도를 추가하는 것에 압도적으로 찬성합니다.

해설 뒤의 to와 어울리는 어휘를 찾는 문제이다. 고민할 필요도 없이 according to가 정답임을 알 수 있다.

어휘 overwhelmingly 압도적으로 in favor of ~에 찬성하여 along 따라서 including 포함하여 concerning 관하여 considering 고려할 때

ACTUAL TEST 06 ACTUAL TEST 07 ACTUAL TEST 08 ACTUAL TEST 09 ACTUAL TEST 10

247

119

One ------- of today's sales meeting is to report the increased market share to the president.
(A) aim
(B) aims
(C) will aim
(D) aiming

오늘 판매미팅의 목표는 시장에서 증가된 시장 점유율을 보고하는 것이다.

해설 빈칸은 one 뒤에 어울리는 명사자리이다. 동사가 is이므로 주어가 단수여야 한다. 정답 후보로는 aim(목적, 목표), aiming(겨냥, 조준) 등이 가능하다. of 이하가 '오늘 판매미팅의 ~'이므로 정답은 aim이다. one aim of today's sales meeting 오늘 판매미팅의 목적

어휘 increased 증가된 market share 시장 점유율 aim 목적, 목표 aiming 겨냥

120

You should notify the lecturer of your anticipated absences ------- alternate dates can be scheduled.
(A) despite
(B) ever since
(C) due to
(D) so that

당신은 대체 날짜가 잡히기 위해서 예상된 불참을 강연자에게 알려줘야 합니다.

해설 빈칸은 뒤에 문장을 받아야 하는 접속사자리이다. despite, due to는 전치사로 오답이다. 뒷문장에 can이 보이므로 so that ~ can구문임을 짐작할 수 있다. 그래서 정답은 (D) so that이다.

어휘 lecturer 강연자 anticipated 예상 되는 absence 불참 alternate date 대체 날짜

121

Steve Jackson has been an authorized stockbroker for more than 25 years and also specializes in overseas -------.
(A) invested
(B) investments
(C) investor
(D) invests

Steve Jackson은 25년 이상 동안 허가된 증권 중개인이었고, 또한 해외투자를 전문으로 합니다.

해설 빈칸은 동사 specializes in(~을 전문으로 하다)과 의미 연결이 되는 명사자리이다. 전문으로 하는 것은 특정 분야를 말하므로 investments(투자), investor(투자자) 중에서 (B) investments가 정답이다.

어휘 authorized 허가된 stockbroker 증권 중개인 specialize 전문으로 하다 overseas 해외의

122

All ------- of a confidential nature will be stored in locked filing cabinets that can be accessed only by designated personnel.
(A) effects
(B) positions
(C) repetitions
(D) documents

기밀 성질의 모든 문서들은 오직 지정된 직원들에 의해서만 접근될 수 있는 잠긴 파일 캐비닛에 저장될 것입니다.

해설 빈칸은 뒤의 of a confidential nature(기밀 성질의)와 의미가 연결되는 명사가 들어갈 자리이다. 해석상 documents(문서)가 적절한 정답이다. all documents of a confidential nature 기밀 성질의 모든 문서들
어휘 confidential 비밀의, 기밀의 nature 특성, 성질 store 보관하다 locked 잠기어진 designated 지정된 repetition 반복

123

On account of his insight as a real estate analyst, Mr. Will is well ------- by his co-workers.
(A) respect
(B) respects
(C) respected
(D) respective

부동산 분석가로서 그의 통찰력 때문에 Will 씨는 그의 직장 동료로부터 아주 존경을 받는다.

해설 빈칸은 be동사 is와 부사 well 뒤에 어울리는 형태의 단어가 들어갈 자리이다. 특히, well은 pp형태의 수식과도 잘 어울린다는 점을 알아둔다면 respected(존경 받는)를 정답으로 선택하기 한결 쉬울 것이다. 형용사인 respective는 '각각의'의 의미이다.
어휘 on account of ~때문에 insight 통찰력 real estate 부동산 respected 존경 받는 respective 각각의

124

Using the survey data, Chef Frank Dols will ------- publish a new book, Famous French Food.
(A) soon
(B) lately
(C) well
(D) once

설문조사 자료를 사용하는 요리사 Frank Dols 씨는 곧 새로운 책인 Famous French Food를 출판할 것입니다.

해설 문장의 시제가 미래이므로 soon(곧)이 어울린다. lately(최근에)는 현재완료, once(한때)는 과거시제와 잘 어울린다.
어휘 survey 설문

125

If you can prove that what a landlord is charging for rent is too high, you may be able to ------- the rent payment.
(A) negotiates
(B) negotiate
(C) negotiated
(D) negotiating

만약 집주인이 임대료를 너무 높게 부과한다는 것을 입증한다면 임대 지불을 협의할 수 있을지도 모른다.

해설 빈칸은 be able to 뒤에 어울리는 단어가 들어갈 자리이다. <be able to + 동사>구조를 알고 있다면 쉽게 해결되는 문제이다. 정답은 (B) negotiate(협상하다)이다.

어휘 prove 입증하다 landlord 주인, 임대주 payment 지불 금액

126

Southbank Park's plans to build a movie studio and a fancy hotel should bring ------- revenue to the city.
(A) increased
(B) designated
(C) renovated
(D) managed

영화 스튜디오나 화려한 호텔을 건설하는 Southbank Park의 계획은 증가된 수익을 도시에 가져온다.

해설 빈칸은 뒤의 명사 revenue(수익)와 의미연결이 자연스러운 형용사자리이다. 선택지 중에서 의미가 자연스럽게 연결되는 단어는 increased(증가된)이다. bring increased revenue to the city 증가된 수익을 도시에 가져오다

어휘 studio 제작소 fancy 화려한, 고급의 revenue 수익 increased 증가된 designated 지정된 renovated 수리된

127

Today's businesses have large volumes of critical data that must be protected and ------- at a moment's notice.
(A) constant
(B) useful
(C) competent
(D) accessible

오늘날의 회사들은 순식간에 보호되고 접근될 수 있는 대량의 중대한 정보를 가진다.

해설 빈칸은 관계대명사 that 앞의 선행사인 critical data(자료)와 의미 연결이 적절한 형용사가 들어갈 자리이다. '자료는 보호되고 바로 접근 가능해야 한다'는 의미가 적절하므로 (D) accessible(접근 가능한)이 정답이다.

어휘 volume 양 critical 중요한 at a moment's notice 순식간에, 즉시, 곧바로 constant 지속적인 useful 유용한 competent 유능한, 능력 있는

128

The inventory system, ------- is used to keep track of items in stock, enables warehouse supervisors to order out of stock items immediately online.
(A) that
(B) who
(C) whom
(D) which

재고가 있는 물건을 추적하는데 사용되는 재고시스템은, 창고관리자가 재고 없는 아이템을 즉시 온라인으로 주문하는 것을 가능하게 합니다.

해설 빈칸은 명사 system을 선행사로 취하는 관계대명사자리이다. 사물 주격 관계대명사로 which와 that이 가능하지만, 관계대명사 that은 콤마 뒤에 쓸 수 없으므로 탈락이다. 그래서 정답은 (D) which이다.

어휘 inventory 재고 keep track of 추적하다 in stock 재고가 있는 out of stock 재고가 없는

129

If you require ------- information concerning Mr. Brady's eligibility as a candidate for the senior managerial position, please contact our office without any hesitation.
(A) one
(B) many
(C) every
(D) more

만약 당신이 부서 매니저 직책을 위한 지원자로서 Brady 씨의 적격성에 대한 더 많은 정보를 요구한다면, 우리 사무실에 주저 없이 연락 주십시오.

해설 빈칸은 information 앞에 의미가 어울리는 형용사가 들어갈 자리이다. information(정보)은 셀 수 없는 명사로, 수치 개념의 one, many, every와 연결될 수 없다. 그래서 (D) more(더 많은)가 정답이다.

어휘 concerning ~에 관한 eligibility 적임, 적격 senior 선임 without hesitation 주저 없이

130

As a director of sales and marketing, Mr. Richards has often travelled to Taiwan, ------- to Taipei.
(A) relatively
(B) primarily
(C) temporarily
(D) yet

판매와 마케팅이사로서, Richards 씨는 자주 Taiwan으로 여행을 갔지만 대부분은 Taipei로 여행을 갔다.

해설 빈칸은 의미가 적절한 부사가 들어갈 자리이다. 빈칸 앞에 Taiwan(대만) 그리고 뒤에 to Taipei(타이베이로)라고 되므로, 이 사이에 의미가 어울리는 부사는 primarily(주로)이다.

어휘 relatively 상대적으로 primarily 주로 temporarily 일시적으로, 임시로

Questions 131-134 refer to the following report.

Kelvin Hotels has successfully ------- from a local, family-owned
131.
hotel to a nationally known franchise of luxury business-class
hotels. ------- the business started, its low rates and proximity
132.
to major interstates attracted many truck drivers and long-
distance motorists. -------. Capital Hotels then refurbished all
133.
the rooms, built new hotels near major airports in the state,
and raised rates by about 50%. Since that time, about 60% of
Kelvin Hotel's guests have been from the corporate sector. The
business is highly profitable and plans to expand to the Midwest
and Western areas of the country soon. Partnerships with travel
agencies ------- this expansion.
134.

Kelvin Hotels는 지방의 가족 소유 호텔에서 전국의 호화로운 프랜차이즈 호텔로 성공적으로 변했다. 사업을 시작했을 때, 적은 비용과 주간 도로로의 인접성은 많은 트럭 운전자들과 장거리 운전자들에게 매력적이었다. 하지만 8년간의 침체된 수입 끝에, 소유주들은 그 사업을 Capital Hotels Group에 매각하기로 결정했다. Capital Hotels는 모든 방을 재단장했고 그 주에서 주요 공항과 가까운 곳에 새로운 호텔을 지었고 비용을 50% 가까이 올렸다. 그때 이후로 약 60%에 가까운 Kelvin Hotel의 손님들이 기업 분야로부터 생겨났다. 그 사업은 매우 수익성이 높아서 곧 중서부와 서부 지역으로 확장할 계획이다. 여행사와의 제휴관계는 이러한 확장을 촉진시켰다.

어휘 family-owned 가족에 의해 운영되는 proximity 가까움, 근접 interstate 주간도로 refurbish 재단장하다 sector 분야 profitable 수익성 expansion 확장

131
(A) used
(B) operated
(C) differed
(D) changed

해설 빈칸 뒤로 전치사 from이 이어지고 있기 때문에 빈칸에는 자동사가 와야 한다. 선택지 중 자동사의 쓰임도 있으며 특히 빈칸 뒤의 구조 from A to B와 상응하는 선택지는 (D)이다. change from A to B는 'A에서 B로 변화하다'로 해석한다.

132
(A) When
(B) Although
(C) However
(D) During

해설 빈칸 뒤로 문장이 이어지고 있으므로 빈칸은 접속사자리이다. 전치사인 (D)와 접속부사인 (C)는 제외한다. 물론 (C) however는 접속사의 쓰임이 있긴 하지만 그 경우 형용사나 부사가 바로 뒤에 따라야 하므로 여기서는 정답이 될 수 없다. 나머지 접속사 (A)와 (B) 중에서 문맥상 사업이 시작할 때 당시의 상황이 설명되고 있기 때문에 정답은 (A) When이 적절하다.

133

(A) However, after 8 consecutive years of sagging revenues, the owners decided to sell the business to Capital Hotels Group Co.
(B) After talking with Boston Consulting Group, Kelvin Hotel has recently decided to upgrade its facility.
(C) All the staff of Kelvin Hotel were extremely friendly and eager to make customers comfortable.
(D) Kelvin Hotel became much more popular to residents and tourists alike.

해설 빈칸 앞으로는 매각되기 전의 호텔에 대한 설명이 있었고 빈칸 뒤로는 매각되고 난 후의 호텔에 대한 설명이 이어지므로 빈칸에서는 매각이 이어지게 된 이유와 과정이 들어가야 한다.

(A) 하지만 8년간의 침체된 수입 끝에, 소유주들은 그 사업을 Capital Hotels Group에 매각하기로 결정했다.
(B) Boston Consulting Group과 대화를 마친 후, Kelvin Hotel은 최근에 시설을 업그레이드하기로 결정했다.
(C) Kelvin Hotel의 모든 직원들은 매우 친절하고 고객들을 편안하게 만들기를 원했다.
(D) Kelvin Hotel은 주민들과 관광객들에게 훨씬 더 인기가 많아졌다.

134

(A) facilitates
(B) are facilitated
(C) will be facilitated
(D) have facilitated

해설 문장의 주어인 Partnerships와 우선 수일치를 하여 단수동사인 (A)를 제외시킨다. 빈칸 뒤로 this expansion이라는 명사 목적어가 따라 나오고 있으므로 능동태 동사인 (D)가 정답이 된다.

ACTUAL TEST 06 ACTUAL TEST 07 ACTUAL TEST 08 ACTUAL TEST 09 ACTUAL TEST 10

Caldwell Motors has distributed a maintenance manual for its new Camry sedan. The Camry 3.2 liter model has been recalled ------- an issue related to its transmission system. In this latest
135.
model, the engine seems to speed up ------- when the car is
136.
shifted into neutral gear.

Representatives of Caldwell point out that the problem is not hazardous and that no accidents or injuries have happened as a result of the malfunction, but they encourage owners to bring their cars to the nearest Caldwell service center. Caldwell technicians have been trained to fix the problem.

-------. Free rental vehicles will be provided while the cars are
137.
at the service center. Caldwell has issued an official apology to its customers. Owners of the affected cars will receive a written notice ------- the next month.
138.

Caldwell Motors는 새로운 Camry 세단용 유지관리 매뉴얼을 배포했다. Camry 3.2리터 모델은 변속기 시스템 문제 때문에 회수되었다. 이 최신 모델에서 엔진이 중립 기어로 이동할 때 엔진이 불필요하게 속도를 올리는 것처럼 보인다.

Caldwell의 직원들은 그 문제가 위험하지 않고 오작동의 결과로 사고나 부상은 일어나지 않았다고 지적했으나 소유주들이 차를 가장 가까운 Caldwell 서비스센터로 가져가도록 장려한다. Caldwell 기술자들은 이 문제를 고치기 위해 훈련받았다.

제조업체는 이 리콜과 관련된 모든 비용을 부담할 것이다. 차들이 서비스센터에 있는 동안 무료 렌트카가 제공될 것이다. Caldwell은 고객들에게 공식적인 사과를 했다. 이 문제가 있는 차들의 소유주들은 다음 달 안으로 서면 통지서를 받게 될 것이다.

어휘 maintenance 유지, 보수관리 related to ~와 관련 있는 transmission 전파, 전달 shift 바꾸다 neutral 중립, 중립의 representative 대표 hazardous 위험한 malfunction 고장, 기능 불량

135
(A) since
(B) due to
(C) as for
(D) among

해설 적절한 전치사 어휘를 고르는 문제이다. 자동차가 리콜 된 것은 변속기와 관련된 문제 때문이므로 이유의 전치사 (B)가 정답이다. (A) since는 접속사일 때 '~ 이래로'와 '~ 때문에'라는 의미이지만 전치사일 때는 '~이래로'라는 의미밖에 없다는 점에 주의하자.

136
(A) unnecessariness
(B) unnecessarily
(C) unnecessity
(D) unnecessary

해설 빈칸 앞의 speed up은 그 자체로 '가속하다'라는 의미의 자동사이므로 빈칸 뒤에 목적어는 불필요하다. 자동사 뒤에 위치할 수 있는 부사인 (B)가 정답이다.

137

(A) The manufacturer isn't responsible for technical flaws at all.
(B) Therefore, fixing the vehicle may require your expense.
(C) The manufacturer will cover all expenses associated with this recall.
(D) Unfortunately, the Caldwell service center in your area was closed only last year.

해설 전체적으로 차량의 리콜에 관한 내용이 주를 이루고 있다. 특정 자동차 모델에 제조상의 결함이 있어 리콜을 하므로 제조업체가 모든 비용을 지불하겠다는 내용이 적절하다.

(A) 제조업체는 기술적 결함에 대해 전혀 책임이 없다.
(B) 따라서 차량을 수리하는 데에는 비용이 들 수 있다.
(C) 제조업체는 이 리콜과 관련된 모든 비용을 부담할 것이다.
(D) 불행하게도 당신 지역의 Caldwell 서비스센터는 작년에 문을 닫았다.

138

(A) between
(B) among
(C) along
(D) within

해설 빈칸 뒤로 기간명사인 the next month가 있다. 그러므로 빈칸은 기간을 나타내는 전치사 (D)가 적절하다. 나머지 오답들은 모두 전치사이기는 하지만 기간 앞 전치사로는 사용하지 않는다.

Questions 139-142 refer to the following e-mail.

To: Nicole Cassidy

From: Murphey Harison

Date: April 6

Subject: Re: Recommendations

Nicole,

I'll be glad to assist you as much as I can. I'm assuming that you're intending to do a bit of research on London before you leave. When you get there, you should really try to go to a couple of places that are of cultural and historical importance. This will give you an ------- to have some interesting and
139.
pleasant conversations with your business colleagues.

-------. You should always keep this in mind because it is crucial
140.
that you are always on time for your appointments.

------- your negotiations start, be ready to ------- them with a
141.   **142.**
generous spirit of give and take. Perhaps you should determine beforehand - with the help of your supervisor - exactly what sort of compromises you are prepared to make.

Have a wonderful trip. We'll see you at the next staff meeting.

수신: Nicole Cassidy

발신: Murphey Harison

날짜: 4월 6일

제목: Re: 추천

Nicole,

내가 할 수 있는 한 기꺼이 도와줄게. 나는 네가 떠나기 전에 런던에 대해 약간의 조사를 할 거라고 생각해. 그곳에 도착했을 때, 너는 반드시 문화적으로 그리고 역사적으로 중요한 몇 곳을 가봐야 해. 이것은 너에게 사업 동료들과 즐겁고 흥미로운 대화를 나눌 기회를 줄 거야.

난 런던에서 교통이 가끔 큰 문제가 될 수 있다고 주의를 줘야겠어. 네가 항상 약속에 제시간에 도착하는 것은 중요하기 때문에 이 점을 항상 유의해야 해. 일단 협상이 시작되면, 너그러운 마음으로 그것들을 실행할 준비가 되어있어야 해. 아마도 너는 미리 결정해야 할 거야 – 상사의 도움과 함께 – 정확히 어떤 종류의 타협을 할 준비를 해야 하는지를.

즐거운 여행이 되길 바란다. 다음 직원회의 때 봐.

어휘 assume 추정하다 importance 중요성 crucial 중대한 negotiation 협상 conduct 하다 generous 너그러운 spirit 마음

139
(A) observation
(B) operation
(C) originality
(D) opportunity

해설 빈칸 뒤의 to부정사가 단서표현으로 사용되었다. 선택지의 명사들 중 to부정사의 수식을 받을 수 있는 명사는 (D)가 유일하다. an opportunity to do는 '~할 기회'로 해석된다. 그 외에 to부정사의 수식을 받는 명사로는 chance(기회), ability(능력), time(시간), way(방법) 등이 있다.

140
(A) I enjoyed the holidays with my family in London.
(B) Please let me know if you have problems with traffic.
(C) London is such a wonderful city, and there are many amazing places to visit.
(D) I should warn you that traffic can sometimes be a great problem in London.

해설 빈칸 뒤로 약속시간을 엄수하는 것이 아주 중요하다는 언급이 있다. 그렇기 때문에 반드시 명심해야(keep in mind) 할 것은 (D)로 런던에서의 교통이 큰 문제가 될 수 있다는 점이다.

(A) 나는 런던에서 가족들과 휴가를 즐겼어.
(B) 교통 체증에 문제가 생기면 알려줘.
(C) 런던은 정말 멋진 도시고 방문할 만한 멋진 장소들이 많아.
(D) 나는 런던에서 교통이 가끔 큰 문제가 될 수 있다고 주의를 줘야겠어.

141
(A) whereas
(B) once
(C) provided
(D) however

해설 빈칸 뒤로 문장이 이어지고 있기 때문에 빈칸은 접속사자리가 되며 형용사나 부사가 뒤따르지 않고는 접속사로 사용할 수 없는 (D)는 우선 제외된다. 문맥상 '일단 협상이 시작하고 나면 너그러운 마음으로 협상을 진행하라'고 연결하는 것이 매끄러우므로 정답은 (B)가 된다. 참고로 접속사 once는 '일단 ~하고 나서'라는 의미로 단순히 '~하면'이라고 기억해 if와 혼동하지 않도록 유의한다.

142
(A) install
(B) repair
(C) conduct
(D) acquaint

해설 빈칸 다음에 them을 목적어로 취하는 동사어휘를 선택하는 문제이다. 목적격 them은 negotiations(협상)이므로 '협상을 실행하다'가 적절하므로 정답은 (C) conduct이다.

Questions 143-146 refer to the following letter.

February 5, 2020
 	
Ms. Mia Grathan
 	
BMC Motors Incorporation
 	
Oxford St., London, England
 	
Dear Madam
 	
Thank you very much for bringing this matter to our attention. The message ------- in your letter truly inspired us to do better.
    143.
------- the management and staff, I personally apologize for
144.
the incorrect information that was published on January 13 in Today's News. I assure you that we will publish a corrected article and apologize to you in print.
 	
We hope this will ------- all your concerns regarding this matter
    145.
and we will ensure this will not happen again in the future.
-------. Just send us a copy of your advertisement and the
146.
specific date you intended to publish it.
 	
Respectfully yours,
 	
Tess Carter
 	
Editor-in–Chief
 	
Today's News
	2020년 2월 5일
	Mia Grathan 씨
	BMC Motors Incorporation
	Oxford St., London, England
	
	부인께,
	
	이 문제에 우리가 주의를 기울이도록 해주셔서 감사드립니다. 당신의 편지에 포함된 메시지는 우리가 더 잘 하도록 진심으로 격려를 해주었습니다. 경영진과 직원들을 대신하여, 1월 13일, Today's news에 발표된 잘못된 정보에 대해 개인적으로 사과를 드립니다. 저는 우리가 수정된 기사를 출간할 것이고 지면으로 당신에게 사과드릴 것을 보장합니다.
	
	저희는 이것이 이 문제에 대한 당신의 모든 우려를 해결하길 바라고 이러한 일이 미래에는 다시는 일어나지 않도록 확실히 할 것입니다.
	
	이번에는 당신의 사업 요구사항에 맞는 무료 광고 공간을 제공하고자 합니다. 광고의 사본과 구체적으로 원하는 출간 날짜를 저희에게 보내주시기 바랍니다.
	
	존경을 담아
	
	Tess Carter
	편집장
	Today's News

어휘 inspire 격려하다 assure 장담하다, 확인하다 mean ~을 의도하다 concern 염려하다 ensure 보장하다 specific 구체적인 intend to ~할 작정이다, ~하려고 생각하다

143
(A) was contained
(B) is to be contained
(C) contained
(D) to contain

해설 빈칸이 속한 문장에서 동사는 inspired이기 때문에 빈칸은 동사자리가 될 수 없다. 그러므로 일단 동사인 선택지 (A)와 (B)는 제외한다. 빈칸은 명사 the message를 후치 수식하는 형용사자리인데 빈칸 뒤로 목적어가 없기 때문에 목적어가 필요한 to부정사 (D)는 정답이 될 수 없다. 그러므로 전치사구를 이끌고 명사를 후치 수식할 수 있는 과거분사 (C)가 정답이다.

144
(A) Instead
(B) Despite
(C) On behalf of
(D) Owing to

해설 회사를 대표하여 회사의 실수를 사과하고 있으므로 '~를 대신하여', 혹은 '~를 대표하여'라는 의미의 (C) On behalf of가 가장 잘 어울린다.

145
(A) approximate
(B) address
(C) streamline
(D) satisfy

해설 목적어인 concerns(우려, 관심)와 어울리는 동사어휘를 찾는다. 회사 측의 실수에 대한 사과와 해결 방법을 앞서 언급했으므로 이것이 당신의 '우려를 해결하다'라는 의미로 연결하는 것이 가장 적절하다. 특히 정답인 동사 address는 명사로 '주소'라는 의미가 있긴 하지만 토익에서는 주로 동사로 '(문제나 우려 따위를) 해결하다' 또는 '연설하다'라는 의미로 사용된다.

146
(A) Also, you can get some discounts at our local shops when you present the coupon accompanied with this flyer.
(B) We recognized that your advertisement was eligible to be posted in Today's News.
(C) We specialize in designing advertisement at reasonable prices.
(D) At this time we would also like to offer you a complimentary advertising space of 1 column for your business needs.

해설 빈칸 앞으로는 잘못된 정보에 대한 사과를 전하며 수정 기사를 내고 지면상으로 사과를 전하겠다는 내용만 볼 수 있고 광고에 관한 언급은 찾을 수 없다. 하지만 빈칸 뒤로 광고와 그 광고를 발행할 구체적인 날짜를 전달해달라고 언급하고 있다. 빈칸에는 사과의 의미로 무료로 광고를 내주겠다는 내용이 들어가야 적절하다.

(A) 또한, 당신은 이 전단지에 있는 쿠폰을 제시할 때 저희 지역 매장에서 할인을 받을 수 있습니다.
(B) 우리는 당신의 광고가 Today's news에 게재될 자격이 있다는 것을 인식했습니다.
(C) 우리는 합리적인 가격으로 광고를 디자인하는 것을 전문으로 합니다.
(D) 이번에는 당신의 사업 요구사항에 맞는 무료 광고 공간을 제공하고자 합니다.

259

Actual Test 01

101	(C)	108	(A)	115	(A)	122	(A)	129	(D)	136	(A)	143	(B)
102	(A)	109	(D)	116	(A)	123	(C)	130	(A)	137	(D)	144	(C)
103	(C)	110	(A)	117	(A)	124	(B)	131	(B)	138	(C)	145	(D)
104	(D)	111	(C)	118	(C)	125	(A)	132	(A)	139	(C)	146	(C)
105	(B)	112	(A)	119	(A)	126	(D)	133	(C)	140	(B)		
106	(B)	113	(C)	120	(B)	127	(C)	134	(D)	141	(C)		
107	(B)	114	(B)	121	(A)	128	(A)	135	(C)	142	(D)		

Actual Test 02

101	(B)	108	(C)	115	(A)	122	(B)	129	(B)	136	(C)	143	(C)
102	(A)	109	(D)	116	(A)	123	(B)	130	(D)	137	(C)	144	(D)
103	(D)	110	(D)	117	(A)	124	(A)	131	(A)	138	(C)	145	(D)
104	(B)	111	(A)	118	(B)	125	(C)	132	(D)	139	(A)	146	(C)
105	(A)	112	(D)	119	(C)	126	(D)	133	(A)	140	(A)		
106	(B)	113	(B)	120	(B)	127	(C)	134	(D)	141	(C)		
107	(B)	114	(C)	121	(B)	128	(D)	135	(A)	142	(B)		

Actual Test 03

101	(B)	108	(A)	115	(B)	122	(A)	129	(A)	136	(A)	143	(D)
102	(C)	109	(D)	116	(A)	123	(C)	130	(D)	137	(D)	144	(B)
103	(C)	110	(A)	117	(C)	124	(A)	131	(A)	138	(C)	145	(A)
104	(C)	111	(B)	118	(A)	125	(B)	132	(D)	139	(D)	146	(B)
105	(D)	112	(C)	119	(A)	126	(D)	133	(D)	140	(A)		
106	(D)	113	(A)	120	(D)	127	(B)	134	(B)	141	(B)		
107	(C)	114	(A)	121	(C)	128	(D)	135	(C)	142	(B)		

Actual Test 04

101	(A)	108	(C)	115	(B)	122	(A)	129	(A)	136	(A)	143	(A)
102	(D)	109	(B)	116	(A)	123	(B)	130	(A)	137	(C)	144	(B)
103	(C)	110	(D)	117	(D)	124	(C)	131	(C)	138	(B)	145	(C)
104	(D)	111	(D)	118	(B)	125	(B)	132	(A)	139	(C)	146	(A)
105	(C)	112	(D)	119	(C)	126	(D)	133	(D)	140	(B)		
106	(C)	113	(C)	120	(B)	127	(A)	134	(A)	141	(A)		
107	(C)	114	(A)	121	(A)	128	(A)	135	(A)	142	(B)		

Actual Test 05

101	(C)	108	(D)	115	(B)	122	(B)	129	(C)	136	(C)	143	(A)
102	(B)	109	(C)	116	(C)	123	(A)	130	(A)	137	(C)	144	(D)
103	(C)	110	(A)	117	(D)	124	(B)	131	(A)	138	(D)	145	(C)
104	(A)	111	(B)	118	(D)	125	(D)	132	(C)	139	(A)	146	(C)
105	(A)	112	(A)	119	(A)	126	(D)	133	(C)	140	(B)		
106	(A)	113	(D)	120	(B)	127	(A)	134	(C)	141	(A)		
107	(C)	114	(C)	121	(D)	128	(C)	135	(A)	142	(B)		

Actual Test 06

No.	Ans	No.	Ans	No.	Ans	No.	Ans	No.	Ans	No.	Ans	No.	Ans
101	(A)	108	(A)	115	(B)	122	(B)	129	(D)	136	(D)	143	(C)
102	(D)	109	(A)	116	(D)	123	(A)	130	(B)	137	(A)	144	(A)
103	(C)	110	(D)	117	(D)	124	(C)	131	(C)	138	(B)	145	(D)
104	(C)	111	(A)	118	(A)	125	(D)	132	(A)	139	(A)	146	(A)
105	(D)	112	(A)	119	(B)	126	(D)	133	(C)	140	(B)		
106	(D)	113	(C)	120	(D)	127	(D)	134	(B)	141	(A)		
107	(C)	114	(A)	121	(C)	128	(A)	135	(C)	142	(C)		

Actual Test 07

No.	Ans	No.	Ans	No.	Ans	No.	Ans	No.	Ans	No.	Ans	No.	Ans
101	(B)	108	(B)	115	(B)	122	(D)	129	(B)	136	(A)	143	(B)
102	(D)	109	(B)	116	(C)	123	(B)	130	(D)	137	(D)	144	(B)
103	(B)	110	(B)	117	(B)	124	(B)	131	(A)	138	(A)	145	(D)
104	(B)	111	(B)	118	(A)	125	(A)	132	(A)	139	(B)	146	(A)
105	(B)	112	(D)	119	(D)	126	(D)	133	(C)	140	(D)		
106	(C)	113	(D)	120	(A)	127	(B)	134	(A)	141	(B)		
107	(D)	114	(A)	121	(D)	128	(A)	135	(A)	142	(D)		

Actual Test 08

No.	Ans	No.	Ans	No.	Ans	No.	Ans	No.	Ans	No.	Ans	No.	Ans
101	(C)	108	(D)	115	(D)	122	(C)	129	(D)	136	(D)	143	(D)
102	(C)	109	(A)	116	(D)	123	(B)	130	(D)	137	(C)	144	(C)
103	(D)	110	(D)	117	(A)	124	(A)	131	(D)	138	(A)	145	(B)
104	(C)	111	(A)	118	(D)	125	(D)	132	(B)	139	(B)	146	(D)
105	(B)	112	(A)	119	(C)	126	(A)	133	(B)	140	(C)		
106	(A)	113	(C)	120	(C)	127	(C)	134	(D)	141	(C)		
107	(C)	114	(A)	121	(D)	128	(B)	135	(D)	142	(A)		

Actual Test 09

No.	Ans	No.	Ans	No.	Ans	No.	Ans	No.	Ans	No.	Ans	No.	Ans
101	(C)	108	(B)	115	(D)	122	(A)	129	(A)	136	(C)	143	(C)
102	(B)	109	(A)	116	(A)	123	(C)	130	(A)	137	(D)	144	(A)
103	(B)	110	(B)	117	(A)	124	(B)	131	(A)	138	(B)	145	(B)
104	(A)	111	(A)	118	(D)	125	(B)	132	(D)	139	(B)	146	(A)
105	(C)	112	(C)	119	(B)	126	(D)	133	(D)	140	(B)		
106	(A)	113	(C)	120	(D)	127	(A)	134	(C)	141	(C)		
107	(C)	114	(D)	121	(D)	128	(C)	135	(B)	142	(C)		

Actual Test 10

No.	Ans	No.	Ans	No.	Ans	No.	Ans	No.	Ans	No.	Ans	No.	Ans
101	(C)	108	(D)	115	(B)	122	(D)	129	(D)	136	(B)	143	(C)
102	(A)	109	(D)	116	(B)	123	(C)	130	(B)	137	(C)	144	(C)
103	(B)	110	(A)	117	(D)	124	(A)	131	(D)	138	(D)	145	(B)
104	(B)	111	(B)	118	(D)	125	(B)	132	(A)	139	(D)	146	(D)
105	(B)	112	(B)	119	(A)	126	(A)	133	(A)	140	(D)		
106	(D)	113	(C)	120	(D)	127	(D)	134	(D)	141	(B)		
107	(A)	114	(D)	121	(B)	128	(D)	135	(B)	142	(C)		

ANSWER SHEET

Reading Comprehension Part V, Part VI

No.	A	B	C	D	No.	A	B	C	D	No.	A	B	C	D	No.	A	B	C	D	No.	A	B	C	D
101	Ⓐ	Ⓑ	Ⓒ	Ⓓ	111	Ⓐ	Ⓑ	Ⓒ	Ⓓ	121	Ⓐ	Ⓑ	Ⓒ	Ⓓ	131	Ⓐ	Ⓑ	Ⓒ	Ⓓ	141	Ⓐ	Ⓑ	Ⓒ	Ⓓ
102	Ⓐ	Ⓑ	Ⓒ	Ⓓ	112	Ⓐ	Ⓑ	Ⓒ	Ⓓ	122	Ⓐ	Ⓑ	Ⓒ	Ⓓ	132	Ⓐ	Ⓑ	Ⓒ	Ⓓ	142	Ⓐ	Ⓑ	Ⓒ	Ⓓ
103	Ⓐ	Ⓑ	Ⓒ	Ⓓ	113	Ⓐ	Ⓑ	Ⓒ	Ⓓ	123	Ⓐ	Ⓑ	Ⓒ	Ⓓ	133	Ⓐ	Ⓑ	Ⓒ	Ⓓ	143	Ⓐ	Ⓑ	Ⓒ	Ⓓ
104	Ⓐ	Ⓑ	Ⓒ	Ⓓ	114	Ⓐ	Ⓑ	Ⓒ	Ⓓ	124	Ⓐ	Ⓑ	Ⓒ	Ⓓ	134	Ⓐ	Ⓑ	Ⓒ	Ⓓ	144	Ⓐ	Ⓑ	Ⓒ	Ⓓ
105	Ⓐ	Ⓑ	Ⓒ	Ⓓ	115	Ⓐ	Ⓑ	Ⓒ	Ⓓ	125	Ⓐ	Ⓑ	Ⓒ	Ⓓ	135	Ⓐ	Ⓑ	Ⓒ	Ⓓ	145	Ⓐ	Ⓑ	Ⓒ	Ⓓ
106	Ⓐ	Ⓑ	Ⓒ	Ⓓ	116	Ⓐ	Ⓑ	Ⓒ	Ⓓ	126	Ⓐ	Ⓑ	Ⓒ	Ⓓ	135	Ⓐ	Ⓑ	Ⓒ	Ⓓ	146	Ⓐ	Ⓑ	Ⓒ	Ⓓ
107	Ⓐ	Ⓑ	Ⓒ	Ⓓ	117	Ⓐ	Ⓑ	Ⓒ	Ⓓ	127	Ⓐ	Ⓑ	Ⓒ	Ⓓ	137	Ⓐ	Ⓑ	Ⓒ	Ⓓ					
108	Ⓐ	Ⓑ	Ⓒ	Ⓓ	118	Ⓐ	Ⓑ	Ⓒ	Ⓓ	128	Ⓐ	Ⓑ	Ⓒ	Ⓓ	138	Ⓐ	Ⓑ	Ⓒ	Ⓓ					
109	Ⓐ	Ⓑ	Ⓒ	Ⓓ	119	Ⓐ	Ⓑ	Ⓒ	Ⓓ	129	Ⓐ	Ⓑ	Ⓒ	Ⓓ	139	Ⓐ	Ⓑ	Ⓒ	Ⓓ					
110	Ⓐ	Ⓑ	Ⓒ	Ⓓ	120	Ⓐ	Ⓑ	Ⓒ	Ⓓ	130	Ⓐ	Ⓑ	Ⓒ	Ⓓ	140	Ⓐ	Ⓑ	Ⓒ	Ⓓ					

ANSWER SHEET

Reading Comprehension Part V, Part VI

No.	A	B	C	D	No.	A	B	C	D	No.	A	B	C	D	No.	A	B	C	D	No.	A	B	C	D
101	Ⓐ	Ⓑ	Ⓒ	Ⓓ	111	Ⓐ	Ⓑ	Ⓒ	Ⓓ	121	Ⓐ	Ⓑ	Ⓒ	Ⓓ	131	Ⓐ	Ⓑ	Ⓒ	Ⓓ	141	Ⓐ	Ⓑ	Ⓒ	Ⓓ
102	Ⓐ	Ⓑ	Ⓒ	Ⓓ	112	Ⓐ	Ⓑ	Ⓒ	Ⓓ	122	Ⓐ	Ⓑ	Ⓒ	Ⓓ	132	Ⓐ	Ⓑ	Ⓒ	Ⓓ	142	Ⓐ	Ⓑ	Ⓒ	Ⓓ
103	Ⓐ	Ⓑ	Ⓒ	Ⓓ	113	Ⓐ	Ⓑ	Ⓒ	Ⓓ	123	Ⓐ	Ⓑ	Ⓒ	Ⓓ	133	Ⓐ	Ⓑ	Ⓒ	Ⓓ	143	Ⓐ	Ⓑ	Ⓒ	Ⓓ
104	Ⓐ	Ⓑ	Ⓒ	Ⓓ	114	Ⓐ	Ⓑ	Ⓒ	Ⓓ	124	Ⓐ	Ⓑ	Ⓒ	Ⓓ	134	Ⓐ	Ⓑ	Ⓒ	Ⓓ	144	Ⓐ	Ⓑ	Ⓒ	Ⓓ
105	Ⓐ	Ⓑ	Ⓒ	Ⓓ	115	Ⓐ	Ⓑ	Ⓒ	Ⓓ	125	Ⓐ	Ⓑ	Ⓒ	Ⓓ	135	Ⓐ	Ⓑ	Ⓒ	Ⓓ	145	Ⓐ	Ⓑ	Ⓒ	Ⓓ
106	Ⓐ	Ⓑ	Ⓒ	Ⓓ	116	Ⓐ	Ⓑ	Ⓒ	Ⓓ	126	Ⓐ	Ⓑ	Ⓒ	Ⓓ	135	Ⓐ	Ⓑ	Ⓒ	Ⓓ	146	Ⓐ	Ⓑ	Ⓒ	Ⓓ
107	Ⓐ	Ⓑ	Ⓒ	Ⓓ	117	Ⓐ	Ⓑ	Ⓒ	Ⓓ	127	Ⓐ	Ⓑ	Ⓒ	Ⓓ	137	Ⓐ	Ⓑ	Ⓒ	Ⓓ					
108	Ⓐ	Ⓑ	Ⓒ	Ⓓ	118	Ⓐ	Ⓑ	Ⓒ	Ⓓ	128	Ⓐ	Ⓑ	Ⓒ	Ⓓ	138	Ⓐ	Ⓑ	Ⓒ	Ⓓ					
109	Ⓐ	Ⓑ	Ⓒ	Ⓓ	119	Ⓐ	Ⓑ	Ⓒ	Ⓓ	129	Ⓐ	Ⓑ	Ⓒ	Ⓓ	139	Ⓐ	Ⓑ	Ⓒ	Ⓓ					
110	Ⓐ	Ⓑ	Ⓒ	Ⓓ	120	Ⓐ	Ⓑ	Ⓒ	Ⓓ	130	Ⓐ	Ⓑ	Ⓒ	Ⓓ	140	Ⓐ	Ⓑ	Ⓒ	Ⓓ					

ANSWER SHEET

Reading Comprehension Part V, Part VI

No.	A	B	C	D	No.	A	B	C	D	No.	A	B	C	D	No.	A	B	C	D	No.	A	B	C	D
101	Ⓐ	Ⓑ	Ⓒ	Ⓓ	111	Ⓐ	Ⓑ	Ⓒ	Ⓓ	121	Ⓐ	Ⓑ	Ⓒ	Ⓓ	131	Ⓐ	Ⓑ	Ⓒ	Ⓓ	141	Ⓐ	Ⓑ	Ⓒ	Ⓓ
102	Ⓐ	Ⓑ	Ⓒ	Ⓓ	112	Ⓐ	Ⓑ	Ⓒ	Ⓓ	122	Ⓐ	Ⓑ	Ⓒ	Ⓓ	132	Ⓐ	Ⓑ	Ⓒ	Ⓓ	142	Ⓐ	Ⓑ	Ⓒ	Ⓓ
103	Ⓐ	Ⓑ	Ⓒ	Ⓓ	113	Ⓐ	Ⓑ	Ⓒ	Ⓓ	123	Ⓐ	Ⓑ	Ⓒ	Ⓓ	133	Ⓐ	Ⓑ	Ⓒ	Ⓓ	143	Ⓐ	Ⓑ	Ⓒ	Ⓓ
104	Ⓐ	Ⓑ	Ⓒ	Ⓓ	114	Ⓐ	Ⓑ	Ⓒ	Ⓓ	124	Ⓐ	Ⓑ	Ⓒ	Ⓓ	134	Ⓐ	Ⓑ	Ⓒ	Ⓓ	144	Ⓐ	Ⓑ	Ⓒ	Ⓓ
105	Ⓐ	Ⓑ	Ⓒ	Ⓓ	115	Ⓐ	Ⓑ	Ⓒ	Ⓓ	125	Ⓐ	Ⓑ	Ⓒ	Ⓓ	135	Ⓐ	Ⓑ	Ⓒ	Ⓓ	145	Ⓐ	Ⓑ	Ⓒ	Ⓓ
106	Ⓐ	Ⓑ	Ⓒ	Ⓓ	116	Ⓐ	Ⓑ	Ⓒ	Ⓓ	126	Ⓐ	Ⓑ	Ⓒ	Ⓓ	135	Ⓐ	Ⓑ	Ⓒ	Ⓓ	146	Ⓐ	Ⓑ	Ⓒ	Ⓓ
107	Ⓐ	Ⓑ	Ⓒ	Ⓓ	117	Ⓐ	Ⓑ	Ⓒ	Ⓓ	127	Ⓐ	Ⓑ	Ⓒ	Ⓓ	137	Ⓐ	Ⓑ	Ⓒ	Ⓓ					
108	Ⓐ	Ⓑ	Ⓒ	Ⓓ	118	Ⓐ	Ⓑ	Ⓒ	Ⓓ	128	Ⓐ	Ⓑ	Ⓒ	Ⓓ	138	Ⓐ	Ⓑ	Ⓒ	Ⓓ					
109	Ⓐ	Ⓑ	Ⓒ	Ⓓ	119	Ⓐ	Ⓑ	Ⓒ	Ⓓ	129	Ⓐ	Ⓑ	Ⓒ	Ⓓ	139	Ⓐ	Ⓑ	Ⓒ	Ⓓ					
110	Ⓐ	Ⓑ	Ⓒ	Ⓓ	120	Ⓐ	Ⓑ	Ⓒ	Ⓓ	130	Ⓐ	Ⓑ	Ⓒ	Ⓓ	140	Ⓐ	Ⓑ	Ⓒ	Ⓓ					

ANSWER SHEET

Reading Comprehension Part V, Part VI

No.	A	B	C	D	No.	A	B	C	D	No.	A	B	C	D	No.	A	B	C	D	No.	A	B	C	D
101	Ⓐ	Ⓑ	Ⓒ	Ⓓ	111	Ⓐ	Ⓑ	Ⓒ	Ⓓ	121	Ⓐ	Ⓑ	Ⓒ	Ⓓ	131	Ⓐ	Ⓑ	Ⓒ	Ⓓ	141	Ⓐ	Ⓑ	Ⓒ	Ⓓ
102	Ⓐ	Ⓑ	Ⓒ	Ⓓ	112	Ⓐ	Ⓑ	Ⓒ	Ⓓ	122	Ⓐ	Ⓑ	Ⓒ	Ⓓ	132	Ⓐ	Ⓑ	Ⓒ	Ⓓ	142	Ⓐ	Ⓑ	Ⓒ	Ⓓ
103	Ⓐ	Ⓑ	Ⓒ	Ⓓ	113	Ⓐ	Ⓑ	Ⓒ	Ⓓ	123	Ⓐ	Ⓑ	Ⓒ	Ⓓ	133	Ⓐ	Ⓑ	Ⓒ	Ⓓ	143	Ⓐ	Ⓑ	Ⓒ	Ⓓ
104	Ⓐ	Ⓑ	Ⓒ	Ⓓ	114	Ⓐ	Ⓑ	Ⓒ	Ⓓ	124	Ⓐ	Ⓑ	Ⓒ	Ⓓ	134	Ⓐ	Ⓑ	Ⓒ	Ⓓ	144	Ⓐ	Ⓑ	Ⓒ	Ⓓ
105	Ⓐ	Ⓑ	Ⓒ	Ⓓ	115	Ⓐ	Ⓑ	Ⓒ	Ⓓ	125	Ⓐ	Ⓑ	Ⓒ	Ⓓ	135	Ⓐ	Ⓑ	Ⓒ	Ⓓ	145	Ⓐ	Ⓑ	Ⓒ	Ⓓ
106	Ⓐ	Ⓑ	Ⓒ	Ⓓ	116	Ⓐ	Ⓑ	Ⓒ	Ⓓ	126	Ⓐ	Ⓑ	Ⓒ	Ⓓ	135	Ⓐ	Ⓑ	Ⓒ	Ⓓ	146	Ⓐ	Ⓑ	Ⓒ	Ⓓ
107	Ⓐ	Ⓑ	Ⓒ	Ⓓ	117	Ⓐ	Ⓑ	Ⓒ	Ⓓ	127	Ⓐ	Ⓑ	Ⓒ	Ⓓ	137	Ⓐ	Ⓑ	Ⓒ	Ⓓ					
108	Ⓐ	Ⓑ	Ⓒ	Ⓓ	118	Ⓐ	Ⓑ	Ⓒ	Ⓓ	128	Ⓐ	Ⓑ	Ⓒ	Ⓓ	138	Ⓐ	Ⓑ	Ⓒ	Ⓓ					
109	Ⓐ	Ⓑ	Ⓒ	Ⓓ	119	Ⓐ	Ⓑ	Ⓒ	Ⓓ	129	Ⓐ	Ⓑ	Ⓒ	Ⓓ	139	Ⓐ	Ⓑ	Ⓒ	Ⓓ					
110	Ⓐ	Ⓑ	Ⓒ	Ⓓ	120	Ⓐ	Ⓑ	Ⓒ	Ⓓ	130	Ⓐ	Ⓑ	Ⓒ	Ⓓ	140	Ⓐ	Ⓑ	Ⓒ	Ⓓ					

ANSWER SHEET

Reading Comprehension Part V, Part VI

No.	A	B	C	D	No.	A	B	C	D	No.	A	B	C	D	No.	A	B	C	D	No.	A	B	C	D
101	Ⓐ	Ⓑ	Ⓒ	Ⓓ	111	Ⓐ	Ⓑ	Ⓒ	Ⓓ	121	Ⓐ	Ⓑ	Ⓒ	Ⓓ	131	Ⓐ	Ⓑ	Ⓒ	Ⓓ	141	Ⓐ	Ⓑ	Ⓒ	Ⓓ
102	Ⓐ	Ⓑ	Ⓒ	Ⓓ	112	Ⓐ	Ⓑ	Ⓒ	Ⓓ	122	Ⓐ	Ⓑ	Ⓒ	Ⓓ	132	Ⓐ	Ⓑ	Ⓒ	Ⓓ	142	Ⓐ	Ⓑ	Ⓒ	Ⓓ
103	Ⓐ	Ⓑ	Ⓒ	Ⓓ	113	Ⓐ	Ⓑ	Ⓒ	Ⓓ	123	Ⓐ	Ⓑ	Ⓒ	Ⓓ	133	Ⓐ	Ⓑ	Ⓒ	Ⓓ	143	Ⓐ	Ⓑ	Ⓒ	Ⓓ
104	Ⓐ	Ⓑ	Ⓒ	Ⓓ	114	Ⓐ	Ⓑ	Ⓒ	Ⓓ	124	Ⓐ	Ⓑ	Ⓒ	Ⓓ	134	Ⓐ	Ⓑ	Ⓒ	Ⓓ	144	Ⓐ	Ⓑ	Ⓒ	Ⓓ
105	Ⓐ	Ⓑ	Ⓒ	Ⓓ	115	Ⓐ	Ⓑ	Ⓒ	Ⓓ	125	Ⓐ	Ⓑ	Ⓒ	Ⓓ	135	Ⓐ	Ⓑ	Ⓒ	Ⓓ	145	Ⓐ	Ⓑ	Ⓒ	Ⓓ
106	Ⓐ	Ⓑ	Ⓒ	Ⓓ	116	Ⓐ	Ⓑ	Ⓒ	Ⓓ	126	Ⓐ	Ⓑ	Ⓒ	Ⓓ	135	Ⓐ	Ⓑ	Ⓒ	Ⓓ	146	Ⓐ	Ⓑ	Ⓒ	Ⓓ
107	Ⓐ	Ⓑ	Ⓒ	Ⓓ	117	Ⓐ	Ⓑ	Ⓒ	Ⓓ	127	Ⓐ	Ⓑ	Ⓒ	Ⓓ	137	Ⓐ	Ⓑ	Ⓒ	Ⓓ					
108	Ⓐ	Ⓑ	Ⓒ	Ⓓ	118	Ⓐ	Ⓑ	Ⓒ	Ⓓ	128	Ⓐ	Ⓑ	Ⓒ	Ⓓ	138	Ⓐ	Ⓑ	Ⓒ	Ⓓ					
109	Ⓐ	Ⓑ	Ⓒ	Ⓓ	119	Ⓐ	Ⓑ	Ⓒ	Ⓓ	129	Ⓐ	Ⓑ	Ⓒ	Ⓓ	139	Ⓐ	Ⓑ	Ⓒ	Ⓓ					
110	Ⓐ	Ⓑ	Ⓒ	Ⓓ	120	Ⓐ	Ⓑ	Ⓒ	Ⓓ	130	Ⓐ	Ⓑ	Ⓒ	Ⓓ	140	Ⓐ	Ⓑ	Ⓒ	Ⓓ					

ANSWER SHEET

Reading Comprehension Part V, Part VI

No.	A	B	C	D	No.	A	B	C	D	No.	A	B	C	D	No.	A	B	C	D	No.	A	B	C	D
101	Ⓐ	Ⓑ	Ⓒ	Ⓓ	111	Ⓐ	Ⓑ	Ⓒ	Ⓓ	121	Ⓐ	Ⓑ	Ⓒ	Ⓓ	131	Ⓐ	Ⓑ	Ⓒ	Ⓓ	141	Ⓐ	Ⓑ	Ⓒ	Ⓓ
102	Ⓐ	Ⓑ	Ⓒ	Ⓓ	112	Ⓐ	Ⓑ	Ⓒ	Ⓓ	122	Ⓐ	Ⓑ	Ⓒ	Ⓓ	132	Ⓐ	Ⓑ	Ⓒ	Ⓓ	142	Ⓐ	Ⓑ	Ⓒ	Ⓓ
103	Ⓐ	Ⓑ	Ⓒ	Ⓓ	113	Ⓐ	Ⓑ	Ⓒ	Ⓓ	123	Ⓐ	Ⓑ	Ⓒ	Ⓓ	133	Ⓐ	Ⓑ	Ⓒ	Ⓓ	143	Ⓐ	Ⓑ	Ⓒ	Ⓓ
104	Ⓐ	Ⓑ	Ⓒ	Ⓓ	114	Ⓐ	Ⓑ	Ⓒ	Ⓓ	124	Ⓐ	Ⓑ	Ⓒ	Ⓓ	134	Ⓐ	Ⓑ	Ⓒ	Ⓓ	144	Ⓐ	Ⓑ	Ⓒ	Ⓓ
105	Ⓐ	Ⓑ	Ⓒ	Ⓓ	115	Ⓐ	Ⓑ	Ⓒ	Ⓓ	125	Ⓐ	Ⓑ	Ⓒ	Ⓓ	135	Ⓐ	Ⓑ	Ⓒ	Ⓓ	145	Ⓐ	Ⓑ	Ⓒ	Ⓓ
106	Ⓐ	Ⓑ	Ⓒ	Ⓓ	116	Ⓐ	Ⓑ	Ⓒ	Ⓓ	126	Ⓐ	Ⓑ	Ⓒ	Ⓓ	135	Ⓐ	Ⓑ	Ⓒ	Ⓓ	146	Ⓐ	Ⓑ	Ⓒ	Ⓓ
107	Ⓐ	Ⓑ	Ⓒ	Ⓓ	117	Ⓐ	Ⓑ	Ⓒ	Ⓓ	127	Ⓐ	Ⓑ	Ⓒ	Ⓓ	137	Ⓐ	Ⓑ	Ⓒ	Ⓓ					
108	Ⓐ	Ⓑ	Ⓒ	Ⓓ	118	Ⓐ	Ⓑ	Ⓒ	Ⓓ	128	Ⓐ	Ⓑ	Ⓒ	Ⓓ	138	Ⓐ	Ⓑ	Ⓒ	Ⓓ					
109	Ⓐ	Ⓑ	Ⓒ	Ⓓ	119	Ⓐ	Ⓑ	Ⓒ	Ⓓ	129	Ⓐ	Ⓑ	Ⓒ	Ⓓ	139	Ⓐ	Ⓑ	Ⓒ	Ⓓ					
110	Ⓐ	Ⓑ	Ⓒ	Ⓓ	120	Ⓐ	Ⓑ	Ⓒ	Ⓓ	130	Ⓐ	Ⓑ	Ⓒ	Ⓓ	140	Ⓐ	Ⓑ	Ⓒ	Ⓓ					

ANSWER SHEET

Reading Comprehension Part V, Part VI

No.	ANSWER A B C D	No.	ANSWER A B C D	No.	ANSWER A B C D	No.	ANSWER A B C D	No.	ANSWER A B C D
101	Ⓐ Ⓑ Ⓒ Ⓓ	111	Ⓐ Ⓑ Ⓒ Ⓓ	121	Ⓐ Ⓑ Ⓒ Ⓓ	131	Ⓐ Ⓑ Ⓒ Ⓓ	141	Ⓐ Ⓑ Ⓒ Ⓓ
102	Ⓐ Ⓑ Ⓒ Ⓓ	112	Ⓐ Ⓑ Ⓒ Ⓓ	122	Ⓐ Ⓑ Ⓒ Ⓓ	132	Ⓐ Ⓑ Ⓒ Ⓓ	142	Ⓐ Ⓑ Ⓒ Ⓓ
103	Ⓐ Ⓑ Ⓒ Ⓓ	113	Ⓐ Ⓑ Ⓒ Ⓓ	123	Ⓐ Ⓑ Ⓒ Ⓓ	133	Ⓐ Ⓑ Ⓒ Ⓓ	143	Ⓐ Ⓑ Ⓒ Ⓓ
104	Ⓐ Ⓑ Ⓒ Ⓓ	114	Ⓐ Ⓑ Ⓒ Ⓓ	124	Ⓐ Ⓑ Ⓒ Ⓓ	134	Ⓐ Ⓑ Ⓒ Ⓓ	144	Ⓐ Ⓑ Ⓒ Ⓓ
105	Ⓐ Ⓑ Ⓒ Ⓓ	115	Ⓐ Ⓑ Ⓒ Ⓓ	125	Ⓐ Ⓑ Ⓒ Ⓓ	135	Ⓐ Ⓑ Ⓒ Ⓓ	145	Ⓐ Ⓑ Ⓒ Ⓓ
106	Ⓐ Ⓑ Ⓒ Ⓓ	116	Ⓐ Ⓑ Ⓒ Ⓓ	126	Ⓐ Ⓑ Ⓒ Ⓓ	135	Ⓐ Ⓑ Ⓒ Ⓓ	146	Ⓐ Ⓑ Ⓒ Ⓓ
107	Ⓐ Ⓑ Ⓒ Ⓓ	117	Ⓐ Ⓑ Ⓒ Ⓓ	127	Ⓐ Ⓑ Ⓒ Ⓓ	137	Ⓐ Ⓑ Ⓒ Ⓓ		
108	Ⓐ Ⓑ Ⓒ Ⓓ	118	Ⓐ Ⓑ Ⓒ Ⓓ	128	Ⓐ Ⓑ Ⓒ Ⓓ	138	Ⓐ Ⓑ Ⓒ Ⓓ		
109	Ⓐ Ⓑ Ⓒ Ⓓ	119	Ⓐ Ⓑ Ⓒ Ⓓ	129	Ⓐ Ⓑ Ⓒ Ⓓ	139	Ⓐ Ⓑ Ⓒ Ⓓ		
110	Ⓐ Ⓑ Ⓒ Ⓓ	120	Ⓐ Ⓑ Ⓒ Ⓓ	130	Ⓐ Ⓑ Ⓒ Ⓓ	140	Ⓐ Ⓑ Ⓒ Ⓓ		

ANSWER SHEET

Reading Comprehension Part V, Part VI

No.	ANSWER A B C D	No.	ANSWER A B C D	No.	ANSWER A B C D	No.	ANSWER A B C D	No.	ANSWER A B C D
101	Ⓐ Ⓑ Ⓒ Ⓓ	111	Ⓐ Ⓑ Ⓒ Ⓓ	121	Ⓐ Ⓑ Ⓒ Ⓓ	131	Ⓐ Ⓑ Ⓒ Ⓓ	141	Ⓐ Ⓑ Ⓒ Ⓓ
102	Ⓐ Ⓑ Ⓒ Ⓓ	112	Ⓐ Ⓑ Ⓒ Ⓓ	122	Ⓐ Ⓑ Ⓒ Ⓓ	132	Ⓐ Ⓑ Ⓒ Ⓓ	142	Ⓐ Ⓑ Ⓒ Ⓓ
103	Ⓐ Ⓑ Ⓒ Ⓓ	113	Ⓐ Ⓑ Ⓒ Ⓓ	123	Ⓐ Ⓑ Ⓒ Ⓓ	133	Ⓐ Ⓑ Ⓒ Ⓓ	143	Ⓐ Ⓑ Ⓒ Ⓓ
104	Ⓐ Ⓑ Ⓒ Ⓓ	114	Ⓐ Ⓑ Ⓒ Ⓓ	124	Ⓐ Ⓑ Ⓒ Ⓓ	134	Ⓐ Ⓑ Ⓒ Ⓓ	144	Ⓐ Ⓑ Ⓒ Ⓓ
105	Ⓐ Ⓑ Ⓒ Ⓓ	115	Ⓐ Ⓑ Ⓒ Ⓓ	125	Ⓐ Ⓑ Ⓒ Ⓓ	135	Ⓐ Ⓑ Ⓒ Ⓓ	145	Ⓐ Ⓑ Ⓒ Ⓓ
106	Ⓐ Ⓑ Ⓒ Ⓓ	116	Ⓐ Ⓑ Ⓒ Ⓓ	126	Ⓐ Ⓑ Ⓒ Ⓓ	135	Ⓐ Ⓑ Ⓒ Ⓓ	146	Ⓐ Ⓑ Ⓒ Ⓓ
107	Ⓐ Ⓑ Ⓒ Ⓓ	117	Ⓐ Ⓑ Ⓒ Ⓓ	127	Ⓐ Ⓑ Ⓒ Ⓓ	137	Ⓐ Ⓑ Ⓒ Ⓓ		
108	Ⓐ Ⓑ Ⓒ Ⓓ	118	Ⓐ Ⓑ Ⓒ Ⓓ	128	Ⓐ Ⓑ Ⓒ Ⓓ	138	Ⓐ Ⓑ Ⓒ Ⓓ		
109	Ⓐ Ⓑ Ⓒ Ⓓ	119	Ⓐ Ⓑ Ⓒ Ⓓ	129	Ⓐ Ⓑ Ⓒ Ⓓ	139	Ⓐ Ⓑ Ⓒ Ⓓ		
110	Ⓐ Ⓑ Ⓒ Ⓓ	120	Ⓐ Ⓑ Ⓒ Ⓓ	130	Ⓐ Ⓑ Ⓒ Ⓓ	140	Ⓐ Ⓑ Ⓒ Ⓓ		

ANSWER SHEET

Reading Comprehension Part V, Part VI

No.	ANSWER A B C D	No.	ANSWER A B C D	No.	ANSWER A B C D	No.	ANSWER A B C D	No.	ANSWER A B C D
101	Ⓐ Ⓑ Ⓒ Ⓓ	111	Ⓐ Ⓑ Ⓒ Ⓓ	121	Ⓐ Ⓑ Ⓒ Ⓓ	131	Ⓐ Ⓑ Ⓒ Ⓓ	141	Ⓐ Ⓑ Ⓒ Ⓓ
102	Ⓐ Ⓑ Ⓒ Ⓓ	112	Ⓐ Ⓑ Ⓒ Ⓓ	122	Ⓐ Ⓑ Ⓒ Ⓓ	132	Ⓐ Ⓑ Ⓒ Ⓓ	142	Ⓐ Ⓑ Ⓒ Ⓓ
103	Ⓐ Ⓑ Ⓒ Ⓓ	113	Ⓐ Ⓑ Ⓒ Ⓓ	123	Ⓐ Ⓑ Ⓒ Ⓓ	133	Ⓐ Ⓑ Ⓒ Ⓓ	143	Ⓐ Ⓑ Ⓒ Ⓓ
104	Ⓐ Ⓑ Ⓒ Ⓓ	114	Ⓐ Ⓑ Ⓒ Ⓓ	124	Ⓐ Ⓑ Ⓒ Ⓓ	134	Ⓐ Ⓑ Ⓒ Ⓓ	144	Ⓐ Ⓑ Ⓒ Ⓓ
105	Ⓐ Ⓑ Ⓒ Ⓓ	115	Ⓐ Ⓑ Ⓒ Ⓓ	125	Ⓐ Ⓑ Ⓒ Ⓓ	135	Ⓐ Ⓑ Ⓒ Ⓓ	145	Ⓐ Ⓑ Ⓒ Ⓓ
106	Ⓐ Ⓑ Ⓒ Ⓓ	116	Ⓐ Ⓑ Ⓒ Ⓓ	126	Ⓐ Ⓑ Ⓒ Ⓓ	135	Ⓐ Ⓑ Ⓒ Ⓓ	146	Ⓐ Ⓑ Ⓒ Ⓓ
107	Ⓐ Ⓑ Ⓒ Ⓓ	117	Ⓐ Ⓑ Ⓒ Ⓓ	127	Ⓐ Ⓑ Ⓒ Ⓓ	137	Ⓐ Ⓑ Ⓒ Ⓓ		
108	Ⓐ Ⓑ Ⓒ Ⓓ	118	Ⓐ Ⓑ Ⓒ Ⓓ	128	Ⓐ Ⓑ Ⓒ Ⓓ	138	Ⓐ Ⓑ Ⓒ Ⓓ		
109	Ⓐ Ⓑ Ⓒ Ⓓ	119	Ⓐ Ⓑ Ⓒ Ⓓ	129	Ⓐ Ⓑ Ⓒ Ⓓ	139	Ⓐ Ⓑ Ⓒ Ⓓ		
110	Ⓐ Ⓑ Ⓒ Ⓓ	120	Ⓐ Ⓑ Ⓒ Ⓓ	130	Ⓐ Ⓑ Ⓒ Ⓓ	140	Ⓐ Ⓑ Ⓒ Ⓓ